Lecture Notes in Computer Science 13255

More information about this series at https://link.springer.com/bookseries/558

Owolabi Legunsen · Grigore Rosu (Eds.)

Model Checking Software

28th International Symposium, SPIN 2022
Virtual Event, May 21, 2022
Proceedings

Editors
Owolabi Legunsen
Cornell University
Ithaca, NY, USA

Grigore Rosu 🔟
University of Illinois Urbana-Champaign
Urbana, IL, USA

ISSN 0302-9743   ISSN 1611-3349 (electronic)
Lecture Notes in Computer Science
ISBN 978-3-031-15076-0   ISBN 978-3-031-15077-7 (eBook)
https://doi.org/10.1007/978-3-031-15077-7

This Springer imprint is published by the registered company Springer Nature Switzerland AG
The registered company address is: Gewerbestrasse 11, 6330 Cham, Switzerland

Preface

This volume contains the proceedings of the 28th International Symposium on Model Checking Software, SPIN 2022, held online from Chicago, Illinois, on May 21, 2022. Since 1995, the event has evolved and has been consolidated as a reference symposium in the area of formal methods related to model checking. The previous edition of the SPIN symposium took place in Leiden, the Netherlands, with a record number of submissions and participants.

The SPIN 2022 edition requested regular papers, short papers, and tool demos in the following areas: formal verification techniques for automated analysis of software; formal analysis for modeling languages, such as UML/state charts; formal specification languages, temporal logic, and design-by-contract; model checking and automated theorem proving, including SAT and SMT; verifying compilers; abstraction and symbolic execution techniques; static analysis and abstract interpretation; combination of verification techniques; modular and compositional verification techniques; verification of timed and probabilistic systems; automated testing using advanced analysis techniques; combination of static and dynamic analyses; derivation of specifications, test cases, or other useful material via formal analysis; case studies of interesting systems or with interesting results; engineering and implementation of software verification and analysis tools; benchmark and comparative studies for formal verification and analysis tools; formal methods education and training; and insightful surveys or historical accounts on topics of relevance to the symposium.

The symposium attracted 11 submissions that were each carefully reviewed by three Program Committee (PC) members. The selection process included further online discussion open to all PC members. As a result, eight papers were selected for presentation at the symposium and publication in Springer's proceedings. The program consisted of eight regular papers and two invited talks.

We would like to thank all the authors who submitted papers, the Steering Committee, the PC, the additional reviewers, the invited speakers, the participants, and the organizers of the cohosted events for making SPIN 2022 a successful event. We also thank all the sponsors that provided online facilities and financial support to make the symposium possible.

May 2022

Owolabi Legunsen
Grigore Rosu

Organization

Program Committee Chairs

Owolabi Legunsen	Cornell University, USA
Grigore Rosu	University of Illinois at Urbana-Champaign, USA

Steering Committee

Dragan Bosnacki (Chair)	Eindhoven University of Technology, The Netherlands
Susanne Graf	Verimag, France
Gerard Holzmann	Nimble Research, USA
Stefan Leue	University of Konstanz, Germany
Jaco van der Pol	Aarhus University, Denmark
Neha Rungta	Amazon Web Services, USA
Willem Visser	Stellenbosch University, South Africa

Program Committee

Axel Legay	UCLouvain, Belgium
Cristina Seceleanu	Mälardalen University, Sweden
Doron Peled	Bar Ilan University, Israel
Jaco van de Pol	Aarhus University, Denmark
Kyungmin Bae	Pohang University of Science and Technology, South Korea
Stefan Leue	University of Konstanz, Germany
Neeraj Suri	Lancaster University, UK
Georgiana Caltais	University of Konstanz, Germany
Madalina Erascu	West University of Timisoara, Romania
Richard DeFrancisco	Augusta University, USA
Christian Schilling	Aalborg University, Denmark
Gerard Holzmann	Nimble Research, USA
Corina Pasareanu	Carnegie Mellon University and NASA, USA
Sandeep Kulkarni	Michigan State University, USA
Klaus Havelund	Jet Propulsion Laboratory, USA
Alberto Lluch Lfuente	Technical University of Denmark, Denmark
Andrei Stefanescu	University of Illinois at Urbana-Champaign, USA
Allison Sullivan	University of Texas at Arlington, USA

Kuen-Bang Hou Favnia   University of Minnesota, USA
Dragan Bosnacki   Eindhoven University of Technology,
                              The Netherlands
Liyi Li   University of Maryland, USA

Local Organization Committee

Neil Zhao   University of Illinois at Urbana-Champaign, USA
Xiaohong Chen   University of Illinois at Urbana-Champaign, USA
Maryam Rostamigiv   TU Dresden, Germany

Additional Reviewers

Fabien Duchene
Martin Kölbl
Tiberiu Seceleanu
Andrew Sogokon
Fabian Bauer-Marquart

Contents

Automated Consistency Analysis
for Legal Contracts

Alan Khoja[2], Martin Kölbl[1($\boxtimes$)], Stefan Leue[1], and Rüdiger Wilhelmi[2]

[1] Department of Computer Science, University of Konstanz, Konstanz, Germany
`Martin.Koelbl@uni-konstanz.de`, `Stefan.Leue@uni-konstanz.de`
[2] Department of Law, University of Konstanz, Konstanz, Germany
`Alan.Khoja@uni-konstanz.de`, `Wilhelmi@uni-konstanz.de`

Abstract. Contracts in business life, and in particular company purchase agreements, often comprise a large number of provisions and are correspondingly long and complex. In practice, it is therefore a great challenge to keep track of their regulatory context and to identify and avoid inconsistencies in such contracts. Against this background, we propose a semi-formal as well as a formal logical modeling of this type of contracts, using decidable first-order theories. We also present the tool *ContractCheck*, which performs fully automated inconsistency analyses on the considered contracts using Satisfiability Modulo Theories (SMT) solving.

1 Introduction

Contracts are indispensable in business. They enable the contracting parties to arrange their legal relationships by giving legal effect to their common will and establishing mutual claims. A prominent example is the purchase of a company in a share purchase agreement (SPA). Like any purchase contract, an SPA must specify at least the indispensable *essentialia negotii*: the purchaser and the seller, as well as the purchase object and the purchase price to be transferred. In practice, SPAs regulate all relevant legal issues in the contract and exclude references to statutory law as far as possible. As a consequence, SPAs have a very local semantics that is almost entirely based on the contractual duties agreed upon in the SPA.

Contracts, and especially SPAs, are often very long and complex. This is due, in particular, to the large number and complexity of the issues to be regulated. In addition, a large number of persons are often involved in the drafting. Moreover, the negotiations and the drafting may take long and comprise a large number of amendments of the draft. Length, complexity and frequent changes make a contract prone to errors and inconsistencies, such as references being wrong, missing essentials or unfulfillable claims. Inconsistencies in the form of missing essentials can be found by a simple syntactic analysis. It is significantly more complex to find inconsistencies in the dynamics of several claims. Claims should not contradict each other and be performable in the context of legal facts described in

O. Legunsen and G. Rosu (Eds.): SPIN 2022, LNCS 13255, pp. 1–23, 2022.
https://doi.org/10.1007/978-3-031-15077-7_1

the contract. Also, the combination of several due dates can be unexpectedly restricted by a statute of limitations. For instance, assume an SPA contains a warranty claim that must be asserted within 14 days after the closing on day 28, then subsequent performance must be made within 28 days, and otherwise damages must be paid within another 14 days. Further assume, that the contract contains a provision that warranty claims are limited to 42 days after closing. In this example, the warranty clause provides that performance can continue until day 84, while the limitation period ends on day 70. The timing in the SPA is inconsistent.

In this paper we propose a concept to model and automatically analyze a textual SPA. As its main contributions, we present a meta-model for the entities of an SPA using a class diagram from the Unified Modeling Language (UML) [Obj17] in Sect. 3, give the modeling a semantics in decidable fragments of first-order logic in Sect. 4 and automatically analyze the SPA for inconsistencies using Satisfiability Modulo Theory (SMT) technology in Sect. 5. The aim is a red-flag system to highlight errors that we compute in a two-step analysis:

- First, our syntactic analysis checks whether the fundamental elements are part of the SPA and every referenced claim does also exist.
- Second, we provide a dynamic analysis to check whether every claim can be performed and whether a feasible execution of the SPA exists.

We have implemented the analyses in a tool called *ContractCheck*, and demonstrate its ability to detect and explain inconsistencies using a case study in Sect. 6. In this paper, we develop the concept and the tool using an SPA under German law, but this does not preclude adaptation to contracts with a different subject matter or under other jurisdictions, as they might be more complex but basically have a comparable structure with similar elements.

When considering examples of SPAs, it can be observed that they often consist of very similar blocks of text that only vary in certain parameters, for instance the agreed price. In the case of international company purchases, it is estimated that about half of the text of the provisions is changed little or not at all [HS16]. In order to obtain a formal logical representation of the SPA, as part of our approach and tool we provide a library of parameterized structured English text blocks that can be freely combined and used to compose the contract textually. These blocks allow greater flexibility than conventional approaches, in which the creation of contracts is dialog-driven and based on decision trees. Each of these blocks has a formal semantics expressed using formulae from a decidable fragment of first-order logic. The conjunction of these conditions then constitutes the logical representation of the contract. The analysis method that we describe in this paper generalizes to the class of all concrete contracts that can be formulated by composing and parameterizing the provided text blocks.

Related Work. We review works addressing the logical modeling and analysis of legal artefacts. We consider the verification of smart contracts [BK19,PF19] which are, in effect, described by executable program code, outside the scope of this paper, since their analysis has more similarity with program analysis.

Several meta-models of various legal domains describing legal entities and their relations have been proposed. A first work representing contracts with UML has been proposed in [EGB+01]. A multi-level hierarchical ontology to model a contract is described in [KJ03], which is expressed using UML class diagrams. A modeling of contracts as business processes has been suggested in [Kab05, WS05]. In [DNS08], a business process is translated into state machines to check whether it is always beneficial for the contracting parties to fulfill their claims while the contract is being executed. LegalRuleML [PGR+11, OAS21, Gru18] is a specialization of the general language RuleML [BPS10] designed to express relationships between legal entities by rules. We are not aware of any extension of Legal-RuleML towards the analysis of contract executions for inconsistencies. The Contract Specification Language (CSL) is a modeling language that represents claims as actions in a contract. In [HKZ12], an execution of a given CSL expression is computed as a sequence of actions, which is then analyzed to determine whether any specified commitments are met. In [HLM20], a contract is interpreted and analyzed as a composition of commitments. In [MKK14], the natural language sentences of an e-contract are translated into a dependency graph in order to check whether individual regulations contradict each other.

Deontic logic [VW51] is a family of modal logics designed to express the semantics of claims with operators for obligation, permission, and prohibition. Deontic logic is translated into propositional logic in [CM07] and analyzed for inconsistencies using a tableau calculus in [CM08]. Further analyses using tableau constructions are proposed in [BBB09]. These analyses find contradictions inside of a contract but do not compute potential contract executions. The Contract Lanugage *CL* [PS07, PS12] encompasses Deontic logic. In [PPS07], a contract given in *CL* is translated into a transition system, which is then analyzed by the model checker NuSMV for inconsistencies. In [CS17], a *C-O diagram* [MDCS10], which is a graphical extension of *CL*, is expressed by state machines and analyzed using the real-time model checker UPPAAL. The analyses find syntactic inconsistencies and prove a dynamic inconsistency by one execution but needs an expert to encode a contract as a *C-O diagram*. An extension of *CL* to *RCL* in [MB15, BM21] allows to reason about the persons between whom claims exist using the tool *RECALL*. A further system supporting a Deontic logic based approach is the Linear Time Temporal Logic (LTL) based language *FL* [GMS10, GMS11] together with the model checker *FormaLex* [GMS11, FMS+17]. In the above cited approaches, claims can only be logically connected, so that a prioritization of primary and secondary duties, which are central concepts in SPAs, is impossible.

Comparison to Related Work. The approach that we propose in this paper focuses on the use of SAT and SMT technology in discovering inconsistencies in SPAs. While many of the approaches cited above do have the ability to detect inconsistencies, they do not have the ability to produce models revealing reasons for inconsistencies that lie in data rather than in the execution of actions, which is one of the aspects that we will focus on. Also, only finite executions are of interest in an SPA which is why LTL-style model checking capabilities of infinite behaviors are not required. In comparison to the approaches relying on Deontic logics, while we do consider claims, they are only one of the many logical facets of contracts that we are interested in. SAT- and SMT-based modeling and analysis turns out to be very flexible in allowing us to directly represent claims in the formalization of SPAs without requiring the overhead of model checking or tableau constructions required to analyze deontic logic fomulae.

Contributions. This paper presents the following main contributions:

1. We propose an ontology for SPAs using the UML.
2. We provide a logical formalization of SPAs using a decidable fragment of first order logic. By this we contribute to the extensive research area addressing the use of formal logics in the representation of legal artefacts.
3. We define a number of consistency analyses that are applicable to SPAs.
4. We describe a tool that uses a collection of parameterized natural language building blocks from which textual SPAs can be composed.
5. We present the prototypical tool *ContractCheck* that uses SAT, SMT and satisfiability core technology to perform the consistency analyses and which produces diagnostic information explaining identified inconsistencies.
6. We illustrate the application of this approach to an example SPA.

2   Preliminaries

We describe the modeling of an SPA using class diagrams from the UML and encode both the consistency requirements as well as the consistency analyses in decidable theories of first-order logic.

Modeling. The entities of an SPA are depicted as classes in a class diagram of UML [Obj17]. A class contains attributes and operations. An attribute describes a property of an object and has a name and a type. A class diagram graphically represents classes by rectangles and their associations to each other by lines. The relationship between different classes are described by associations between the classes. An association *generalization* describes the relationship between an abstract class and a more specific class. The generalization is graphically represented by an arrow with a triangle, pointing to the abstract class. The association *aggregation* represents an affiliation and is marked using a diamond symbol attached to the associated object. A set relation can be annotated by an integer value range indicating how many objects of one class are related to how many objects of the other class.

Formalization in Logic. We formalize an SPA and the analyses in decidable fragments of first-order logic. The formalization uses the logic of linear real arithmetic, equality, integers and uninterpreted functions [KS16]. For these fragments, efficient SMT solvers [KS16] exist that automatically decide whether a logical formula from the fragment is satisfiable. In case of satisfiability, they return a satisfying assignment which is also called a model, and otherwise, they return unsat.

For example, an SMT solver calculates that the formula $(x > 0) \land (x + y < 0)$ is satisfiable and returns, for instance, the variable assignment $x = 0.9$ and $y = -2.0$ as a possible model.

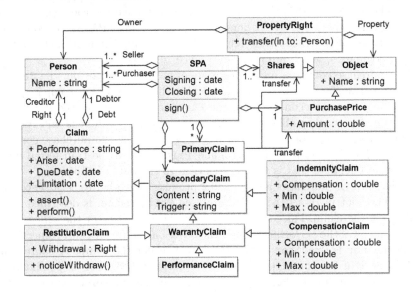

Fig. 1. Class diagram of a Sales Purchase Agreement (SPA)

3 Contract Modeling

We propose the use of UML class diagrams in the ontological modeling of an abstract view on an SPA. An instance of a class diagram describes an legal contract and will be the basis for the analyses encoding in the next sections. We concretize this modeling approach by applying it to the modeling of a concrete SPA for the purchase of a pretzel bakery.

3.1 Modeling of an SPA

For modeling purposes, it is necessary to determine the typical provisions in an SPA. These can be found in numerous legal template books [GS22, MSJ22, Sei18a, WAB20, WK22]. For the present project, we analyzed a wide variety of these books (regarding German law) [vH20a, vH20b, MS22a, MS22b, Pfi22, Sei18b, Sei18c, Sei18d, Sei18e]. We have identified the following provisions as typical for an SPA: contracting parties, purchase object, purchase price provisions, conditions and execution, warranties and indemnities, liability, final provisions. Based on this, an SPA was developed that contains the typical provisions. In this paper, we are primarily concerned with the provisions on *warranties*, *indemnities* and *liability*[1], supplemented by the indispensable provisions on the contracting parties (*purchaser* and *seller*), the *purchase object* and the *purchase price*.

From these provisions, we derive an ontology that is given as a UML class diagram, depicted in Fig. 1. It represents the typical provisions of an SPA in the form of classes. Notice that this ontology can be extended to other types of contracts. In this paper, we restrict ourselves to considering SPAs since, compared to other types of contracts, they rely much less on implicit legal facts implied by legal dogmatics, which are typically waived in SPAs.

As a purchase contract, an SPA consists of at least one person, the `Seller`, who has to transfer an `Object`, in particular the `Shares` of a company, as a *purchase object* to a second person, the `Purchaser`. In return, the `Purchaser` has to transfer another `object`, an `Amount` of money, as `PurchasePrice`. An SPA becomes effective on the date of `Signing`, on which the purchase contract is `signed`. The `Shares` and the `Purchase Price` have to be transferred when due on date `DueDate`, that is usually identical to the date of `Closing`.

In the SPA, the purchaser and the seller promise each other to *perform* certain *claims*. The content of a `Claim`, the promised `Performance`, is described as an attribute in the claim. For each *claim*, either the *purchaser* or the *seller* is the *debtor*, who owes the *performance*, and the other one is the *creditor*, respectively. The `Purchaser` is `Creditor` of the *claim* to transfer the company *shares* and the `Seller` is a `Debtor` of the same. Vice versa, the `Seller` is `Creditor` of the *claim* to transfer the `PurchasePrice` and the `Purchaser` is `Debtor` of the same. A `claim` arises on date `Arise`. The creditor can `assert` that the debtor does `perform` the *claim* in rendering the `Performance`. S/he can `assert` the claim from the `DueDate` until the `Limitation` date. Any `claim` expires on the day of `Limitation`. In order to fulfill these *claims*, we also need to model the *property rights*. The seller can *perform* the *claim*, when s/he is the `Owner` of the `PropertyRight` on the `Shares` and `transfers` this right to the purchaser.

The *claims* to transfer the *shares* and *purchase price* are `PrimaryClaims`. A *primary claim* is a *claim* in a contract that has to be performed from the outset by the *due date*. In this, it differs from a `SecondaryClaim`, that only arises with the breach of another *claim* or of separately listed circumstances. A *secondary claim* refers to another claim by a `Trigger`, and we model its circumstances by an attribute `Content`. We call a *secondary claim* without a `Trigger` an *independent claim*.

Within *secondary claims* in an SPA, a distinction is made between a *warranty claim* and an *indemnity claim* [Wil22]. A `WarrantyClaim` refers to an unknown risk due to a breach of a *primary claim*, or of listed circumstances that are not expected but considered likely enough to require regulation. A *warranty* consists of the *warranty content* as the prerequisite and one or more *warranty claims* as consequence of a breach of warranty. The warranty `content` includes the existence or non-existence of certain circumstances, which usually concern the *purchase object* and especially its properties. The warranty claims are usually *claims* of the *purchaser* for compensation in money, irrespective

---

[1] We set legal terms in italics and terms referring to UML diagrams in teletype font.

of fault. It is also possible to agree on a *claim* for subsequent performance (PeformanceClaim) or a right of Withdrawal that in case of a notice of withdrawal (noticeWithdraw) terminates the contract and can give the purchaser a *claim* for restitution of the *purchase price* and the seller a *claim* for restitution of the *shares* (RestitutionClaims). A CompensationClaim is often limited in the way that the amount of Compensation must reach a minimum value Min and may not exceed a maximum value Max. The limitation may apply only to individual *claims* or to all *claims* under the contract. If the purchaser has a *claim* for compensation, this can be offset against the purchase price claim, so that the total amount of money to be paid is reduced accordingly. An *indemnity* refers to a known risk due to an expected breach of a *primary claim* or listed circumstances. In case of such a breach, it gives the purchaser an IndemnityClaim for indemnification by means of an appropriate compensation in money.

Example 1 (Bakery SPA). As a running example, we use an SPA for the fictitious sale of a bakery from the seller Eva to the purchaser Chris. We instantiate this example by the UML class diagram presented in Fig. 2. In the bakery SPA, Chris agrees to pay the purchase price of €40,000 (PayClaim), and Eva agrees to give Chris ownership of the bakery Shares Bakery (TransferClaim). Both claims are due at the agreed closing 28 days after signing. In case the pretzel bakery is not transferred or the purchase price is not paid at closing, then the other contracting party may withdraw from the purchase contract. In addition to the *primary claims*, Eva warranties in a WarrantyClaim PretzelWarranty that the bakery can bake 10,000 of pretzels a day. If the bakery in the example cannot bake 10,000 of pretzels, then the warranty is breached and Chris has to assert this breach within the DueDate of 14 days of closing. In case of assertion, Eva has to make good within 28 days because of the PerformanceClaim Claim1, otherwise she has to pay within 14 days a compensation of €1,000 per 100 of pretzels that cannot be baked, due to the CompensationClaim Claim2. Claim2 has a minimal compensation of €1000. Any claim under the warranty has a Limitation of 42 days of closing. Further crucial facts are represented in the bakery SPA. Due to debts of the Eva, a local bank Bank has ownership by way of security in the shares in the bakery SecurityOwnership.

Manual inspection reveals the following inconsistencies in the SPA: Eva's *primary claim* according to the SPA is to transfer the bakery to Chris. In order to fulfill her claim, she must be the owner. However, consider that Bank is the owner of the bakery due to the transfer of ownership by way of security. Eva cannot fulfill her claim as she is not the owner of the Bakery, which we consider an inconsistency, or at least a loophole. Another inconsistency is due to the timing of the claims. The PretzelWarranty has a Limitation of 42 days after Closing, even if an assertion occurs within 14 days after Closing, then followed by the 28 days of Claim1 and 14 days of Claim2. This implies that Claim2 can take up to 56 days after closing, contradicting the Limitation of 42 days.

4 Formalization

We present the logical encoding of the objects of an SPA in decidable fragments of first-order logic and demonstrate the encoding using the bakery SPA case study. A model representing a satisfying assignment of the formalization represents a possible execution of the considered SPA.

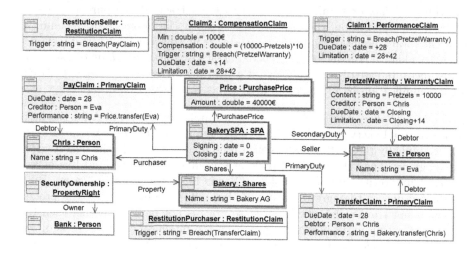

Fig. 2. Object diagram of Bakery SPA

We intend the consistency analyses in Sect. 5 to occur before signing when facts of life are only partially known. In an SPA, for example, a claim can define the performance of a transfer, whereas it is unknown whether and on which day the property relations will change. We use variables to model legal facts, and constrain their possible values according to the constraints specified in the SPA. We formalize an SPA using decidable fragments of first-order logic since it turns out to be ideally suited to accommodate incomplete legal facts.

4.1 Logical Formalization of Contract Entities

An SPA consists of a set of claims with which an execution of the SPA has to comply. Whether a claim is performed in an execution depends on the objective situation and the behavior of the contracting parties that we call *legal facts*. We define an *execution* of an SPA as a combination of legal facts such that for every *primary claim* or *independent claim*, the claim itself or one of its associated *secondary claims* is performed. Notice, that not every claim in an SPA needs to be performed in a specific execution. First, we formalize the legal facts, then the claims and lastly, combine the claims such that a satisfying assignment of the formalization is a possible SPA execution.

Formalization of Legal Facts. An SPA according to the class diagram in Fig. 1 contains a set $\mathcal{P}$ of persons and a set $\mathcal{O}$ of objects. In the formalization, we reference a person p or an object o by the index of p in $\mathcal{P}$ and the index of o in $\mathcal{O}$, which yields unique identifiers.

Dates in an SPA are usually given by calendar dates. Calendar dates are complicated to process due to the many rules that govern them, such as the treatment of a leap year. In the formalization, we simplify the processing and represent dates using integer variables. An execution of an SPA begins on date $d_S = 0$ with the signature of all contract parties and the closing is performed on date d_C by the transfer of the business ownership. For each claim c in an SPA, we create a date d_c for its performance date.

An ownership can only be transferred from the owner to a new owner. Property relations can be explicitly depicted by the class `PropertyRight`, with an association `Owner` towards a `Person` p and an association `Property` towards an `Object` o. We define a set PR and add to it a tuple (p, o) for every instance of `PropertyRight`. We formalize the property rights by an uninterpreted function $owner(Object) : Person$. ϕ_{owner} represents the property relations stated in the SPA.

$$\phi_{owner} = \bigwedge_{(p,o) \in PR} (owner(o) = p) \tag{1}$$

Formalization of the Claims. Having formalized the legal facts in the SPA, we are now ready to formalize the claims in the SPA. We define a set $\mathcal{C}$ which contains the claims in an SPA. The set $\mathcal{C}_I$ contains the *primary claims* and *independent warranty claims* of an SPA. For every *claim* c, the set $\mathcal{C}(c)$ contains every *secondary claim* s with a `Trigger` to c. In the following, we refer to a claim in $\mathcal{C}(c)$ as a *consequence claim* of c.

Each claim c in the SPA contains a `Performance` l_c, which must be performed for the claim to be performed. Either l_c is a logical formula or the name of an operation in Fig. 1. In the latter case, l_c is replaced with the formalization of the pre- and postconditions of the corresponding operation. For example, the conditions of a property transfer p of an object o from the debtor d to a creditor is represented by the constraint $l_c^p \equiv owner(o) = d$. For every claim c there exists a performance date d_c. The value of d_c is either -1, which represents non-performance, or in the interval $[\texttt{DueDate}, \texttt{Limitation}]$. If `DueDate` is undefined, then its default value is the value of date `Arise` of the claim. In case `DueDate` starts with the sign $+$, then we replace it with $\texttt{Arise} + \texttt{DueDate}$. We formalize a claim r with $\phi_c \equiv (d_c = -1) \vee ((c.\texttt{DueDate} \leq d_c \leq c.\texttt{Limitation}) \Rightarrow l_c)$.

A `WarrantyClaim` w is a special *secondary claim* since it is independent. For this reason, in our formalization, the constraint $d_w = -1$ encodes that w is met, and otherwise it is breached on a date $d_w \geq 0$. A warranty w is formalized by $\phi_w \equiv (d_w = -1 \Rightarrow l_w) \vee (w.\texttt{DueDate} \leq d_w \leq w.\texttt{Limitation})$.

If a *primary claim* or an *independent claim* is not performed, the `Debtor` is obliged to perform a consequence claim s that is associated to the *claim*. A *primary claim* is breached when it is not performed ($d_c = -1$), while a warranty is breached on the date d_w of the notification that the warranty Content is not met. For the formalization of their consequence claims, we introduce a fresh integer variable d'_c with value -1 when the associated *claim* is performed. The value of d'_c is c.DueDate for a breached *primary claim* and the value of d_c for a breached warranty. In case s is a performance claim, its formalization with a performance date d_s and a Performance l_c which is defined as $\phi_s \equiv (d'_c < d_s \leq s.$Limitation$) \Rightarrow l_c$. In case s is a restitution claim, the SPA is withdrawn, formally $\phi_s \equiv d'_c < d_s \leq s.$Limitation. In case s is a compensation claim, the debtor pays a positive compensation l_s to the creditor. The value of l_s is the Compensation that specifies the amount of the compensation. The compensation is paid only above a minimum value Min and cannot be more than the maximum value Max. In the other cases, $l_s = $ *Compensation* applies, as shown in Formula 2. In every of the above cases, the compensation is performed.

$$\phi_{Compensation} \equiv l_s = \begin{cases} 0, & \textit{if Compensation} < \texttt{Min} \\ \texttt{Max} & \textit{if Compensation} > \texttt{Max} \\ Compensation, & \textit{otherwise} \end{cases} \qquad (2)$$

The compensation claim is formally a constraint $\phi_s \equiv \phi_{Compensation} \wedge ((d_s = -1 \Rightarrow Compensation = 0) \vee (d'_c < d_s \leq s.$Limitation$))$.

Execution of an SPA. We are now prepared to give the formalization ϕ_{SPA} of SPA executions. ϕ_{SPA} encodes the property rights and the claims in an SPA, and that in an execution of an SPA, for every *primary claim* and *independent claim*, either the claim or one of its consequence claims need to be performed.

$$\phi_{SPA} \equiv \phi_{owner} \wedge \bigwedge_{c \in \mathcal{C}} \phi_c \wedge \bigwedge_{c \in \mathcal{C}_I} (d_c \geq 0 \vee \bigvee_{\forall s \in \mathcal{C}(c)} d_s \geq 0). \qquad (3)$$

An SMT solver, such as Z3 [dMB08], can produce a satisfiable model for ϕ_{SPA} in case an execution of the SPA exists. This model then represents an execution of the SPA that is consistent with all constraints specified in the SPA.

For a contracting party, it is preferable to perform the *primary claims* and *independent claims*, and not their consequence claims. We formalize this preference with the help of a special set ϕ_{soft} that is encoded in Z3 using soft-asserts. A constraint in ϕ_{soft} is satisfied if the model still satisfies ϕ_{SPA}, otherwise the constraint is not unsatisfied.

$$\phi_{soft} \equiv \bigwedge_{c \in \mathcal{C}_I} d_c \geq 0 \wedge \bigwedge_{s \in \mathcal{C}(c)} d_s = -1 \qquad (4)$$

The SMT solver Z3 computes an optimal solution for the partially satisfiable MaxSMT problem $\phi_v \wedge \phi_{soft}$ in which the *primary claims* and *independent claims* are preferably performed. Z3 returns as a model an execution of the SPA that satisfies as few consequence claims as possible.

4.2   Formalization of the Bakery SPA

Legal Facts in the Bakery SPA. The bakery SPA B describes a set of persons $\mathcal{P}^B = \{\texttt{Eva}, \texttt{Chris}, \texttt{Bank}\}$ and an object set $\mathcal{O}^B = \{\texttt{Bakery}, \texttt{Price}\}$ with the shares of the Bakery and the purchase price Price. Bakery is a property of Bank due to the transfer of ownership by way of security, therefore:

$$\phi^B_{owner} \equiv owner(Bakery) = Bank \tag{5}$$

Claims in the Bakery SPA. Eva is obliged by the *TransferClaim* to transfer the shares of the bakery on a day d_u. She has to perform the *TransferClaim* on the day of Closing (28) and if she misses that date, Chris has a claim on her delivery. Eva can only perform the transfer if she is the owner of Bakery. The formalization is the constraint

$$\phi_{TransferClaim} \equiv (-1 = d_u) \vee ((28 \le d_u) \Rightarrow (owner(Bakery) = Eva)). \tag{6}$$

Furthermore, Chris is obliged by *PayClaim* to pay Price to Eva. The condition for the transfer is formally captured by the constraint $owner(Price) = Chris$. The transfer is performed on a day d_z and is due on day 28. The formalization of the *PayClaim* is

$$\phi_{PayClaim} \equiv (-1 = d_z) \vee ((28 \le d_z) \Rightarrow owner(PurchasePrice) = Chris). \tag{7}$$

If one of these two *primary claims* is not performed, then the related restitution (shorthand: Res.) claim allows the respective creditor on a date ≥ 0 to withdraw from the SPA, formally

$$\phi_{Res.Purchaser} \equiv d_{Res.Purchaser} = -1 \vee PayClaim.DueDate < d_{Res.Purchaser} \tag{8}$$
$$\phi_{Res.Seller} \equiv d_{Res.Seller} = -1 \vee TransferClaim.DueDate < d_{Res.Purchaser}. \tag{9}$$

If the *warranty claim* *PretzelWarranty* is breached, then Chris notifies this breach on a day $d_g \ge 0$. $d_g = -1$ means that there is no indication of a non-performance and therefore the warranty Condition $Pretzels = 10,000$ is met. The formalization for the *PretzelWarranty* is

$$\phi_{PretzelWarranty} \equiv (d_g = -1 \Rightarrow Pretzels = 10000) \vee (28 \le d_g \le 28 + 14). \tag{10}$$

In the bakery SPA, the warranty has the consequence Claim1, so that the seller can subsequently perform the pretzel guarantee on a date d_n.

$$\phi_{Claim1} \equiv (d_n = -1) \vee (d_g < d_n \le d_g + 28 \Rightarrow Pretzels = 10000) \tag{11}$$

On the other hand, it may be more advantageous for the debtor to pay a compensation l_s on a date d_s for the Compensation. The value of l_s is constrained by the formula $\phi^s_{Compensation}$. If no compensation occurs ($d_s = -1$), then l_s is 0. The formalization of the *compensation claim* Claim2 is

$$\phi_{Claim2} \equiv \phi^s_{Compensation} \wedge ((d_s = -1 \Rightarrow l_s = 0) \vee (d_g < d_s \leq d_g + 28 + 14)) \tag{12}$$

For a *compensation claim*, l_s is either 0 or lies in the range of values between a minimum value Min and a maximum value Max of the compensation. For a paid pretzel compensation, l_s must exceed the value of €1,000 and an upper limit Max is not specified. l_s of the compensation claim is calculated according to the constraint $\phi^s_{Compensation}$.

$$\phi^s_{Compensation} \equiv l_s = \begin{cases} 0, & if \ (10.000 - Pretzels/100) * 1000 \leq 1.000 \\ (10.000 - Pretzels/100) * 1000, & otherwise \end{cases} \tag{13}$$

Execution of Bakery SPA. An execution of the bakery SPA does not need to perform every *primary claim* but can also perform an associated consequence claim. The overall encoding of the claims in the bakery SPA is

$$\phi^B_{SPA} \equiv \phi^B_{owner} \wedge (\phi_{TransferClaim} \vee \phi_{Res.Purchaser}) \wedge (\phi_{PayClaim} \vee \tag{14}$$
$$\phi_{Res.Seller}) \wedge (\phi_{PretzelWarranty} \vee \phi_{Claim1} \vee \phi_{Claim2}) \tag{15}$$

A model of ϕ^B_{SPA} should preferably perform *primary claims* or *independent claims*. This is formalized by

$$\phi^B_{soft} \equiv d_u \geq 0 \wedge d_z \geq 0 \wedge d_{Res.Purchaser} = -1 \wedge \tag{16}$$
$$d_{Res.Seller} = -1 \wedge d_g = -1 \wedge d_n = -1 \tag{17}$$

The bakery SPA is formalized by the constraint $\phi^B_{SPA} \wedge \phi^B_{soft}$. Each satisfying model of this constraint represents a possible execution of the bakery SPA.

5   Contract Analyses

We now propose static and dynamic analyses that find inconsistencies in the object diagram of an SPA.

5.1   Static Analyses

In an SPA, legal elements can be missing. For instance, an SPA does legally not exist if one of the essential entities (*essentialia negotii*) is missing. For instance, according to the German civil code [BGB, §433], the contract of sale must contain, for example, the contracting parties, the purchase object as well as the purchase price. In an SPA, every *primary claim* also needs at least one consequence claim and every claim needs a DueDate by which it is to be performed.

We say a contract is *statically inconsistent* if one of these legal elements is missing. When an SPA is drawn up according to the class diagram in Fig. 1, it is possible to statically check whether every essential legal element is present in the SPA. A static inconsistency analysis is easy to implement using static analyses and can be performed during the parsing (syntactic processing of the contract text) of an SPA.

5.2   Dynamic Analyses

It is more complicated to find a dynamic inconsistency in a contract. An SPA describes both legal facts and claims that the respective contracting parties have agreed upon. For example, Eva agrees to transfer the shares of the bakery. In order to transfer ownership of the shares, she must be the owner. This contradicts the fact that the Bank is the owner of the bakery shares. Despite this fact, the overall SPA can be fulfilled, since Chris can withdraw from the contract. However, an SPA where Chris always has to withdraw is not desirable. For an SPA, it is therefore essential, that each claim can be fulfilled individually, and at least one execution of the SPA exists. We propose two semantic analyses for an SPA:

Analysis I Can each claim be performed?
Analysis II Does there exist an execution of the SPA?

Formalization of the Dynamic Consistency Analyses. We now encode analyses I and II for a given SPA using the constraints defined in Sect. 4. If an encoded analysis is satisfiable, then an SMT solver returns a satisfying variable assignment. If it is unsatisfiable, the SMT solver Z3 can return an unsatisfiability core, which is a minimal subset of conditions that contradicts satisfiability. This subset indicates which claims in the SPA contradict another and, hence, causes an inconsistency in the SPA. These claims need to be changed in the SPA in order to obtain a consistent contract. Remember, a *primary claim* c is performed on its date d_c and a *warranty* w is asserted on day d_w. In the following, we abuse notation and ignore that warranties behave differently to simplify the presentation.

Analysis I is encoded in the constraints Φ_c and Φ_s for every claim in $\mathcal{C}$. We already formalized a claim c by a constraint ϕ_c, which has to perform on a date d_c. For every claim, in addition the property relation represented by ϕ_{owner} has to hold. A *primary claim* or an *independent claim* $c \in \mathcal{C}_I$ can be performed when the following constraint is satisfiable.

$$\Phi_c \equiv \phi_{owner} \wedge \phi_c \wedge d_c \geq 0. \tag{18}$$

A consequence claim $s \in \mathcal{C}(c)$ in an SPA usually needs to be performed if, at the same time, the claim c that is the `Trigger` of s is not performed:

$$\Phi_s \equiv \phi_{owner} \wedge (d_c = -1) \wedge \phi_c \wedge \phi_s \wedge d_s \geq 0. \tag{19}$$

If every constraint Φ_c and Φ_s is satisfiable, then every claim of the considered formalized SPA can be performed.

Analysis II checks whether an execution of the SPA exists by assessing the satisfiability of

$$\Phi_{SPA} \equiv \phi_{SPA} \wedge \phi_{soft}. \tag{20}$$

In addition, Analysis II recognizes whether all *primary claims* and *independent claims* can be performed in the same execution. In this case, every constraint in ϕ_{soft} is satisfied.

Dynamic Consistency Analyses of the Bakery SPA. The bakery SPA is given by the object diagram in Fig. 2. *ContractCheck* generates the following analyses and checks them for satisfiability by the SMT solver Z3.

Analysis I checks whether the individual *primary claims* and *independent claims* are fulfillable. The *TransferClaim* is formalized in the Eq. 6 and the corresponding Analysis I is

$$\Phi_{TransferClaim} \equiv \phi_{owner}^{B} \wedge \phi_{TransferClaim} \wedge d_u \geq 0 \tag{21}$$

$$\equiv owner(Bakery) = Bank \wedge (d_u = -1 \vee \tag{22}$$

$$(28 \leq d_u \Rightarrow owner(Bakery) = Eva)) \wedge d_u \geq 0. \tag{23}$$

owner is a function, therefore the two constraints $owner(Bakery) = Bank$ and $owner(Bakery) = Eva$ are mutually exclusive. As a consequence, the claim cannot be *performed*, which indicates that the contract contains a logical inconsistency. The SMT solver returns these two inconsistent constraints as an unsatisfiability core.

Analysis I for the *PayClaim* (Eq. 7) is

$$\Phi_{PayClaim} \equiv owner(Bakery) = Bank \wedge (d_z = -1 \vee \tag{24}$$

$$(28 \leq d_z \Rightarrow owner(Price) = Chris)) \wedge d_z \geq 0. \tag{25}$$

The SPA states that the closing should be performed on day $d_z = 28$. A possible model that an SMT solver computes contains the assignments $d_z = 28$ and $owner(Price) = Chris$. We can conclude that the PayClaim can be *performed*.

Analysis I for the *PretzelWarranty* (Eq. 10) is

$$\Phi_{PretzelWarranty} \equiv owner(Bakery) = Bank \wedge 28 \leq d_g \leq 28 + 14 \wedge \tag{26}$$

$$(d_g = -1 \Rightarrow pretzels = 10000) \wedge d_g = -1. \tag{27}$$

$\Phi_{PretzelWarranty}$ is satisfiable for $d_g = -1$ and $pretzels = 10000$. Thus, Pretzel-Warranty can be *performed*.

The Analysis II is encoded in the constraint Φ^B_{SPA}. It can be used to check whether an execution of the bakery SPA exists.

$$\Phi^B_{SPA} \equiv \phi^B_{SPA} \wedge \phi^B_{soft} \tag{28}$$

The SMT solver that we use in our automated analysis searches for a satisfiable assignment and computes, for instance, a model with the date assignments: $d_u = -1, d_z = 28, d_g = -1, d_n = -1, d_s = -1, d_{ResitutionSeller} = -1, d_{ResitutionPurchaser} = 29$. This means that the bakery SPA can be performed, even though it is inconsistent since the *primary claim TransferClaim* cannot be performed. This exemplifies that inconsistency of an SPA does not mean that it cannot be performed. Furthermore, as the SMT solver confirms, if the bakery is not assigned by way of security but instead *owner*(Bakery) = *Eva* holds, the pretzel bakery SPA would be consistent.

Further Dynamic Analyses

Time Analyses. The *due date* and *limitation* of a claim can refer to other time events in the contract. In the bakery SPA, for instance, the DueDate of Claim1 depends on the assert date of PetzelWarranty. The combination of several *due dates* and *limitations* can result in an inconsistency where the *due date* of a claim is after the claim expired because of its *limitation*. Analysis $\Phi_{Limitation\text{-}c}$ checks this inconsistency for every *claim* $c \in \mathcal{C}$ with a Limitation. For this analysis, we need to substitute $c.\text{DueDate} \le d_c \le c.\text{Limitation}$ with $c.\text{DueDate} \le d_c$.

$$\Phi_{Limitation\text{-}c} \equiv \phi_{SPA}[c.\text{DueDate} \le d_c / c.\text{DueDate} \le d_c \le c.\text{Limitation}] \wedge \tag{29}$$
$$c.Limitation < c.DueDate \tag{30}$$

In the bakery SPA, the claims Claim1 and Claim2 have a Trigger to Pretzel-Warranty and a Limitation of 70 days.

The SMT solver Z3 computes that $\Phi_{Limitation\text{-}}Claim1$ is unsatisfiable, which entails that the time constraints are consistent. For $\Phi_{Limitation\text{-}}Claim2$, Z3 computes a model that, for instance, contains the following assignments: $d_{Claim1} = -1, d_{PretzelWarranty} = 30$ and $d_{Claim2} = 71$. With this execution, Chris asserts PretzelWarranty on day 29, then Eva tries to perform Claim1 for 28 days but fails. In this model, the compensation claim is due after 71 days, even the legal basis of the claim is outdated already after 70 days. This shows that there is an inconsistency in the timing between the due dates and the Limitation of the PretzelWarranty.

6   The *ContractCheck* Tool

An SPA is usually created in natural language and is not formalized. Natural language processing to automatically obtain a semantic model for the SPA is beyond the scope of this paper. Instead, we provide parameterized structured

English text blocks to the user. We provide a formal semantics of these textblocks within the tool *ContractCheck* [CCT22] that we developed to support the SPA formalization and analysis, so that the user is relieved from the need to provide the formalization manually.

The workflow of the tool is depicted in the diagram in Fig. 3. The user only needs to manually select, combine and parameterize the text blocks. A set of blocks represents a contract and is the input into *ContractCheck*. The inconsistency analyses are performed automatically by *ContractCheck*. *ContractCheck* parses the blocks and translates them into an object diagram. The tool extracts the formal representation of the SPA from this object diagram and generates the analysis code as described in Sect. 5, which Z3 then checks for satisfiability. Finally, *ContractCheck* outputs the results.

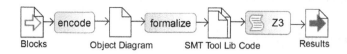

Blocks   Object Diagram   SMT Tool Lib Code   Results

Fig. 3. Tool analysis workflow, modeled using BPMN [Obj14]

ID:	Block1
Text:	The seller $seller.Name hereby sells shares of $shares.Name, with all rights and obligations pertaining thereto, to the Purchaser $purchaser.Name, who accepts such sale.
Object:	"spa:SPA", "seller:Person", "purchaser:Person", "share:Share", "transfer:PrimaryClaim"
Assignment:	"seller.name=Eva", "purchaser.name=Chris", "spa.Seller=$seller", "transfer.Performance=$shares.transfer($purchaser)", ...

Fig. 4. Excerpt from text block encoding of Bakery SPA

SPA Creation by Text Blocks. A user can create and analyze an SPA in the web interface of *ContractCheck*. For every text block, a mapping from text to the elements of the class diagrams in Fig. 1 is defined. A text block consists of a unique *ID*, a natural language *Text* that is parameterized by *Objects* and value *Assignments* to them. Since the variables in Fig. 1 are of a class type, they represent the formalization of an SPA.

A text block example of the bakery SPA in JSON format is given in Fig. 4. The text block with the ID *Block1* defines the essential components of an SPA: A seller, a buyer, the shares to be sold and a price. The $-character in the text indicates the assignment of a variable value, such as the attribute Name for a person. For instance, the assignment to *$seller.name* is currently *Eva*, as defined in the *Assignment* section of the block. A block may reference the variables of another block by using the $-character. For instance, can the property right *prop* assign to its attribute **Property** the value $Block1_share, which references the variable *share* in *Block1*. The library of formalized text blocks can easily be extended. Using the defined text blocks, a user can create an SPA and have it checked automatically using the above devined analyses in *ContractCheck*.

Representation of Results. The results of the analyses are also depicted in the web interface of *ContractCheck*.

The syntactic analysis outputs text messages for each missing legal entity. The result of a dynamic analysis is either a satisfying model, or an unsatisfiability core. *ContractCheck* depicts a satisfying model by a sequence diagram. For the bakery SPA, a computed execution is depicted in Fig. 5. The constraints contained in the unsatisfiability core

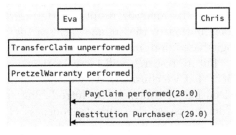

Fig. 5. Bakery SPA execution

are being added due to certain blocks, which *ContractCheck* draws side by side in the web interface, as shown in Fig. 6. The figure shows *Block1* and the block with the chattel mortgage. These are the text blocks that created constraints contained in the unsatisfiability core of $\Phi_{TransferClaim}$. The depicted claims help the user to identify the claims that contradict each other.

Fig. 6. Inconsistence output for the Bakery SPA.

Quantitative Evaluation. We analyzed with *ContractCheck* the bakery SPA and run the dynamic analyses for the claims *TransferClaim, PayClaim, PretzelWarranty, RestitutionSeller RestitutionBuyer, Claim1, Claim2* and the overall contract. The SMT constraint systems that encode the analyses contain at most 21 variables and 63 constraints. The memory demand of the SMT-solver was for every analysis below 18 MB and a model was found within 2 ms. These results show that our analyses encoding is efficient for small SPAs. An analysis of a more realistic size SPA is currently being undertaken.

7   Conclusion

We presented a method for the logical modeling and consistency analysis of legal contracts using the example of an SPA. We provided an ontology for SPAs using UML class diagrams and illustrated the refinement of this ontology to a UML object diagram for a case study. We discussed the logical formalization of the SPA using decidable fragments of first-order logic via SMT solving. We finally introduced the tool *ContractCheck* which allows textual editing of contracts using building blocks, performs the automated derivation of the logical encoding of the contract and the consistency conditions, invokes the Z3 SMT solver, and returns the analysis results to the user. We view this work as an innovative contribution to the enhancement of the quality of complex legal artifacts using logic-based, automated analysis methods.

Future research will increase the scope and complexity of the contract artifacts that we consider. We will also further develop the analysis of the dynamic execution of contracts by introducing state-machine models, among others in order to assess the advantageousness of the contract for different contractual parties in light of the possible dynamic execution scenarios.

Appendix

Text of Bakery SPA

§1 Main Content

1.1 The Seller Anna hereby sells the shares of Bakery AG with all rights and obligations pertaining thereto (including the dividend right for the current financial year), to the Purchaser Chris who accepts such sale. 1.2 The purchaser pays the purchase price 40.000€ to the seller.

1.3 If the transfer is not performed, the Purchaser has the right to withdraw.

1.4 If the pay is not performed, the Seller has the right to withdraw.

§2 The Seller hereby represents and warrants to the Purchaser in the form of an independent guarantee pursuant to Sect. 311 (1) of the German Civil Code and exclusively in accordance with the provisions of this Agreement that the following statements (the "Warranties") are true and correct as of the date of this Agreement and that the warranties set forth in this paragraph will also be true and correct as of the Closing Date:

2.1 The company can produce at least the 10.000 of Pretzels every day (Pretzel Warranty). In case of the breach of the warranty, it needs to be asserted within 14 days.

§3 The Purchaser's rights arising from any inaccuracy of any of the Warranties contained in §1 shall be limited to supplementary performance claims and compensation claims against the Seller, subject to the provisions of

3.1 In case the Pretzel Warranty is not met and then the creditor may demand subsequent performance within 28 business days from the debtor after having transfered the shares.

3.2 In case the Pretzel Warranty is not met and the damage is above 1000€ then a compensation of 100€ per 100 pretzels not baked pretzels is paid within 14 business days.

§4 Claims of §3 expire after 42 business days.

§5 The Bakery AG is transferred by way of security to Bank B.

Text Blocks of Bakery SPA

ID:	Block1
Text:	The seller $seller.Name hereby sells shares of $shares.Name, with all rights and obligations pertaining thereto (including the dividend right for the current financial year), to the Purchaser $purchaser.Name, who accepts such sale.
Object:	"spa:SPA", "seller:Person", "purchaser:Person", "shares:Shares", "transfer:PrimaryClaim"
Assignment:	"purchaser.Name=Chris", "seller.Name=Eva", "spa.Seller=$seller", "spa.Purchaser=$purchaser", "shares.Name=Bakery AG", "spa.Object=$shares", "spa.Claim=$transfer", "spa.Closing=28", "transfer.Performance=Bakery.transfer($purchaser)", "transfer.Debtor=$seller", "transfer.Creditor=$purchaser", "transfer.DueDate=28"

ID:	Block2
Text:	The purchaser pays the purchase price $price.Amount € to the seller on date $payment.DueDate.
Object:	"spa:$SPA", "price:PurchasePrice", "payment:PrimaryClaim"
Assignment:	"spa=$Block1_spa", "spa.Price=$price", "price.Amount=40000", "payment.Debtor=Block1_Purchaser", "spa.Claim=$payment", "payment.Creditor=Block1_Seller", "payment.DueDate=28", "payment.Performance=price.transfer($seller)"

ID:	Block3
Text:	If the $claim is not performed, the $withdraw.Creditor has the right to withdraw.
Object:	"claim:$Claim", "withdraw:RestitutionClaim"
Assignment:	"claim=$Block1_transfer", "withdraw.Name=Restitution Purchaser", "withdraw.Trigger=$claim", "withdraw.Debtor=$claim.Creditor", "withdraw.Creditor=$claim.Debtor"

ID:	Block4
Text:	If the $claim is not performed, the $withdraw.Creditor has the right to withdraw.
Object:	"claim:$Claim", "withdraw:RestitutionClaim"
Assignment:	"claim=$Block2_payment", "withdraw.Name=Restitution Seller", "withdraw.Trigger=$claim", "withdraw.Debtor=$claim.Creditor", "withdraw.Creditor=$claim.Debtor"

ID:	Block5
Text:	The Seller hereby represents and warrants to the Purchaser in the form of an independent guarantee pursuant to Section 311 (1) of the German Civil Code and exclusively in accordance with the provisions of this Agreement that the following statements (the "Warranties) are true and correct as of the date of this Agreement and that the Warranties set forth in this paragraph will also be true and correct as of the Closing Date:

ID:	Block6
Text:	The company can produce at least the $amount of $thing every day. In case of the breach of the warranty, it needs to be asserted within $warranty.Limitation days.
Object:	"warranty:WarrantyClaim", "count:Integer", "amount:Integer", "thing:String"
Assignment:	"warranty.Name=PretzelWarranty", "warranty.Debtor=$Block1_seller", "warranty.DueDate=$Block1_spa.Closing", "thing=Pretzels", "warranty.Creditor=$Block1_purchaser", "warranty.Limitation = +14", "warranty.Performance=(Block6_count=Block6_amount)", "amount=10000", "Block1_spa.Claim=$warranty"

ID:	Block7
Text:	The Purchasers rights arising from any inaccuracy of any of the Warranties contained in $block shall be limited to supplementary performance claims and compensation claims against the Seller, subject to the provisions of
Object:	"claim:$Claim", "per:PerformanceClaim", "block:$Block"
Assignment:	"block=$Block6", "claim=$Block6_warranty", "per.Trigger=$claim", "per.Name=Claim1", "per.DueDate=+28", "per.Debtor=$claim.Debtor", "per.Creditor=$claim.Creditor"

ID:	Block8
Text:	In case the $claim is not met and then the creditor may demand subsequent performance within $per.DueDate business days from the debtor after having transfered the shares.
Object:	"claim:$Claim", "per:PerformanceClaim"
Assignment:	"claim=$Block6_warranty", "per.Name=Claim1", "per.Trigger=$claim", "per.DueDate=+28", "per.Performance=$claim.Performance", "per.Debtor=$claim.Debtor", "per.Creditor=$claim.Creditor"

ID:	Block9
Text:	In case the $claim is not met and the damage is above $comp.Min €then a compensation $claim.Performance is paid within $comp.DueDate days.
Object:	"claim:$Claim", "comp:CompensationClaim"
Assignment:	"claim=$Block6_warranty", "comp.Name=Claim2", "comp.Min=1000", "comp.DueDate=+42", "comp.Trigger=$claim", "comp.Compensation=((Block6_amount-Block6_count)/100)*1000", "comp.Debtor=$claim.Debtor", "comp.Creditor=$claim.Creditor"

ID:	Block10
Text:	Claims in $block expire after $d business days.
Objects:	"claim:$Claim", "d:Date", "block:Block"
Assignment:	"block=Block8", "d=28+42", "${//$block//Claim}.Limitation=$d"

ID:	Block11
Text:	The $object is transferred by way of security to $owner.Name.
Objects:	"owner:Person", "object:$Object", "prop:PropertyRight"
Assignment:	"owner.Name=Bank", "object=$Block1_shares", "prop.Owner=$owner", "prop.Property=$object"'

References

[BBB09] Balbiani, P., Broersen, J.M., Brunel, J.: Decision procedures for a deontic logic modeling temporal inheritance of obligations. Electron. Notes Theor. Comput. Sci. **231**, 69–89 (2009)

[BGB] Bürgerliches Gesetzbuch, German Civil Code

[BK19] Braegelmann, T., Kaulartz, M.: Rechtshandbuch Smart Contracts. C. H. Beck, Munich (2019)

[BM21] Bonifacio, A.L., Della Mura, W.A.: Automatically running experiments on checking multi-party contracts. Artif. Intell. Law **29**(3), 287–310 (2020). https://doi.org/10.1007/s10506-020-09276-y

[BPS10] Boley, H., Paschke, A., Shafiq, O.: RuleML 1.0: the overarching specification of web rules. In: Dean, M., Hall, J., Rotolo, A., Tabet, S. (eds.) RuleML 2010. LNCS, vol. 6403, pp. 162–178. Springer, Heidelberg (2010). https://doi.org/10.1007/978-3-642-16289-3_15

[CCT22] ContractCheck (2022). https://github.com/sen-uni-kn/ContractCheck

[CM07] Castro, P.F., Maibaum, T.S.E.: A complete and compact propositional deontic logic. In: Jones, C.B., Liu, Z., Woodcock, J. (eds.) ICTAC 2007. LNCS, vol. 4711, pp. 109–123. Springer, Heidelberg (2007). https://doi.org/10.1007/978-3-540-75292-9_8

[CM08] Castro, P.F., Maibaum, T.S.E.: A tableaux system for deontic action logic. In: van der Meyden, R., van der Torre, L. (eds.) DEON 2008. LNCS (LNAI), vol. 5076, pp. 34–48. Springer, Heidelberg (2008). https://doi.org/10.1007/978-3-540-70525-3_4

[CS17] Camilleri, J.J., Schneider, G.: Modelling and analysis of normative documents. J. Log. Algebraic Methods Program. **91**, 33–59 (2017)

[dMB08] de Moura, L., Bjørner, N.: Z3: an efficient SMT solver. In: Ramakrishnan, C.R., Rehof, J. (eds.) TACAS 2008. LNCS, vol. 4963, pp. 337–340. Springer, Heidelberg (2008). https://doi.org/10.1007/978-3-540-78800-3_24

[DNS08] Desai, N., Narendra, N.C., Singh, M.P.: Checking correctness of business contracts via commitments. In: AAMAS (2), pp. 787–794. IFAAMAS (2008)

[EGB+01] Engers, T., Gerrits, R., Boekenoogen, M., Glassée, E., Kordelaar, P.: Power: using UML/OCL for modeling legislation - an application report. In: 8th International Conference on Artificial Intelligence and Law, pp. 157–167. Association for Computing Machinery (2001)

[FMS+17] Faciano, C., et al.: Performance improvement on legal model checking. In: ICAIL, pp. 59–68. ACM (2017)

[GMS10] Gorín, D., Mera, S., Schapachnik, F.: Model checking legal documents. In: JURIX, Frontiers in Artificial Intelligence and Applications, vol. 223, pp. 151–154. IOS Press (2010)

[GMS11] Gorín, D., Mera, S., Schapachnik, F.: A software tool for legal drafting. In: FLACOS, EPTCS, vol. 68, pp. 71–86 (2011)

[Gru18] Grupp, M.: Wie baut man einen rechtsautomaten? In: Hartung, M., Bues, M.-M., Halbleib, G. (eds.) Legal Tech, edge number: 1110. C.H. Beck (2018)

[GS22] Gebele, A., Scholz, K.-S. (eds.): Beck'sches Formularbuch Bürgerliches, Handels- und Wirtschaftsrecht, 14th edn. C.H. Beck (2022)

[HKZ12] Hvitved, T., Klaedtke, F., Zalinescu, E.: A trace-based model for multiparty contracts. J. Log. Algebraic Methods Program. **81**(2), 72–98 (2012)

[HLM20] Henglein, F., Larsen, C.K., Murawska, A.: A formally verified static analysis framework for compositional contracts. In: Bernhard, M., et al. (eds.) FC 2020. LNCS, vol. 12063, pp. 599–619. Springer, Cham (2020). https://doi.org/10.1007/978-3-030-54455-3_42

[HS16] Hill, C.A., Solomon, S.D.: Research Handbook on Mergers and Acquisitions. Edward Elgar Publishing, Cheltenham (2016)

[Kab05] Kabilan, V.: Contract workflow model patterns using BPMN. In: EMMSAD, CEUR Workshop Proceedings, vol. 363, pp. 171–182 (2005). CEUR-WS.org

[KJ03] Kabilan, V., Johannesson, P.: Semantic representation of contract knowledge using multi tier ontology. In: Cruz, I.F. Kashyap, V., Decker, S., Eckstein, R. (eds.) Proceedings of SWDB 2003, The First International Workshop on Semantic Web and Databases, Co-Located with VLDB 2003, Humboldt-Universität, Berlin, Germany, 7–8 September 2003, pp. 395–414 (2003)

[KS16] Kroening, D., Strichman, O.: Decision Procedures - An Algorithmic Point of View. Texts in Theoretical Computer Science. An EATCS Series, 2nd edn. Springer, Heidelberg (2016). https://doi.org/10.1007/978-3-540-74105-3

[MB15] Mura, W.A.D., Bonifácio, A.L.: Devising a conflict detection method for multi-party contracts. In: SCCC, pp. 1–6. IEEE (2015)

[MDCS10] Martínez, E., Díaz, G., Cambronero, M.-E., Schneider, G.: A model for visual specification of e-contracts. In: IEEE SCC, pp. 1–8. IEEE Computer Society (2010)

[MKK14] Madaan, N., Radha Krishna, P., Karlapalem, K.: Consistency detection in e-contract documents. In: ICEGOV, pp. 267–274. ACM (2014)

[MS22a] Meyer-Sparenberg, W.: Unternehmenskaufvertrag (gmbh-anteile) - käuferfreundlich. In: Gebele, A., Scholz, K.-S. (eds.) Beck'sches Formularbuch Bürgerliches, Handels- und Wirtschaftsrecht. C.H. Beck (2022)

[MS22b] Meyer-Sparenberg, W.: Unternehmenskaufvertrag (gmbh-anteile) - verkäuferfreundlich. In: Gebele, A., Scholz, K.-S. (eds.) Beck'sches Formularbuch Bürgerliches, Handels- und Wirtschaftsrecht. C.H. Beck (2022)

[MSJ22] Meyer-Sparenberg, W., Jäckle, C. (eds.): Beck'sches M&A-Handbuch: Planung, Gestaltung, Sonderformen, regulatorische Rahmenbedingungen und Streitbeilegung bei Mergers & Acquisitions, 2nd edn. C.H. Beck (2022)

[OAS21] OASIS Standard: LegalRuleML, version 1.0 (2021). https://docs.oasis-open.org/legalruleml/legalruleml-core-spec/v1.0/os/legalruleml-core-spec-v1.0-os.pdf

[Obj14] Object Management Group: Business Process Model and Notation 2014. https://www.omg.org/spec/BPMN

[Obj17] Object Management Group: Unified Modelling Language, Specification 2.5.1 (2017). http://www.omg.org/spec/UML

[PF19]   Boris, P.: Paal and Martin Fries. Smart Contracts, Mohr Siebeck (2019)
[Pfi22]   Pfisterer, B.: Share deal. In: Weise, S., Krauß, H.-F. (eds.) Beck'sche Online-Formulare. C.H. Beck (2022)
[PGR+11] Palmirani, M., Governatori, G., Rotolo, A., Tabet, S., Boley, H., Paschke, A.: LegalRuleML: XML-based rules and norms. In: Olken, F., Palmirani, M., Sottara, D. (eds.) RuleML 2011. LNCS, vol. 7018, pp. 298–312. Springer, Heidelberg (2011). https://doi.org/10.1007/978-3-642-24908-2_30
[PPS07] Pace, G., Prisacariu, C., Schneider, G.: Model checking contracts – a case study. In: Namjoshi, K.S., Yoneda, T., Higashino, T., Okamura, Y. (eds.) ATVA 2007. LNCS, vol. 4762, pp. 82–97. Springer, Heidelberg (2007). https://doi.org/10.1007/978-3-540-75596-8_8
[PS07]   Prisacariu, C., Schneider, G.: A formal language for electronic contracts. In: Bonsangue, M.M., Johnsen, E.B. (eds.) FMOODS 2007. LNCS, vol. 4468, pp. 174–189. Springer, Heidelberg (2007). https://doi.org/10.1007/978-3-540-72952-5_11
[PS12]   Prisacariu, C., Schneider, G.: A dynamic deontic logic for complex contracts. J. Log. Algebraic Methods Program. 81(4), 458–490 (2012)
[Sei18a] Seibt, C.H. (ed.): Beck'sches Formularbuch Mergers & Acquisitions, 3rd edn. C.H. Beck (2018)
[Sei18b] Seibt, C.H.: GmbH-Anteilskaufvertrag - ausführlich, käuferfreundlich. In: Beck'sches Formularbuch Mergers & Acquisitions, pp. 324–456. C.H. Beck (2018)
[Sei18c] Seibt, C.H.: Gmbh-anteilskaufvertrag - ausführlich, verkäuferfreundlich, deutsch. In: Beck'sches Formularbuch Mergers & Acquisitions, pp. 233–323. C.H. Beck, München (2018)
[Sei18d] Seibt, C.H.: Gmbh-anteilskaufvertrag - knapp, ausgewogen. In: Beck'sches Formularbuch Mergers & Acquisitions, pp. 515–525. C.H. Beck (2018)
[Sei18e] Seibt, C.H.: Gmbh-anteilskaufvertrag - knapp, verkäuferfreundlich. In: Beck'sches Formularbuch Mergers & Acquisitions, pp. 457–514. C.H. Beck (2018)
[vH20a] von Hoyenberg, P.: Share deal (GmbH, fester kaufpreis). In: Weipert, L., Arnhold, P., Baltus, M. (eds.) Münchener Vertragshandbuch, pp. 228–233. C.H. Beck (2020)
[vH20b] von Hoyenberg, P.: Share deal (GmbH, mit stichtagsbilanzierung). In: Weipert, L., Arnhold, P., Baltus, M. (eds.) Münchener Vertragshandbuch, Beck-online Bücher, pp. 203–227. C.H. Beck (2020)
[VW51]   Wright, G.H.V.: Deontic logic. Mind 60(237), 1–15 (1951)
[WAB20] Weipert, L., Arnhold, P., Baltus, M. (eds.): Münchener Vertragshandbuch: Band 2, 8th edn. C.H. Beck (2020)
[Wil22]   Wilhelmi, R.: §453. In: Gsell, B., Krüger, W., Lorenz, S., Reymann, C. (eds.) Beck'scher Online Großkommentar, edge note: 744–782. C.H. Beck (2022)
[WK22]   Weise, S., Krauß, H.-F. (eds.): Beck'sche Online-Formulare: Vertrag. C.H. Beck (2022)
[WS05]   Wan, F., Singh, M.P.: Formalizing and achieving multiparty agreements via commitments. In: AAMAS, pp. 770–777. ACM (2005)

Monitoring Cyber-Physical Systems Using a Tiny Twin to Prevent Cyber-Attacks

Fereidoun Moradi[1]([envelope]), Maryam Bagheri[2], Hanieh Rahmati[3], Hamed Yazdi[4], Sara Abbaspour Asadollah[1], and Marjan Sirjani[1]

[1] School of Innovation, Design and Engineering, Mälardalen University, Västerås, Sweden
{fereidoun.moradi,sara.abbaspour,marjan.sirjani}@mdu.se
[2] Tehran Institute for Advanced Studies, Khatam University, Tehran, Iran
mbagheri@ce.sharif.edu
[3] University of Tehran, Tehran, Iran
rahmati_hanie@ut.ac.ir
[4] Chavoosh ICT, Isfahan, Iran
h.yazdi@chavoosh.com

Abstract. We propose a method to detect attacks on sensors and controllers in cyber-physical systems. We develop a monitor that uses an abstract digital twin, Tiny Twin, to detect false sensor data and faulty control commands. The Tiny Twin is a state transition system that represents the observable behavior of the system from the monitor point of view. At runtime, the monitor observes the sensor data and the control commands, and checks whether the observed data and commands are consistent with the state transitions in the Tiny Twin. The monitor produces an alarm when an inconsistency is detected. We model the components of the system and the physical processes in the Rebeca modeling language and use its model checker to generate the state space. The Tiny Twin is built automatically by reducing the state space, keeping the observable behavior of the system, and preserving the trace equivalence. We demonstrate the method and evaluate it in detecting attacks using a temperature control system.

Keywords: Monitoring · Model checking · Abstraction · Cyber-physical systems · Attack detection and prevention · Cyber-security

1 Introduction

Cyber-Physical Systems (CPSs) are mostly safety-critical systems that integrate physical processes in the industrial plants (e.g., thermal power plants or smart water treatment plants) with sensors, actuators and controller components. Since these components are integrated via a communication network (usually wireless), a CPS is vulnerable to malicious cyber-attacks that may cause catastrophic damage to the physical infrastructure and processes. Cyber-attacks may be performed over a significant number of attack points and in a coordinated way. So, detecting and preventing attacks in CPSs are of significant importance.

O. Legunsen and G. Rosu (Eds.): SPIN 2022, LNCS 13255, pp. 24–43, 2022.
https://doi.org/10.1007/978-3-031-15077-7_2

Intrusion Detection Systems (IDSs) are deployed in communication networks to defend the system against cyber-attacks. Regular IDSs cannot easily catch complex attacks. They need to be equipped with complicated logic, based on human (safety and security engineers) reasoning [26]. In rule-based IDSs [26], a set of properties that are extracted from the system design specification are considered as a rule-set to detect attacks. Indeed, if an IDS finds a deviation between the observed packets in the network and the defined rules, it produces an alarm and takes a predefined action such as dropping the packets. The key challenge is the effort required to specify the correct system behavior as rules.

In this paper, we propose a method to detect cyber-attacks on sensors and controllers of a CPS. We model the system components, the progress of time and the interactions between components, and then abstract the model based on the observable behavior of the system. The observable behavior is the set of events that can be observed (sensor data) and controlled (control commands) by the controllers. We develop a monitor module as an IDS that employs the created abstract model to detect the cyber-attacks. The monitor walks over the abstract model at runtime to check whether the behavior of the system is consistent with the model generated at design time. Our approach is similar to using MAPE-K architecture and models@runtime that support the monitoring and adaptation at runtime [6]. Digital Twins [10] are used as digital representation of the system to advance the system monitoring. We call our abstract model a Tiny Twin as it resembles an abstract version of a Digital Twin, and we use it as models@runtime in our method.

To build the Tiny Twin, we start with developing a Timed Rebeca model [32] of the system, and create the state space using a model checker tool. The state space is often huge and usually contains state transitions reflecting the events that are not observable for the controllers, therefore it cannot be directly used in the monitoring. We then reduce the state space using our abstraction tool while preserving the trace equivalence between the original transition system and its abstracted version. In the abstraction process, we consider the observable actions to be receiving sensor data by the controllers, and sending commands to the actuators. These actions are related to the labels of the corresponding transitions in the state space. Using our abstraction tool, the state variables in the controller that store the receiving sensor data as well as the state variables in the actuators that reflect the changes on the state of the actuators will stay observable.

There is a rich literature on using formal models to detect and prevent cyber-attacks on CPSs (e.g., [5,7,11,14,21,34]). For instance, authors in [21] define the behavior of the system using an automaton and employ it to detect man-in-the-middle attacks. Authors in [5] build automaton models, determine the set of unsafe system states, and check whether the system under attacks reaches these states. Authors in [19] model the system as finite state machines and verify the system behavior at runtime. In our work, we integrate the system monitoring with a state space model to detect attacks. The advantage of our method is that the model used by the monitor (the Tiny Twin) is automatically derived from the Timed Rebeca model [32], not purely a specification, and then reduced based on the observable state transitions. To simulate and check the attack detection process, the Timed Rebeca model is mapped to an executable code in Lingua Franca [23]. The mapping does not require much effort because both languages use the same actor-based semantics. Building an actor-based model based on the specification and requirements, then model check and debug it, can reveal the inconsistencies and ambiguities in the specification. Going all the way to the executable code and apply the necessary revisions, helps in reflecting back the necessary details in the model.

In different situations, we may decide differently, for example keeping the signals passed between different controllers as the observable events in the abstract state transition system of a distributed system. We also include logical time in the Tiny Twin model which is related to the physical time with a limited amount of deviation (guaranteed by Lingua Franca framework). Some of the meta-rules regarding the system can be captured in the Tiny Twin. For example, the fact that "seeing extreme changes in the temperature in a short period of time is not possible" can be captured in the way we model the environment, and then reflected in the state space and its abstracted version (Tiny Twin).

Contribution. We develop an abstraction tool that 1) reduces the state transition system of a CPS (i.e., the state space which is the output of a model checker tool) based on the observable behavior (a list provided by the modeler). 2) We propose and implement a monitor algorithm that uses the Tiny Twin to detect cyber-attacks. 3) We develop a temperature control system case study in Lingua Franca [23]. 4) We evaluate the method by simulating several attacks and show how the monitor can catch them, and how the Tiny Twin model helps.

Outline. We give an overview of our method in Sect. 2. We introduce Timed Rebeca and Lingua Franca in Sect. 3. We present our abstraction tool and explain our monitor algorithm in Sect. 4. In Sect. 5, we describe a temperature control system and evaluate our method by implementing the monitor module in Lingua Franca. Section 6 covers the related works. The conclusion and future directions of this work are discussed in Sect. 7.

2   Overview of Our Approach

The overview of our approach is shown in Fig. 1. In [28], we explained our method to develop the model of a CPS in Timed Rebeca [32] and use the Afra model checker [1] to verify the model. In [28], it is shown that how entities of a CPS, i.e., sensors, actuators, controllers, and physical plant are modeled as actors, and interactions between them are modeled as messages passed between the actors. In this paper, we develop an abstraction tool (part (A) in Fig. 1) that reduces the state space of the Timed Rebeca model (generated by Afra model checker tool) to create the Tiny Twin based on the observable behavior for the controllers in the system. The state space of a Timed Rebeca model is a state transition system [33], in which a state represents a particular configuration of the system and includes values of state variables of the actors, and a transition represents triggering of an event (handling a message received by an actor) or progressing the logical time of the model. We develop a monitor module that

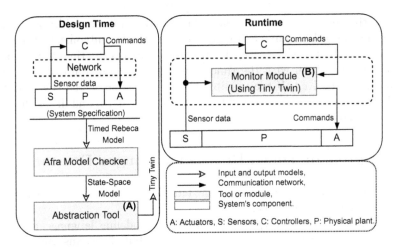

Fig. 1. The overview of our approach. The state space of the Timed Rebeca model of a CPS is generated by the Afra model checker and is reduced by our abstraction tool (see Sect. 4.1). The result is a Tiny Twin that is used by our monitor (see Sect. 4.2) to detect the attacks. The monitor executes together with the system at runtime.

uses the created Tiny Twin to track the order and the timing of events (part (B) in Fig. 1). In safety-critical systems, an isolated and trusted hardware component is leveraged to enhance the security of the complete system [27]. We implement our monitor algorithm as a module that can run on an isolated platform with hardware security support [2].

We implement our monitor module in Lingua Franca [23] that is a language for programming CPSs. In principle, the Lingua Franca code can connect to the physical plant and the controller through the input/output communication channels in the actual system. In this paper, we use Lingua Franca to simulate the system at runtime and evaluate the detection capability of our method by defining compromised components. As shown in Fig. 1, the monitor module observes the sensor data entering the controller, and the control commands leaving to the actuators. We rely on the logical time provided in Lingua Franca when we compare the system execution time with the time represented in the Tiny Twin. Lingua Franca relates logical time to physical time based on the approach introduced in Ptides/Spanner design [8,35]. In the Lingua Franca program we have a network of actors and a scheduler handles the order of events. The scheduler watches the local clock of each actor and hold off processing the message until its measurement of physical time exceeds a threshold. This threshold is defined to align two timelines, logical time and physical time [22].

The Tiny Twin defines the observable behavior of the system in the absence of an attack and contains the order and the time at which the sensor data and control commands are communicated. Transitions in Tiny Twin are tagged by a label that indicates an action or the progress of time. To detect an attack, the monitor receives the sensors data and the control commands at runtime, compares the sensors data with the values of the state variables and checks whether the control commands are consistent with the outgoing transitions in the Tiny Twin. If this is the case, the monitor compares the time of the current state of the Tiny Twin with the time at which the sensor data or the control commands are received. If the monitor observes an unexpected sensor data or control command at an unexpected time, it raises an alarm and drops the faulty control command.

3   Background: Timed Rebeca and Lingua Franca

In this section, we provide an overview on Timed Rebeca and describe the Lingua Franca programming language.

Timed Rebeca. Rebeca [31] is an actor-based modeling language for modeling and formal verification of concurrent and distributed systems. Actors, called *rebecs*, are instances of *reactive classes* and communicate via asynchronous message passing, which is non-blocking for both sender and receiver. Timed Rebeca as an extension of Rebeca has a notion of logical time that is a global time synchronized between all actors. Each actor has a set of variables. Besides, it has a message bag to store the received messages along with their arrival times and their deadlines. The actor takes a message with the least arrival time from its bag and executes the corresponding method that is called *message server*. The actor can change values of its variables and send messages to its *known actors* while executing a message server. In Timed Rebeca, the primitives *delay* and *after* are used to model the progress of time while executing a method. The generated state space of the Timed Rebeca model contains two or more outgoing transitions at the same time for each state in which the value of variables are nondeterministically changed.

Timed Rebeca is supported by the Afra model checker tool [1]. Afra generates the state transition system (i.e., state space model) of the model where states contain values of variables of actors along with the logical time, and transitions represent progressing the logical time of the model or taking a message from an actor's bag and executing the corresponding method [16,30]. The transition in the latter case is labeled with the name of the executed message server. The transition in the first case is labeled with the amount of time progress and is called a timed transition. Note that a model has an unbounded state space when the logical time goes to infinite. In [16], the authors propose an approach, called Shift Equivalence Relation, to make the state space of a Timed Rebeca model bounded, where possible. Afra implements this approach to generate the finite state space of the model.

Lingua Franca. Lingua Franca is a meta language based on the Reactor model for programming CPSs [22,24]. A Reactor model is a collection of *reactors*. A reactor has one or more routines that are called *reactions*. Reactions define the functionality of the reactor, and have access to a *state* shared with other reactions, but only within the same reactor. Reactors have named (and typed) *ports* that allow them to be connected to other reactors. Two reactors can communicate if an *output* port of a reactor is connected to an *input* port of the other reactor. The usage of *ports* establishes a clean separation between the functionality and composition of reactors; a reactor only references its own ports. Reactions are similar to the message handlers in the actor model [12], except rather than responding to messages, reactions are triggered by discrete events and may also produce them. An event relates a value to a *tag* that represents the logical time at which the value is present. An event produced by one reactor is only observed by other reactors that are connected to the port on which the event is produced. Events arrive at input ports, and reactions produce events via output ports.

In Lingua Franca, the logical time does not advance during a reaction. A reactor can have one or more *timers*. Timers are like ports that can trigger reactions. A timer has the form *timer name(offset, period)* that once triggers at the time shown by *offset* (if *offset* is zero, then timer triggers at the start time of the execution), and then triggers every *period*. Lingua Franca has a built-in type for specifying time intervals. A time interval consists of an integer value accompanied with a time unit (e.g., *sec* for seconds or *msec* for milliseconds). Timers are used for specifying periodic tasks, which are very common in embedded computing. Each Lingua Franca program contains a *main reactor* that is an entry point for the execution of the code.

4   Abstraction Tool and Monitor Algorithm

In this section, we first present our developed abstraction tool, which reduces the state space of a Timed Rebeca model based on the observable behavior for the controllers in the system and creates the Tiny Twin. Then, we explain how our monitor detects attacks by checking the consistency between the observed sensor data and control commands and the state transitions in the Tiny Twin.

4.1   Abstraction Tool

Our abstraction method is implemented in a tool[1] by considering the reduction algorithm proposed by Jansen et al. [13]. In order to create an abstract model of a Timed Rebeca model, the modeler provides the tool a list of variables whose values are changed by the observable actions. The tool reduces the state space of a Timed Rebeca model based on the given list. It is applied to the original state space, preserves observable traces (i.e., sequences of actions that represent the observable behavior) where it iteratively refines indistinguishable states, i.e., the classes containing equivalent states, while hides transitions that are called silent transitions. The abstract and original models of the system show the same observable behavior when hiding silent transitions. It begins at the initial state and traverses the outgoing transitions one by one (i.e., BFS graph search). It merges a pair states into an equivalence class if they have the same values for the given variables (the time variable in each state is preserved in the abstraction

---

[1] https://github.com/fereidoun-moradi/Abstraction-tool.

process). All transitions that modify the given variables in the list stay observable and other transitions that do not change the values of these variables become silent transitions.

Example. Figure 2 illustrates how the abstraction tool performs on an example. We depict the transition system of a Timed Rebeca model with the set of variables $\{s, w, h\}$ in Fig. 2(a). We show the values of variables in each state and use $time+ = 10$ to denote that the logical time progresses by 10 units of time over a transition. The transitions that are not timed transitions are labeled with a label of $\{getsense, activate\_h, heating, switchoff\}$. The notation $(a \gg b)$ on each transitions denotes that the source state has the time value a (the value of variable now), which is shifted by the value b and becomes the time value at the leading state. In this system, we may want to check properties such as "the command $activate\_h$ will be issued if $s = 20$ and $h = false$" and "the command $switchoff$ will be issued in less than 10 units of time if $s = 20$ and $h = true$". Two paths $\{activate\_h\}$ and $\{heating, getsense^*, switchoff\}$, respectively, from state $S3$ to state $S4$ and from state $S4$ to state $S2$, satisfy these properties. The action $heating$ is an unobservable action. The tool receives $V = \{s, h\}$ to reduce the transition system of Fig. 2(a). These state variables reflect the changes occur in the system after the observable actions $\{getsense, switchoff\}$ are executed. The equivalence classes created by the tool and the resulting abstract model is shown in Fig. 2(b). Our abstraction tool names each state of Fig. 2(b) with GSi that corresponds to the class e_class_i. For instance, e_class_6 is replaced with $GS6$. Two paths are preserved in the abstract transition system, respectively, from class $GS2$ to class $GS3$ and from $GS3$ to class $GS1$.

4.2 Monitor Algorithm

Algorithm 1 shows the pseudo-code of our *monitor* algorithm. The algorithm observes the sensor data and the control commands transmitted in the network and decides to drop or pass the control commands to the actuators. Suppose that p number of sensors send the sensed data $y = \{y_1, ..., y_p\}$ to the controller. The time k indicates a time value which is derived using Lingua Franca code and it is advanced based on the logical timeline defined in the language. The commands $u = \{u_1, ..., u_n\}$ are issued by the controller for n actuators to maintain the physical plant in the certain desirable state. The sensor data are all within a defined range, i.e., $\forall i \in [1, p], y_i \in [y_i^{min}, y_i^{max}]$.

The algorithm gets (S, T) as an input, where S and T are respectively the sets of states and transitions in the Tiny Twin. The algorithm returns commands u or produces an *alarm*. The monitor starts its observation when the system executes. Upon receiving sensor data y and/or commands u, the algorithm compares y and v (the values stored in the state variables of the model and correspond to the sensors, i.e., $v = \{v_1, v_2..., v_p\}$) at the current state s in the Tiny Twin. If the algorithm finds no differences between them, it proceeds and checks whether the commands u are consistent with the corresponding transitions in the model. If

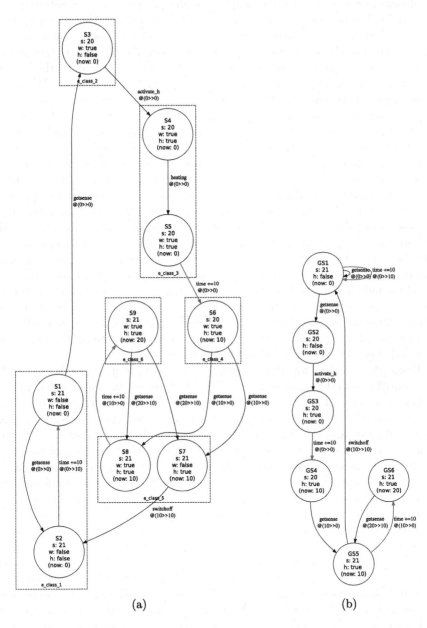

(a)   (b)

Fig. 2. (a) The transition system of an example Timed Rebeca model with the equivalence classes created by the abstraction tool. (b) The Tiny Twin of the transition system is depicted in Fig. 2.(a).

this is the case, the algorithm sends the commands u to the actuators. Otherwise, the algorithm produces an alarm and terminates the process of monitoring.

In the following, we explain the details of the algorithm. The algorithm sets the current state of the system to the initial state of the model that is $s_0 \in S$ (line 2). The algorithm begins its iteration by observing the sensor data y and the commands u (line 3). We use the function $getTime$ to obtain the logical time of the current state and put it in the time variable x (line 4). The algorithm checks the branching states if it observes the sensor data y (lines 6-7). The function $traverse$ returns the next state by traversing the given transitions (line 8). The function $cmpSensorData$ compares the data y and v and the function $cmpTimes$ compares the time k (at which y are observed) with the time x in the model (line 9). If y and v are the same and are observed at time x (the order in which the sensor data is observed is consistent with the order of transitions in the model), the algorithm proceeds and repeats the monitoring process (lines 10). Otherwise, the algorithm returns an alarm (line 11) and terminates the process of monitoring. The algorithm then compares the commands u with the corresponding transitions in the model at time x (line 12). This comparison is performed by the functions $checkTransitions$ and $cmpTimes$ (line 13). The function $checkTransitions$ extracts labels of the outgoing transitions of the current state and checks whether the commands are equal to these labels. If this is the case, the algorithm uses the function $traverse$ to reach the next state and returns the commands u (lines 14-15). Otherwise, it drops the commands and produces an $alarm$ (lines 17-18). The current state is updated if the time k is advanced (lines 19). The algorithm repeats its monitoring.

Example. Let the Tiny Twin of Fig. 2(b) be the input model of Algorithm 1. The algorithm sets the current state to $GS1$. It observes the sensed value 20 and the control command $activate\_h$ at time k, i.e. $k = 0$. The monitor traverses the transition $getSense$ and sets $GS2$ as the current state. The monitor compares the sensed value and the value of the state variable in the current state. If the values are the same and the logical time of the current state is equal to k, i.e. $x = 0$, the monitor proceeds and checks the label of the outgoing transition. It compares the command and the $activate\_h$ label. Since the command and the label are the same, the monitor traverses the outgoing transition and sets the current state to $GS3$. The current state has an outgoing timed transition, the monitor repeats its monitoring and waits to observe the logical time k advances. The monitor observes a new sensed value 21 and control command $switchoff$ at time $k = 10$. The monitor traverses the timed transition and sets the current state to $GS4$. It traverses $getSense$ transition and compares the sensed value and the value of the state variable. It checks whether the values are the same and the logical time of the current state is equal to k, i.e. $x = 10$. The monitor proceeds and checks the label of the outgoing transition, i.e., $switchoff$ label. Since the command and the label are the same, the monitor traverses the outgoing transition $switchoff$ and sets the current state to $GS1$. The monitor repeats the monitoring process. In $GS5$, if the monitor observes a new sensed value 21 at time $k = 20$, without observing a control command, it traverses the timed tran-

---

Algorithm 1: Monitor algorithm

Input: An abstract state space (S, T)
Output: Commands u, or an *alarm*
1 **begin**
2 $\quad$ $s \leftarrow s_0 \in S$;
3 $\quad$ **while** *observes y, u or time k* **do**
4 $\quad\quad$ $x \leftarrow getTime(s)$;
5 $\quad\quad$ **if** y *is present* **then**
6 $\quad\quad\quad$ $s' \leftarrow s$;
7 $\quad\quad\quad$ **for** *each leading state of s'* **do**
8 $\quad\quad\quad\quad$ $s \leftarrow traverse(y, s', S, T)$;
9 $\quad\quad\quad\quad$ **if** $cmpSensorData(y, v)$ *and* $cmpTimes(k, x)$ **then**
10 $\quad\quad\quad\quad\quad$ **break**;
11 $\quad\quad\quad$ **return** *alarm*;
12 $\quad\quad$ **if** u *is present* **then**
13 $\quad\quad\quad$ **if** $checkTransitions(u, s, S, T)$ *and* $cmpTimes(k, x)$ **then**
14 $\quad\quad\quad\quad$ $s \leftarrow traverse(u, s, S, T)$;
15 $\quad\quad\quad\quad$ **return** u;
16 $\quad\quad\quad$ **else**
17 $\quad\quad\quad\quad$ $drops(u)$;
18 $\quad\quad\quad\quad$ **return** *alarm*;
19 $\quad\quad$ $s \leftarrow timeProgress(s, S, T)$;

---

sition and sets the current state to $GS6$. It then traverses *getSense* transition and sets the current state to $GS5$. The monitor updates the logical time with the time value in $GS5$ and the amount of time progress, i.e., $k = 20$ (i.e., shift equivalence relation between states $GS6$ and $GS5$). It compares the sensed value and the value of the state variable in $GS5$. The monitor repeats the same process by observing the sensor data or control commands. The monitor produces an alarm and terminates the monitoring process if it observes a sensed value or a control command inconsistent with the model. It returns an alarm containing a tuple $[k, y^i, u^d, v_1, v_2, ..., v_w]$ where k is a time value showing at which time during system execution an inconsistency is identified, y^i is the inconsistent sensor data, u^d is the dropped control command and v_i are values of state variables in the state GSi where the *monitor* terminated the system execution.

5 Case Study: A Temperature Control System

We evaluate the applicability of our method in detecting and preventing cyber-attacks using a temperature control system. The goal of attacks is to change the temperature out of the desired range or cause damage on the physical infrastructure (i.e., the heating and cooling unit). We assume that attackers can send false sensor data or compromise the controller to alter the commands issued by the controller. We developed the Timed Rebeca model of the temperature control system (see Listing 1(a)) in which four reactive classes are defined to specify the system components and the physical process. We use the Afra model checker to produce the state space of the developed Timed Rebeca model and exploit our abstraction tool to generate the Tiny Twin. We implement both the system and the monitor module in Lingua Franca. We use the mapping between Timed Rebeca and Lingua Franca [33] to write a Lingua Franca code of the system (see Listing 1(b)). This code can be executed on a single core, on multiple cores, or on separate processors connected via a network. In this case study, we configure the number of threads to 1 since the code is mapped form a Rebeca model in which each actor has a single thread of execution. The complete codes of the system and the monitor are available on GitHub[2].

The temperature control system is responsible for maintaining the temperature of a room at a desired range (i.e., the values between 21 and 23). This system includes a sensor, a hc_unit (heating and cooling unit) as an actuator, and a controller (lines 46,56, and 7 in Listing 1(a)). The controller receives sensor data from the sensor and transmits the activate_c, activate_h or switch off command to the hc_unit to respectively activate the cooling or heating process, or switch the heating/cooling process off (lines 10-23). Assume that there is a window inside the room (line 30) and the outside air blows inside when the window is open (line 33). The controller does not know whether the window is open or closed but can activate the heating/cooling process based on the sensed temperature value. The cooling process is activated if the temperature value is higher than the desired range (e.g., the value 24) (line 21). The heating process is activated if the temperature value is lower than the desired range (e.g., the value 20) (line 17). The heating/cooling process is switched off if the temperature value is regulated to the desired range. The physical process is temperature regulation (lines 37-44), and the desired state is a specific range for the temperature. We assume that the temperature of the room is within the desired range at the beginning (i.e., the value 22) (line 1).

Similar to the Timed Rebeca model of the system, the Lingua Franca code implements all components of the system (Listing 1(b)). The input port *getSense* in the reactor *controller* (line 3) is defined to get a sensor value, and three output ports *activate_h*, *activate_c*, and *switchoff* (lines 4-6) are defined to send values as commands to the *hc_unit*. We set the value of *activate_h* to 1 to trigger the heating (line 18), and the value of *switchoff* to 0 to trigger the switch off in the *hc_unit* (line 14). The main reactor instantiates the components and binds their input and output ports to connect the components together (line 67). For example, we connect the output port *out* in the reactor *sensor* to the input port *getSense* in the reactor *controller* (line 70). This way, the new temperature value is transferred from the sensor to the controller. In the main reactor, the use of *after* indicates that a value reaches the input port of the reactor *controller* after 10 units of time (line 70). Note that we use a time function to measure the logical time elapsed since the code started to run (line 37).

---

[2] https://github.com/fereidoun-moradi/RoomTemp.

```
1   env int desiredValue = 22; //environment variables
2   env int timingInterval = 10;
3   reactiveclass Controller(8){
4     knownrebecs{ HC_Unit hc_unit; Sensor sensor;}
5     statevars{ int sensedValue;
6       boolean heating; boolean cooling;}
7     Controller(){
8       sensedValue = desiredValue;
9       heating = false; cooling = false;}
10    msgsrv getSense(int temp){
11      sensedValue = temp;
12      if (temp <= 23 && temp >= 21) { //desired range
13        if (heating == true || cooling == true) {
14          hc_unit.switchoff();
15          heating = false; cooling = false;
16        } else { sensor.start();}
17      } else if (temp < 21) {
18        if (heating == false) { //control command
19          hc_unit.activate_h(); heating = true;
20        } else  { sensor.sense(sensedValue); }
21      } else if (temp > 23) {
22        //...
23      }
24  }
25  reactiveclass Room(8){
26    knownrebecs{ Sensor sensor;}
27    statevars{ int temperature; int outside_air_blowing; }
28    Room(){
29      temperature = 22; //initial value
30      outside_air_blowing = 0; //window is closed
31    }
32    msgsrv status() { //nondeterministic assignment
33      outside_air_blowing = ?(1,0,-1);
34      temperature = temperature - outside_air_blowing;
35      sensor.sense(temperature);
36    }
37    msgsrv heating() {
38      temperature = temperature + 1;
39      self.status();
40    }
41    msgsrv cooling() {
42      temperature = temperature - 1;
43      self.status();
44    }
45  }
46  reactiveclass Sensor(8){
47    knownrebecs{ Room room; Controller controller;}
48    Sensor(){ self.start();}
49    msgsrv start(){
50      room.status();
51    }
52    msgsrv sense(int temp) { //sensing intervals
53      controller.getSense(temp) after(timingInterval);
54    }
55  }
56  reactiveclass HC_Unit(8){
57    knownrebecs{ Room room;}
58    statevars{
59      boolean heater_on;
60      boolean cooler_on;}
61    HC_Unit() { heater_on = false; cooler_on = false;}
62    msgsrv activate_h() {
63      heater_on = true; cooler_on = false;
64      room.heating(); //heating
65    }
66    msgsrv activate_c(){
67      cooler_on = true; heater_on = false;
68      room.cooling(); //cooling
69    }
70    //...
71  }
72  main{
73    Room room(sensor):();
74    Controller controller(hc_unit,sensor):();
75    Sensor sensor(room,controller):();
76    HC_Unit hc_unit(room):();
77  }
```

(a) Timed Rebeca model

```
1   target Cpp {fast: false, threads: 1};
2   reactor Controller { //input and output ports
3     input getSense:int;
4     output activate_h:int;
5     output activate_c:int;
6     output switchoff:int;
7     state heating:bool(false);
8     state cooling:bool(false);
9     reaction(getSense) ->
10    activate_c, activate_h, switchoff {=
11    if(*getSense.get() <= 23 &&
12          *getSense.get() >= 21){
13      if(heating == true || cooling == true) {
14        switchoff.set(0);
15        heating = false; cooling = false;}
16    } else if(*getSense.get() < 21){
17      if(heating == false){
18        activate_h.set(1); heating = true;
19      } else { activate_h.set(0); }
20    } else if(*getSense.get() > 23) {
21      //...
22    }
23    =}
24  }
25  reactor Room {
26    input cooling:int;
27    input heating:int;
28    input status:int;
29    output sensedValue:int;
30    state heating:int(22);
31    state outside_air_blowing:int(0);
32    reaction(status) -> sensedValue {=
33      outside_air_blowing = rand() % 3 + (-1);
34      temperature =
35          temperature - outside_air_blowing;
36      sensedValue.set(temperature);
37      auto elapsed_time =
38          get_elapsed_logical_time();
39    =}
40    reaction(heating) {=
41      temperature = temperature + *heating.get(); =}
42    reaction(cooling) {= //...
43    =}
44  }
45  reactor Sensor {
46    input sensedValue:int;
47    output out:int;
48    output sense:int;
49    timer start(0, 1 sec);
50    reaction(start) -> sensedValue {=
51      sense.set(1); =}
52    reaction(sensedValue) -> out {=
53      out.set(sensedValue.get());=}
54  }
55  reactor HC_Unit {
56    input activate_h:int;
57    input activate_c:int;
58    input switchoff:int;
59    output heating:int;
60    output cooling:int;
61    reaction(activate_h) -> heating {=
62      if (*activate_h.get() == 0){
63        heating.set(0);
64      } else { heating.set(1); }
65    =} //...
66  }
67  main reactor RoomTemp {
68    //...
69    room.sensedValue -> sensor.sensedValue;
70    sensor.out -> controller.getSense  after 10 sec;
71    sensor.sense -> room.status;
72    unit.heating -> room.heating;
73    unit.cooling -> room.cooling;
74    controller.activate_h -> unit.activate_h;
75    controller.activate_c -> unit.activate_c;
76    controller.switchoff -> unit.switchoff;
77  }
```

(b) Lingua Franca code

Listing 1: Timed Rebeca model (a) and Lingua Franca code (b) of the temperature control system.

5.1 Tiny Twin

Figure 3 shows the Tiny Twin of the state space of the developed Timed Rebeca model for the temperature control system. The Tiny Twin is generated by the abstraction tool based on the list V={*sensedValue, cooler_on, heater_on*} of state variables. The original state space of the model includes 76 states and 103 transitions while the generated Tiny Twin contains 21 states (i.e., equivalence classes) and 36 transitions. The Tiny Twin is trace equivalent to the original state space (projected on the variables containing sensors data and control commands). The values of state variables in the list *V* are shown on each state of the model. The variables are indicated by the first letter of the variable names in Figure 3. The variable *now* shows the logical time of the model. The transition between two states is either labeled with an action or the progress of time (i.e., *time+=10*). In the initial state (GS1), the stored temperature value in the controller is within the desired value, i.e., *s: 22*, and the cooling and heating processes have been switched off, i.e., *c: false* and *h: false* (GS1). The logical time of the model progresses by 10 units (GS2). The controller receives a new sensor data that its value depends on the current temperate in the room (GS3 and GS4). The controller begins a new cycle of temperature regulation by reading sensor data that indicates the current temperature value is higher/lower than the desired range (GS8 and GS9). The controller sends *activate_c/activate_h* command to the hc_unit for activating the cooling/heating process, i.e., *c: true* or *h: true* (GS11 and GS12). The temperature value is regulated by the heating/cooling process and reaches the desired range if the window is closed (GS15 and GS17). Otherwise, the temperature value is regulated further by keeping the heating/cooling process activated. In addition to the activation of the heating/-cooling process, the outside air blowing inside through the open window causes the temperature to increase/decrease (GS13 and GS14). The controller sends the *switchoff* command if the new sensor data is within the desired value and the heating/cooling process has been activated (GS16 and GS18). If the sensed temperature value is higher/lower than the desired range, the controller does not send any command to the hc_unit because the cooling/heating process has been activated (GS13 and GS14).

5.2 Attack Types and Detection Capability

We evaluate the capability of the developed *monitor* module in detecting attacks. We consider three types of attacks that target the *integrity* aspect of a CPS. (1) Attackers have the ability of tampering sensor data or injecting any arbitrary values into the vulnerable channel between controller and sensors, i.e., *replay or tampering attack*, (2) attackers are able to manipulate the controller through malicious code injection into the software of the controller, i.e., *fabrication or masquerade attack*, and (3) one or more attackers can perform a coordinated attack to force the system to change its correct functionally. Any of the above attacks could be performed in a stealthy way when attackers try to remain

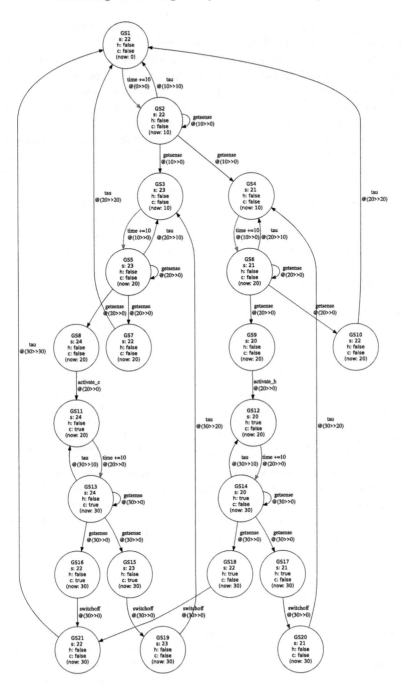

Fig. 3. The Tiny Twin of the temperature control system. The labels on each state show the temperature value s and the status of the cooling c and heating h processes. The variable now shows the logical time on each state. The transition between two states is labeled with an action or the progress of time.

undetected by doing slow damage and keeping the impact of the attack close to the changes in the correct behavior of the system.

According to [28], we model these types of attacks using the defined attack schemes. To implement the attacks, we modify the reactions of the *sensor* and the *controller* reactors in the developed Lingua Franca code. This way, these reactors behave as *compromised components* and respectively send false sensor data and faulty control commands on the output ports.

We consider the number of false sensor data and faulty control commands as the number of attacks. In our experiments, we simulate 20 false sensor data and 12 faulty control commands as listed in Table 1. We also simulate 240 coordinated attacks (combination of the false sensor data and the faulty control commands). For each attack, we execute the Lingua Franca compiler once and generate an executable file. We calculate the detection rate of the monitor with respect to the detected/undetected attacks. In this case study, the detection rate is around 68.8 percent and the average time of the state checking of the monitor is around 0.0008 s.

Table 1. Attacks and detection capability of the monitor module.

System States	# Attacks	False sensor data/ Faulty control commands	Detection Capability (DS/DC)
GS1 and GS2	4	Sensor data (20, 21, 23, or 24)	DS (20 and 24)
GS3 and GS5	4	Sensor data (20, 21, 22, or 24)	DS (20 and 21)
GS4 and GS6	4	Sensor data (20, 22, 23, or 24)	DS (23 and 24)
GS8	2	Command (*activate_h* or *switchoff*)	DC (*activate_h* and *switchoff*)
GS9	2	Command (*activate_c* or *switchoff*)	DC (*activate_c* and *switchoff*)
GS11 and GS13	4	Sensor data (20, 21, 22, or 23)	DS (20 and 21)
GS12 and GS14	4	Sensor data (21, 22, 23, or 24)	DS (23 and 24)
GS15, GS16, GS17, GS18	2	Command (*activate_h* or *activate_c*)	DC (*activate_h* and *activate_c*)

#Attacks.: Number of simulated attacks, *DS*: Detect false sensor data, *DC*: Detect faulty control commands.

Table 1 shows the states with one or more outgoing transitions that correspond to the sensor data or control commands. If the *compromised controller* sends a command that differs from the outgoing transition, the *monitor* module can detect/drop the faulty control command. From states $GS2$, $GS5$, $GS6$, $GS13$ and $GS14$ (see Fig. 3) you may move to different states. For instance, assume that 23 is sensed as the temperature value in $GS2$ but the *compromised sensor* sends the value 20. According to the Tiny Twin of the case study, the value for the next states can be either 21 ($GS4$), 22 ($GS1$ or $GS2$), or 23 ($GS3$) so the *monitor* module detects the false sensor data. Note that the controller should in principle sends *activate_h* to activate the heating process by sensing 20. But this is where in modeling the behavior of the environment, in the Timed Rebeca model, we do not model any jumps in the temperature from 22 to 20. So, this is captured as an unexpected behavior. As another example, assume that the value 22 is sensed as the temperature value in $GS2$ but the *compromised sensor* sends a sensed value 23 or 21. In this case, the *monitor* module can not detect the false sensor data. We are able to use meta-rules to check if the paths between turning the heating (or cooling) unit(s) are taken too quickly, or any of these units stay turned on for a time longer than expected.

Table 2. Alarms of the monitor module in case of attacks.

System States	False sensor data/ Faulty control commands	Alarms list
GS1 and GS2	Sensor data (20)	$[time, y^i : 20, y : 23, s : 22, c : false, h : false]$
GS3 and GS5	Sensor data (21)	$[time, y^i : 21, y : 22, s : 23, c : false, h : false]$
GS4 and GS6	Sensor data (23)	$[time, y^i : 23, y : 22, s : 23, c : false, h : false]$
GS8	Command (*activate_h*)	$[time, u^d : activate\_h, y : 24, s : 24, c : false, h : false]$
GS9	Command (*switchoff*)	$[time, u^d : switchoff, y : 20, s : 20, c : false, h : false]$
GS11 and GS13	Sensor data (21)	$[time, y^i : 21, y : 22, s : 24, c : true, h : false]$
GS12 and GS14	Sensor data (24)	$[time, y^i : 24, y : 22, s : 20, c : false, h : true]$
GS16	Command (*activate_c*)	$[time, u^d : activate\_c, y : 22, s : 22, c : true, h : false]$

time: The logical time which is derived using Lingua Franca code.

Table 2 shows the alarms list returned by the monitor module when a false sensor data or a faulty control command is detected. The alarm is comprised of a time value, a false sensor data or a faulty control command, the status of the physical plant reported by the sensor and the value of the state variables in the state where the monitor module terminated the system execution. Having this report would be very helpful for system testers/developers to find the situation of the system state when the alarm happened and find the actual source of the attack.

In a CPS, there may be several variables involved in the physical process as well as various sensors and actuators. The monitoring approach using the Tiny Twin enables us to consider only variables are affected during an attack (i.e., violation of properties). Tiny Twin provides relevant information about attacks that can be employed in mitigation techniques, backtracking and recovering the system after attacks. We have developed the Timed Rebeca models and the Lingua Franca codes of two case studies (Secure Water Treatment system (SWaT)[3] and Pneumatic Control System (PCS)[4]) available on the GitHub, for which the *monitor* module can properly detect attacks on the system. In these case studies, the original state space model of the Timed Rebeca model of the SWaT contains 614 states and 777 transitions and the original state space model of the PCS has 1388 states and 2686 transitions. The Tiny Twin models of these systems respectively have 85 states and 139 transitions and 120 states and 224 transitions.

6   Related Work

There are interesting works based on formal methods and also using models for detecting attacks at runtime.

Lanotte et al. [18] propose a formal approach based on runtime enforcement to ensure specification compliance in networks of controllers. They define a synthesis algorithm with respect to Ligatti et al.'s edit automata [20]. The algorithm

---

[3] https://github.com/fereidoun-moradi/SWaT-Rebeca-Model.
[4] https://github.com/fereidoun-moradi/Reconfigurable-Pneumatic-System.

takes an alphabet of observable actions and a timed correctness property, and returns an edit automaton as an enforcer. In their work, the enforcers are synthesized regarding deterministic behaviors of the controllers. The network of enforcers preserves weak bisimilarity equivalence in relation to the networks of controllers. The enforcers contain clock variables and specify safe behaviors of controllers. At runtime, they are used to detect the compromised controllers and emit the actions (i.e., faulty control commands) that cause failures on the physical plant. Similar to their approach, we detect/drop faulty control commands if they deviate from the behavioral model of the system. We develop the CPS model as an actor model that contains the progress of time and shows the interactions between the system components. We drive the abstract behavioral model with respect to the trace equivalence that ignores the actions are not observable for the controllers while preserving the actions order in the original model.

Cheng et al. [7] propose a methodology to detect/prevent attacks modifying the data that are used for control decisions in the controllers. These attacks can violate control branches or control integrity (i.e., the number of loop iterations) in the software of the controller. They derive a finite-state automaton (FSA) model in a training phase by monitoring the normal behavior of the program at runtime. They assume sensors data are trustable and therefore they augment the FSA model with the sensors data that report states of the physical plant. In their approach, a controller is considered as a compromised controller when it behaves inconsistently with the corresponding state transitions and the augmented data in the model. In our approach, we perform model checking to generate a model at design time without employing any training phase at runtime. We detect faulty control commands either if they are caused by compromised controllers or the commands are sent based on the receiving false sensor data.

Křikava et al. [17] use data driven models@runtime and create the logic of control systems based on the feedback control loops. They use networks of actors to represent the target system and the adaptation logic. In [3], authors explore the benefits of using the Ptolemy II framework [29] for model-based development of large-scale self-adaptive systems with multiple interacting feedback control loops. They propose a Ptolemy template based on a coordinated actor model to build a self-adaptive system. In their work, model@runtime is used by a coordinator to ensure the satisfaction of the safety properties and to adapt the system by predicting the violation of requirements, e.g. performance degradation. In [33], Sirjani et al. use the Rebeca modeling language to conduct a formal verification of the CPS programs developed in the Lingua Franca language. They study different ways to construct a transition system model for the distributed and concurrent software components of a CPS. They focus on the cyber part and model a faithful interface to the physical part. In our work, we develop executable code that represents system behavior at runtime by mapping the Timed Rebeca to the Lingua Franca, whereas the work in [33] validates a program written in Lingua Franca using model checking.

In [25], authors propose adaptive security policies at runtime. They use ProB model checker to automatically detect the root cause of security violations. They check design models (UML models are transformed to B-method) against security constraints at runtime. The authors in [15] propose monitors expressed as automaton models [4] to detect injection attacks against a system. Their automaton models represent parametric specifications to be checked at runtime. Their monitors support event duplication to prevent the system against attacks. They validate the approach by implementing the monitors and performing attack examples on a program taken from the FISSC benchmark [9].

7   Conclusion and Future Work

In this paper, we proposed a method for detecting cyber-attacks on CPSs. In particular, we used a Tiny Twin to detect the attacks on sensors and controllers. We developed an abstraction tool to build the Tiny Twin, which is an abstract version of a state transition system representing the system correct behavior in the absence of an attack. The abstraction tool reduces the transition system based on a list of state variables. The list of state variables includes the variables that store the receiving sensor data and the state variables in the actuators that reflect the changes on the state of the actuators. In our method, we built a monitor module that executes together with the system. It produces an alarm if the sensor data or the control commands are not consistent with the state transitions in the Tiny Twin. We evaluated the capability of our method in detecting attacks on a temperature control system. As the future work, we aim to build a module to recover the system after attacks based on the adaptation plans. We plan to automatically generate potential protection strategies using reinforcement learning.

Acknowledgment. The work of a subset of authors is partly supported by SSF Serendipity project, KKS DPAC Project (Dependable Platforms for Autonomous Systems and Control), and KKS SACSys Synergy project (Safe and Secure Adaptive Collaborative Systems).

References

1. Afra: An integrated environment for modeling and verifying Rebeca family designs (2021). https://rebeca-lang.org/alltools/Afra. Accessed 09 July 2021
2. Abera, T., et al.: C-FLAT: control-flow attestation for embedded systems software. In: Proceedings of the 2016 ACM SIGSAC Conference on Computer and Communications Security, pp. 743–754 (2016)
3. Bagheri, M., et al.: Coordinated actor model of self-adaptive track-based traffic control systems. J. Syst. Softw. **143**, 116–139 (2018)
4. Barringer, H., Falcone, Y., Havelund, K., Reger, G., Rydeheard, D.: Quantified event automata: towards expressive and efficient runtime monitors. In: Giannakopoulou, D., Méry, D. (eds.) FM 2012. LNCS, vol. 7436, pp. 68–84. Springer, Heidelberg (2012). https://doi.org/10.1007/978-3-642-32759-9_9
5. Carvalho, L.K., Wu, Y.C., Kwong, R., Lafortune, S.: Detection and mitigation of classes of attacks in supervisory control systems. Automatica **97**, 121–133 (2018)

6. Cheng, B.H.C., et al.: Using models at runtime to address assurance for self-adaptive systems. In: Bencomo, N., France, R., Cheng, B.H.C., Aßmann, U. (eds.) Models@run.time. LNCS, vol. 8378, pp. 101–136. Springer, Cham (2014). https://doi.org/10.1007/978-3-319-08915-7_4

7. Cheng, L., Tian, K., Yao, D., Sha, L., Beyah, R.A.: Checking is believing: event-aware program anomaly detection in cyber-physical systems. IEEE Trans. Dependable Secure Comput. **18**(2), 825–842 (2019)

8. Corbett, J.C., et al.: Spanner: Google's globally distributed database. ACM Trans. Comput. Syst. **31**(3), 1–22 (2013)

9. Dureuil, L., Petiot, G., Potet, M.-L., Le, T.-H., Crohen, A., de Choudens, P.: FISSC: a fault injection and simulation secure collection. In: Skavhaug, A., Guiochet, J., Bitsch, F. (eds.) SAFECOMP 2016. LNCS, vol. 9922, pp. 3–11. Springer, Cham (2016). https://doi.org/10.1007/978-3-319-45477-1_1

10. Eckhart, M., Ekelhart, A.: A specification-based state replication approach for digital twins. In: Proceedings of the 2018 Workshop on Cyber-Physical Systems Security and Privacy, pp. 36–47 (2018)

11. Gao, C., Seatzu, C., Li, Z., Giua, A.: Multiple attacks detection on discrete event systems. In: 2019 IEEE International Conference on Systems, Man and Cybernetics (SMC), pp. 2352–2357. IEEE (2019)

12. Hewitt, C.: Viewing control structures as patterns of passing messages. Artif. Intell. **8**(3), 323–364 (1977)

13. Jansen, D.N., Groote, J.F., Keiren, J.J.A., Wijs, A.: An $O(m \log n)$ algorithm for branching bisimilarity on labelled transition systems. In: TACAS 2020. LNCS, vol. 12079, pp. 3–20. Springer, Cham (2020). https://doi.org/10.1007/978-3-030-45237-7_1

14. Kang, E., Adepu, S., Jackson, D., Mathur, A.P.: Model-based security analysis of a water treatment system. In: Proceedings of Software Engineering for Smart Cyber-Physical Systems, pp. 22–28. ACM (2016)

15. Kassem, A., Falcone, Y.: Detecting fault injection attacks with runtime verification. In: Proceedings of the 3rd ACM Workshop on Software Protection, pp. 65–76 (2019)

16. Khamespanah, E., Sirjani, M., Sabahi-Kaviani, Z., Khosravi, R., Izadi, M.: Timed Rebeca schedulability and deadlock freedom analysis using bounded floating time transition system. Sci. Comput. Program. **98**, 184–204 (2015)

17. Křikava, F., Collet, P., France, R.B.: Actor-based runtime model of adaptable feedback control loops. In: Proceedings of the 7th Workshop on Models@ run. time, pp. 39–44 (2012)

18. Lanotte, R., Merro, M., Munteanu, A.: A process calculus approach to detection and mitigation of PLC malware. Theoret. Comput. Sci. **890**, 125–146 (2021)

19. Lee, E., Seo, Y.D., Kim, Y.G.: A cache-based model abstraction and runtime verification for the internet-of-things applications. IEEE Internet Things J. **7**(9), 8886–8901 (2020)

20. Ligatti, J., Bauer, L., Walker, D.: Edit automata: enforcement mechanisms for run-time security policies. Int. J. Inf. Secur. **4**(1), 2–16 (2005)

21. Lima, P.M., Alves, M.V., Carvalho, L.K., Moreira, M.V.: Security against network attacks in supervisory control systems. IFAC-PapersOnLine **50**(1), 12333–12338 (2017)

22. Lohstroh, M., Menard, C., Bateni, S., Lee, E.A.: Toward a Lingua Franca for deterministic concurrent systems. ACM Trans. Embed. Comput. Syst. **20**(4), 1–27 (2021)

23. Lohstroh, M., Menard, C., Schulz-Rosengarten, A., Weber, M., Castrillon, J., Lee, E.A.: A language for deterministic coordination across multiple timelines. In: 2020 Forum for Specification and Design Languages (FDL), pp. 1–8. IEEE (2020)
24. Lohstroh, M., et al.: Reactors: a deterministic model for composable reactive systems. In: Chamberlain, R., Edin Grimheden, M., Taha, W. (eds.) CyPhy/WESE - 2019. LNCS, vol. 11971, pp. 59–85. Springer, Cham (2020). https://doi.org/10.1007/978-3-030-41131-2_4
25. Loulou, H., Saudrais, S., Soubra, H., Larouci, C.: Adapting security policy at runtime for connected autonomous vehicles. In: 2016 IEEE 25th International Conference on Enabling Technologies: Infrastructure for Collaborative Enterprises (WETICE), pp. 26–31. IEEE (2016)
26. Mitchell, R., Chen, I.R.: A survey of intrusion detection techniques for cyber-physical systems. ACM Comput. Surv. 46(4), 1–29 (2014)
27. Mohan, S., Bak, S., Betti, E., Yun, H., Sha, L., Caccamo, M.: S3a: secure system simplex architecture for enhanced security and robustness of cyber-physical systems. In: Proceedings of the 2nd ACM International Conference on High Confidence Networked Systems, pp. 65–74 (2013)
28. Moradi, F., Abbaspour Asadollah, S., Sedaghatbaf, A., Čaušević, A., Sirjani, M., Talcott, C.: An actor-based approach for security analysis of cyber-physical systems. In: ter Beek, M.H., Ničković, D. (eds.) FMICS 2020. LNCS, vol. 12327, pp. 130–147. Springer, Cham (2020). https://doi.org/10.1007/978-3-030-58298-2_5
29. Ptolemaeus, C.: System design, modeling, and simulation: using Ptolemy II, vol. 1. Ptolemy. org Berkeley (2014)
30. Reynisson, A.H., et al.: Modelling and simulation of asynchronous real-time systems using timed Rebeca. Sci. Comput. Program. 89, 41–68 (2014)
31. Sirjani, M., Jaghoori, M.M.: Ten years of analyzing actors: Rebeca experience. In: Agha, G., Danvy, O., Meseguer, J. (eds.) Formal Modeling: Actors, Open Systems, Biological Systems. LNCS, vol. 7000, pp. 20–56. Springer, Heidelberg (2011). https://doi.org/10.1007/978-3-642-24933-4_3
32. Sirjani, M., Khamespanah, E.: On time actors. In: Ábrahám, E., Bonsangue, M., Johnsen, E.B. (eds.) Theory and Practice of Formal Methods. LNCS, vol. 9660, pp. 373–392. Springer, Cham (2016). https://doi.org/10.1007/978-3-319-30734-3_25
33. Sirjani, M., Lee, E.A., Khamespanah, E.: Verification of cyberphysical systems. Mathematics 8(7), 1068 (2020)
34. Zhang, Q., Li, Z., Seatzu, C., Giua, A.: Stealthy attacks for partially-observed discrete event systems. In: 2018 IEEE 23rd International Conference on Emerging Technologies and Factory Automation (ETFA), vol. 1, pp. 1161–1164. IEEE (2018)
35. Zhao, Y., Liu, J., Lee, E.A.: A programming model for time-synchronized distributed real-time systems. In: 13th IEEE Real Time and Embedded Technology and Applications Symposium (RTAS 2007), pp. 259–268. IEEE (2007)

Synthesis of Rigorous Floating-Point Predicates

Thanh Son Nguyen$^{(\boxtimes)}$, Ben Jones , and Zvonimir Rakamarić

School of Computing, University of Utah, Salt Lake City, USA
{thanhson,benjones,zvonimir}@cs.utah.edu

Abstract. A *floating-point predicate* is a routine that returns a boolean value based on a result of a floating-point computation. For example, in computational geometry floating-point predicates determine whether 3 points are collinear or which side of a line a point lies on. Due to floating-point round-off errors, implementing such predicates correctly, while maintaining good performance, requires both domain knowledge and deep understanding of the floating-point standard. Hence, it is usually done by experts that carefully craft them by relying on the floating-point round-off error model and complex mathematical derivations. This paper presents our automatic floating-point predicates synthesis method. Given an input predicate specified over reals, our method synthesizes the corresponding rigorous floating-point predicate by automatically deriving the expression that calculates the round-off error-bound of the input computation. We minimize the number of operations in the error-bound calculation, which is critical to maintain good performance, by judiciously reusing intermediate results, applying absolute-value inequalities, adjusting polynomial coefficients, and performing meta-heuristic grouping. We implemented the method in a prototype tool FPSyn. We evaluated FPSyn on 8 floating-point predicates, and showed that it synthesizes predicates whose performance is on par with optimized manually crafted implementations, while they outperform the straightforward interval arithmetic implementations.

1 Introduction

Floating-point is the most commonly used representation for real numbers in computing. However, because the distribution of floating-point numbers is uneven and the number of supported precisions is limited by the underlying architecture, the exact real-valued result of a calculation is usually not representable in floating-points and hence it must be rounded. Therefore, floating-point round-off error is inevitable in almost all floating-point operations. In

This work was supported in part by the NSF award CCF 1552975.
Z. Rakamarić—The author contributed to this work before joining Amazon Web Services (AWS).

safety-critical domains, such as automated control or medical devices, it is essential to ensure that the round-off errors cannot lead to catastrophic failures. In those domains, rigorous analysis or synthesis of floating-point routines is an important problem.

There are many applications where we have to make a discrete decision (by returning a boolean or integer value) based on branching on a computed floating-point value (using an if-condition for example). We call such routines *floating-point predicates*. For example, in computational geometry, we typically need such branching to determine which side of a line a point lies on, or whether 3 points are collinear. Due to round-off errors, implementing floating-point predicates correctly is very hard—if we are not careful, it is easy to return, for example, that 3 points are collinear, while they are in fact not. Hence, experts rely on manually derived *adaptive* implementations [15], which compute the result in floating-point arithmetic and in addition compute the estimate of the result's round-off error-bound—if the error-bound is greater than the specified threshold, they fall back on exact arithmetic to recompute the result. Such implementations strike a balance between always computing in exact arithmetic, which is extremely slow, and naively computing using floating-points, which can lead to incorrect results being returned. However, coming up with an efficient computation for estimating round-off error-bounds is currently a complex manual task where such computations are derived by experts using pen-and-paper over multiple days or even weeks. The main contribution of this paper is an automatic method for generating round-off error-bound computations for floating-point predicates, thereby replacing the manual pen-and-paper step.

There are many approaches available that either dynamically (e.g., [13,14]) or statically (e.g., [3,5,16,18]) estimate floating-point round-off errors. However, in the context of floating-points predicates, these approaches are inadequate. Static approaches typically generate error-bounds that are overly pessimistic to be effectively used in this setting since they would result in frequent invocations of exact arithmetic, thereby significantly degrading performance. Dynamic approaches incur a significant runtime overhead, which would again lead to degraded performance of a predicate. In this paper, we propose a method for automatic synthesis of performant rigorous floating-point predicates. The method automatically generates a function that calculates an input floating-point expression together with its error-bound with a minimized number of operations. Our work is greatly inspired by manual mathematical methods for estimating error-bound for geometric predicates, in which inequalities are applied to derive simple formulas to estimate error-bound [15]. Our method applies multiple techniques for simplifying the error-bound formula, including absolute value inequalities, coefficient adjusting, common subexpression elimination, and meta-heuristic grouping. At the high-level, we first break up the input expression into binary intermediate steps, and we assign the result of each step to a helper variable. Second, we consecutively derive the error-bound for each variable, and optimize the number of operations of the error-bound formula by substitutions and coefficient adjustments. The substitutions replace candidate intermediate calculations in the error-bound expression by pre-calculated intermediate results, which are saved in the variables. Furthermore, we set the coefficients that are close to each other to the same value, so that the terms can be grouped to reduce the number of operations. After generating the error-bound expression of the final result, we further optimize it by double-substitutions. Finally, we use tabu search to find an optimal grouping of the generated subexpressions.

We implemented the method in a prototype tool called FPSyn (Floating-point Predicate Synthesizer). We demonstrate the effectiveness of FPSyn by synthesizing 8 benchmarks including 4 geometric predicates (Orient2d, Orient3d, InCircle, InSphere) and 4 other common computations (ConvexHullArea, Intersection2D, Intersection3D, Polynomial). We compare the performance and error-bound range of FPSyn's output with that of the manual-derived error-bound formula (for the first 4 predicates) and interval arithmetic. We show that FPSyn synthesizes error-bound computations that compute error-bounds that are almost as precise as the manually derived ones while offering comparable performance. Moreover, the synthesized predicates are several times more performant than the straightforward implementations that use interval arithmetic.

We summarize our contributions as follows:

- We propose a method that optimizes the number of operations needed to calculate the error-bound of an input expression by multiple techniques.
- Our implementation FPSyn takes a predicate over reals as input and synthesizes a rigorous floating-point predicate by calculating the input together with its error-bound.
- We evaluate FPSyn by comparing its output with manually-derived error-bound and interval arithmetic, and demonstrate that the performance of FPSyn's output is close to that of manually-derived error-bound and significantly better than that of interval arithmetic.
- Our results indicate that FPSyn can be efficiently applied to replace human work in generating error-bound formula for geometric floating-point predicates or similar applications.

2 Motivating Example

We first provide the basics of floating-point arithmetic and round-off errors. There are exactly $\frac{1}{2\epsilon}$ floating-point numbers in the range $[2^n, 2^{n+1})$, where $n \in \mathbb{Z}$ such that $2^n, 2^{n+1}$ are representable in the chosen floating-point format and ϵ is the machine epsilon. (When 2^n or 2^{n+1} are not representable, we get an underflow or overflow exception; in this paper, we assume that such exceptions do not occur in our calculations.) The distance between two consecutive floating-point numbers is $2\epsilon \times 2^n$. The result of a floating-point arithmetic operation is obtained by rounding the corresponding real arithmetic result to the nearest floating-point. Hence, the *round-off error* that gets introduced is at most half the distance between the two consecutive floating-points that squeeze the real result. More formally, let t denote the floating-point rounding of a real number $\tilde{t}$; then, the round-off error $|\tilde{t} - t|$ is at most $\frac{1}{2} \times 2\epsilon \times floor\_power\_2(\min(t, \tilde{t})) \le \epsilon|t|$.

Therefore, $\epsilon|t|$ is the round-off error-bound of t. We capture the rounding model as $\tilde{t} = t \pm \epsilon|t|$, which is equivalent to $\tilde{t} \in [t - \epsilon|t|, t + \epsilon|t|]$.

In this section, we use a simple geometric predicate to demonstrate our approach. The predicate determines the orientation of 3 points in a two-dimensional space, and the following is its infinite-precision real arithmetic implementation:

```
bool Orient2D(ax,ay,bx,by,cx,cy) {
  real expr = (ax - cx)*(by - cy) - (ay - cy)*(bx - cx);
  return (expr >= 0);
}
```

The predicate returns *true* if the points are oriented clockwise or are collinear, and *false* otherwise.

Unfortunately, infinite-precision real arithmetic is not readily available to programmers, and hence they typically leverage the common finite-precision floating-point arithmetic standard. However, correctly implementing this predicate using floating-points is a complex task since, due to round-off errors, the sign of the floating-point result does not necessarily match the sign of the real result. Hence, one has to carefully craft an implementation that guards against floating-point round-off errors causing wrong results to be returned. We can safely infer the sign of the real result if the floating-point result is "far enough" from 0, or more precisely, if the absolute value of the floating-point result is greater than an estimated round-off error-bound. One approach to estimating the error-bound is using interval arithmetic [9], but that is typically prohibitively expensive since it needs at least 4 times the number of operations in the original expression, combined with the cost of pipeline flushing caused by the required switching of the floating-point rounding modes. Another approach is to leverage worst-case error analysis tools, such as FPTaylor [16] or Rosa [3], but that typically leads to gross overestimations of the round-off error since there are no restrictions on the inputs (in the form of small intervals), which makes such tools unusable in this context. The current state-of-the-art is to manually derive *adaptive arithmetic* implementations that are correct and also performant, as we describe next.

The manually derived adaptive arithmetic implementation of our motivating example predicate is the following:

```
const double eps = pow(2,-53);
const double orient2Dcoeff = eps*(3+16*eps);
bool Adapt_Orient2D(ax,ay,bx,by,cx,cy) {
  double tmp1 = (ax - cx)*(by - cy), tmp2 = (ay - cy)*(bx - cx);
  double expr = tmp1 - tmp2;
  double bound = orient2Dcoeff*(fabs(tmp1)+fabs(tmp2));
  if (fabs(expr) >= bound) return (expr >= 0);
  else return Orient2DExact(ax,ay,bx,by,cx,cy);
}
```

Here, instead of comparing the absolute value of the floating-point result with the error-bound, we equivalently compare it with the simpler bound expression $(3\epsilon +$

$16\epsilon^2) \otimes (|tmp1| \oplus |tmp2|)$, which can be computed using just 4 operations (note that orient2Dcoeff is a pre-calculated constant). If this comparison succeeds, we can safely return the result computed using floating-points; if it does not, we have to fall back to computing the result using the much more expensive exact arithmetic. Given that this manually derived bound expression is typically tight, falling back to the exact arithmetic computation happens rarely in practice, which leads to a performant implementation.

Shewchuk [15] introduced the manual steps for deriving the bound expression, and the accompanying proof of their correctness. The expression is simplified by reusing the intermediate values and applying inequalities, and we summarize the derivation steps for our example. First, we denote the intermediate values of our expression as $t1 = a_x \ominus c_x$, $t2 = b_y \ominus c_y$, $t3 = t1 \otimes t2$, $t4 = a_y \ominus c_y$, $t5 = b_x \ominus c_x$, $t6 = t4 \otimes t5$, $t7 = t3 \ominus t6$, where $\ominus$ and $\otimes$ are floating-point operations.

The inputs a_x, c_x, b_y, c_y have no round-off error since those are floating-point numbers. Hence, $\tilde{t1} = t1 \pm \epsilon|t1|$ and $\tilde{t2} = t2 \pm \epsilon|t2|$. From these two error-bounds, we derive the error-bound of $t3$ as $\tilde{t3} = \tilde{t1}\,\tilde{t2} = (t1 \pm \epsilon|t1|)(t2 \pm \epsilon|t2|) = t1\,t2 \pm (2\epsilon + \epsilon^2)|t1\,t2| = t3 \pm [\epsilon|t3| + (2\epsilon + \epsilon^2)|t1\,t2|]$. So the error-bound of $t3$ is $\epsilon|t3| + (2\epsilon + \epsilon^2)|t1\,t2|$. Now, from the rounding function, it follows that $t3 = rnd(t1\,t2) \simeq |t1\,t2| \leq (1 + \epsilon)|t3|$. Hence, we can safely substitute $|t1\,t2|$ in the error-bound with $(1 + \epsilon)|t3|$ to get $(3\epsilon + 3\epsilon^2 + \epsilon^3)|t3|$. Similarly, the error-bound of $t6$ is $(3\epsilon + 3\epsilon^2 + \epsilon^3)|t6|$, and of $t7$ is $\epsilon|t7| + (3\epsilon + 3\epsilon^2 + \epsilon^3)(|t3| + |t6|)$. To reduce the computation cost, we can optimize the error-bound further by safely removing operations. Instead of comparing $|t7|$ with the error-bound derived above, we can equivalently compare it with $\frac{3\epsilon+3\epsilon^2+\epsilon^3}{1-\epsilon} \times (|t3| + |t6|)$ because $|t7| > \epsilon|t7| + (3\epsilon + 3\epsilon^2 + \epsilon^3)(|t3| + |t6|)$ is equivalent to $|t7| > \frac{3\epsilon+3\epsilon^2+\epsilon^3}{1-\epsilon} \times (|t3| + |t6|)$.

Note that all of the above computations are in real arithmetic. Next, we need to safely (i.e., making sure that the floating-point computation always results in a larger error-bound) convert them into floating-point arithmetic to be able to implement them in a program. If we temporarily ignore the computations of the constants, we can replace the two remaining $+$ and $\times$ operations with $\oplus$ and $\otimes$ (i.e., their floating-point counterparts) by multiplying the error-bound with $(1 + \epsilon)^2$ because

$$\frac{3\epsilon + 3\epsilon^2 + \epsilon^3}{1 - \epsilon} \times (|t3| + |t6|) \leq \frac{3\epsilon + 3\epsilon^2 + \epsilon^3}{1 - \epsilon}(1 + \epsilon) \times (|t3| \oplus |t6|)$$

$$\leq \frac{3\epsilon + 3\epsilon^2 + \epsilon^3}{1 - \epsilon}(1 + \epsilon)^2 \otimes (|t3| \oplus |t6|)$$

Assuming that $\epsilon \leq 2^{-3}$, which is the case for all common floating-point formats, we can overapproximate $\frac{3\epsilon+3\epsilon^2+\epsilon^3}{1-\epsilon}(1+\epsilon)^2$ with the floating-point number $3\epsilon+16\epsilon^2$. Our final bound is then $\epsilon \otimes (3 \oplus 16 \otimes \epsilon) \otimes (|t3| \oplus |t6|)$, which is what is implemented in the Adapt_Orient2D function above.

Clearly, deriving such bounds manually requires a tremendous amount of expert human effort and ingenuity. In this work, we propose a rigorous algorithm that can synthesize such bounds automatically from the input function. When we apply it on the motivating example, our algorithm automatically synthesizes

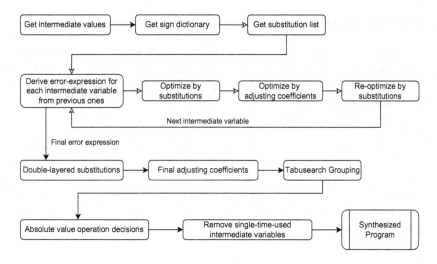

Fig. 1. FPSyn algorithm flowchart.

the following function that calculates the result in floating-points as well as the accompanying rigorous error-bound:

```
void FPPSynt_Orient2D(ax,ay,bx,by,cx,cy,*result,*error_bound) {
    double t1 = (ax - cx)*(by - cy);
    double t2 = (ay - cy)*(bx - cx);
    *result = t1-t2;
    // Calculation of the error-bound
    *error_bound = 1.0000000001 *
                   (4.44089209850063e-16 *(fabs(t1) +fabs(t2)));
}
```

Then, we plug in the synthesized function into the predicate:

```
bool Adapt_Orient2D(ax,ay,bx,by,cx,cy) {
    double result, error_bound;
    FPPSynt_Orient2D(ax,ay,bx,by,cx,cy,&result,&error_bound);
    if (fabs(result) >= error_bound) return (result >= 0);
    else return Orient2DExact(ax,ay,bx,by,cx,cy);
}
```

In this simple example, to compute both the result of the input function and its error-bound, FPSyn uses 12 operations in total, while the manually derived method uses 11, so just one less. Note that FPSyn computes the actual error-bound expression that can be used in other settings as well (e.g., for dynamic error-bound estimation), instead of the customized manually-derived expression that can only be used as a part of the predicate.

3   FPSyn Algorithm

Our synthesis algorithm is inspired by the Shewchuk's manual round-off error-bound derivation method [15]. Our key contribution is a rigorous algorithm that judiciously applies simplifying rewrite rules to reduce the number of operations in the error-bound computation. The rewrite rules are in the form of simplifying substitutions (of intermediate computations) and inequalities, and we formally justify them when needed by proving that they are rigorous. At the high level, our algorithm first splits the input expression into binary-operation subexpressions that compute intermediate values. Then, it derives and optimizes the round-off error-bound expressions of each intermediate value. Finally, it merges the intermediate error-bound expressions to obtain the final one, which is further optimized. Figure 1 shows the flowchart of the algorithm, and we describe the steps in detail next.

3.1   Step 1: Simplify the Input Expression

The goal of this step if to simplify the original expression by breaking it up into smaller (irreducible) subexpressions that are subsequently easier to work with and optimize. First, we identify common subexpressions, and extract and reuse them by introducing intermediate variables. For example, we split the expression $output = a^6 + b^2 + c * d + (a^6 + b^2) * c * d$ into $t_0 = a^6 + b^2$, $output = t_0 + c * d + t_0 * c * d$. Then, we split complex expressions into just binary or unary expressions, again by introducing intermediate variables. Applying this step on our example leads to the following subexpressions: $t_0 = a^6$, $t_1 = b^2$, $t_2 = t_0 + t_1$, $t_3 = c * d$, $t_4 = t_2 + t_3$, $t_5 = t_2 * t_3$, $output = t_4 + t_5$. Finally, we replace all power operations with multiplications of power operations with power-of-2 exponents, followed by rewriting them into binary multiplication operations. Applying this step generates (note that $a^6 = a^4 * a^2$): $t_0 = a * a$, $t_1 = t_0 * t_0$, $t_2 = t_0 * t_1$, $t_3 = b * b$, $t_4 = t_2 + t_3$, $t_5 = c * d$, $t_6 = t_4 + t_5$, $t_7 = t_4 * t_5$, $output = t_6 + t_7$. We generate the floating-point program that calculates the input expression by replacing all real-number operations $+, *$ with their floating-point counterparts $\oplus, \otimes$. (Note that this introduces floating-point errors, which we compensate for by generating the error-bound expression.) To count the number of operations in an expression in the later steps of the algorithm, we first perform this simplification. In other words, we define the number of operations in an expression to be the number of intermediate variables obtained after this simplification step.

3.2   Step 2: Build the Sign Dictionary

Knowing a sign of each intermediate variable allows us to build a more extensive substitution list in the next section, which in turn leads to more opportunities for simplifications. Hence, we infer signs of all intermediate variables using a simple, conservative static analysis step that assigns 1 to non-negative subexpressions, -1 to non-positive, and 0 otherwise ("don't know"). We define the inference as:

- $Sign(t = x) = sign(x)$ if x is a non-zero number; $Sign(t = 0) = 1$
- $Sign(t = x) = 0$ if x is a variable
- $Sign(t = x \otimes x) = 1$ if x is a variable
- $Sign(t = x \oplus y) = Sign(x)$ if $Sign(x) = Sign(y)$; otherwise $Sign(t = x \oplus y) = 0$
- $Sign(t = x \otimes y) = Sign(x) * Sign(y)$

Currently, we only infer signs of intermediate values based on the square terms. For example, we can infer the signs of $x*x, x*x+y*y$, or $-3*x*x-2*y*y$, but not of $x * x + 2 * x + 1$. The sign dictionary for our running example is $Sign[t_0 = output] = [1, 1, 1, 1, 1, 0, 0, 0, 0]$.

3.3   Step 3: Generate the Substitutions List

In this step, we build the list of possible substitutions we use to simplify the error-bound expressions. Note that we make sure that each generated substitution is rigorous by proving that the error-bound obtained after a substitution is strictly greater than the original one. Let $\theta = 1 + 2\epsilon$. Then, we derive the substitutions list from the expression and the sign of each intermediate variable by applying the following rules:

1. For each $t = x \otimes y$, we add a substitution $|x * y| = \theta * |t|$.
2. For each $t = x \oplus y$ and $Sign(t) \neq ?$, we add a substitution $|x| + |y| = \theta * |t|$.
3. For each $t = x \oplus y$ or $t = x \ominus y$, we add a substitution: $|t| = \theta * |x| + \theta * |y|$.

To prove that the substitutions are rigorous, we need the following two lemmas.

Lemma 1. *Given a real number r, $|r| \leq (1 + \epsilon)|rnd(r)|$ for all rounding modes.*

Proof. We start with the standard property of the floating-point rounding function: $|r - rnd(r)| \leq \epsilon |rnd(r)|$. We add $|rnd(r)|$ to both sides to get $|rnd(r)| + |r - rnd(r)| \leq (1 + \epsilon)|rnd(r)|$. Then, we use the inequality $|a + b| \leq |a| + |b|$ to derive $|r| \leq |rnd(r)| + |r - rnd(r)|$, which implies $|r| \leq (1 + \epsilon)|rnd(r)|$.

Lemma 2. *Given a real number r, $|rnd(r)| \leq (1 + \epsilon)|r|$ for all rounding modes.*

Proof. We start with the standard property of the floating-point rounding function: $|r - rnd(r)| \leq \epsilon |r|$. We add $|r|$ to both sides to get $|r| + |r - rnd(r)| \leq (1 + \epsilon)|r|$. Then, we use the inequality $|a - b| \leq |a| + |b|$ to derive $|rnd(r)| \leq |r| + |r - rnd(r)|$, which implies $|rnd(r)| \leq (1 + \epsilon)|r|$.

Theorem 1. *Our substitution rules above are rigorous:*

1. *If $t = x \otimes y$, then $|x * y| \leq \theta * |t|$.*
2. *If $t = x \oplus y$ and $Sign(t) \neq 0$, then $|x| + |y| \leq \theta * |t|$.*
3. *If $t = x \oplus y$ or $t = x \ominus y$, then: $|t| = \theta * |x| + \theta * |y|$.*

Proof. We apply Lemma 1 and Lemma 2 to each substitution rule:

1. $|x * y| \leq (1 + \epsilon)|rnd(x * y)| \leq \theta|t|$

2. $Sign(x) = (y) \neq 0 \simeq |x| + |y| = |x + y| \leq (1 + \epsilon)rnd(x + y) \leq \theta|t|$
3. $|t| = |rnd(x \pm y)| \leq (1 + \epsilon)|x \pm y| \leq \theta * (|x| + |y|)$

Note that $(1 + \epsilon)$ is not representable in floating-points, and θ is the smallest floating-point greater than $(1 + \epsilon)$.

Based on the rules, we generate the following substitutions list for our example:
(1) $|a * a| = \theta * |t_0|$, (2) $|t_0 * t_0| = \theta * |t_1|$, (3) $|t_0 * t_1| = \theta|t_2|$, (4) $|b * b| = \theta * |t_3|$, (5) $|t_2| + |t_3| = \theta * |t_4|$, (6) $|t_4| = \theta * |t_2| + \theta * |t_3|$, (7) $|c * d| = \theta * |t_5|$, (8) $|t_6| = \theta * |t_4| + \theta * |t_5|$, (9) $|t_4 * t_5| = \theta * |t_7|$, (10) $|result| = \theta * |t_6| + \theta * |t_7|$.

3.4   Step 4: Derive and Optimize Error-Bound Subexpressions

This step consists of four substeps. First, we derive the error-bound expressions of the intermediate variables using the following rigorous derivation rules.

Theorem 2. *Let Δt denote the error-bound of an intermediate variable t. Then the following rules are rigorous:*

1. $\Delta(t = x) = 0$ *where x is a number or a variable*
2. $\Delta(t = x \oplus y, x \ominus y) = \Delta(x) + \Delta(y) + \epsilon|t|$
3. $\Delta(t = x \otimes y) = |x|\Delta(y) + |y|\Delta(x) + \Delta(x)\Delta(y) + \epsilon|t|$

Note that all the operations in the right-hand-side are in real arithmetic and the expressions are derived symbolically.

Proof. Let $\tilde{t}$ denote the value of an intermediate variable t if all the calculations are in real arithmetic. An expression is a rigorous error-bound of t if it is greater than or equal to $|\tilde{t} - t|$. We prove the derivation rules above recursively by assuming that the error-bounds of all intermediate values prior to t are rigorous:

1. Trivial base case
2. If $t = x \oplus y$ or $x \ominus y$ then $|\tilde{t} - t| = |\tilde{x} \pm \tilde{y} - (x \pm y) + (x \pm y) - t| = |(\tilde{x} - x) \pm (\tilde{y} - y) + (x \pm y) - rnd(x \pm y)| \leq |(\tilde{x} - x)| + |\tilde{y} - y| + |(x \pm y) - rnd(x \pm y)| \leq \Delta(x) + \Delta(y) + \epsilon|t|$.
3. If $t = x \otimes y$ then $|\tilde{t} - t| = |\tilde{x}\tilde{y} - t| = |x(\tilde{y} - y) + y(\tilde{x} - x) + (\tilde{x} - x)(\tilde{y} - y) + xy - t| \leq |x(\tilde{y} - y)| + |y(\tilde{x} - x)| + |(\tilde{x} - x)(\tilde{y} - y)| + |xy - rnd(xy)| \leq |x|\Delta(y) + |y|\Delta(x) + \Delta(x)\Delta(y) + \epsilon|t|$.

Second, we optimize the error-bound expressions by first applying all multiplication substitutions. Then, we attempt each addition substitution in turn, and reapply multiplication substitutions after each attempt: if the number of operations decreases, we keep the new expression. We repeat this until there are no further improvements.

Third, we adjust the coefficients whenever possible. For each addition in the expression, we adjust the coefficient of each term to the greatest coefficient within a manually specified threshold. In practice, choosing a larger threshold typically leads to better performance of the synthesized predicate, but also to more conservative error-bounds. In our experiments, we use the same threshold of 6ϵ for all benchmarks; we selected the threshold by performing just several simple trial-and-error runs.

Finally, we re-optimize the error-bound expression by performing substitutions one more time (i.e., repeating the second substep). If we cannot apply any new substitution, we reverse the coefficient adjustments to obtain a tighter error-bound. Note that the purpose of the coefficient adjustment substep is not for grouping by the coefficient, but for applying more substitutions.

We demonstrate this step on our running example. By employing the derivation rules, FPSyn derives $\Delta(t_0) = \epsilon * |t_0|$ and $\Delta(t_1) = \epsilon * |t_1| + (2\epsilon + \epsilon^2) * |t_0 * t_0|$. Then, it optimizes $\Delta(t_1)$ using substitution 2 and gets $\Delta(t_1) = (\theta(2\epsilon + \epsilon^2) + \epsilon) * |t_1|$. To simplify the example, we approximate the constant with 3ϵ to get $\Delta(t_1) \approx 3\epsilon * |t_1|$. Next, FPSyn derives $\Delta(t_2) = 4\epsilon|t_0 * t_1| + \epsilon|t_2|$, optimizes it using substitution 3, and gets $\Delta(t_2) \approx 5\epsilon * |t_2|$. FPSyn continues to derive $\Delta(t_3) = \epsilon * |t_3|$ and $\Delta(t_4) = \epsilon * |t_4| + 5\epsilon * |t_2| + \epsilon * |t_3|$. For $\Delta(t_4)$, FPSyn first applies substitution 6 and gets $\epsilon(6 + 2\epsilon) * |t_2| + \epsilon(2 + 2\epsilon) * |t_3|$. Then, it adjusts the coefficients with threshold 6ϵ and gets $\epsilon(6 + 2\epsilon) * (|t_2| + |t_3|)$; finally, it re-optimizes it using substitution 5 and gets $\Delta(t_4) \approx 6\epsilon * |t_4|$. After we perform this step on all the subexpressions, we generate the error-bound of the final result as $\Delta(output) = \epsilon * |output| + 7\epsilon * |t_4| + 2\epsilon * |t_5| + 8\epsilon|t_7|$.

3.5   Step 5: Apply Double-Layered Substitution

We try to escape from a local minima after step 4 by applying two substitutions in sequence, thereby allowing worse result after the first application, but potentially improved results after the second one. For example, the final error-bound we generated in the previous step $\epsilon * |result| + 7\epsilon * |t_4| + 2\epsilon * |t_5| + 8\epsilon|t_7|$ can be simplified if we first apply substitution 10 and then substitution 8 (see Sect. 3.3). After applying substitution 10, we get $7\epsilon * |t_4| + 2\epsilon * |t_5| + \epsilon(1 + 2\epsilon) * |t_6| + \epsilon(9 + 2\epsilon) * |t_7|$ (note that the number of operations increases). Then, after applying substitution 8, we get $\epsilon[7 + (1 + 2\epsilon)^2] * |t_4| + \epsilon[2 + (1 + 2\epsilon)^2] * |t_5| + \epsilon(9 + 2\epsilon) * |t_7|$. We approximate the constants and rewrite the expression as $8\epsilon * |t_4| + 3\epsilon * |t_5| + 9\epsilon * |t_7|$, where the number of operations is less than in the original expression. We perform this step only on the error-bound expression of the final result, and not the intermediate variables, because the calculation is significantly heavier than the previous step.

Next, we again adjust the coefficients as in step 4, but only for the outermost addition since adjusting the coefficients again for inner additions often significantly increases the error-bound. For example, with the threshold of 5ϵ, after this step the previous error-bound becomes $9\epsilon * |t_4| + 3\epsilon * |t_5| + 9\epsilon * |t_7|$. The purpose of this is to prepare the expression for tabu search that follows.

3.6   Step 6: Group Subexpressions Using Tabu Search

When the error-bound expression is an addition of k terms, we employ customized tabu search [7] to find an optimal (in terms of the number of operations) partition and grouping of subexpressions. The tabu search candidates are the different ways we can partition the expression. We define the fitness function as the number of operations in $simplify(partition_1) + simplify(partition_2) + \dots$ where $simplify$ is a function that simplifies an expression by grouping the common factors of addition terms. Besides the standard parameters of the tabu search algorithm, we introduce two additional ones to control random restarts: r is the number of candidates we explore before restarting, and p is the number of restarts we do before increasing the target number of partitions. Our customized algorithm then works as follows. Initially, we set the target number of partitions to 2. We generate a random starting candidate (i.e., partition) and start tabu search. During search, we maintain our best candidate partition we managed to generate so far. If the best candidate partition cannot be improved after r generated candidates, we restart from a new random starting candidate. After p restarts, we increase the number of partitions by 1, generate a starting candidate partition, and restart tabu search. We terminate the search after the total number of generated candidates exceeds a preset threshold. The best partition for our example's error-bound expression is $[9\epsilon * |t_4| + 9\epsilon * |t_7|, 3\epsilon * |t_5|]$, and after this step it becomes $9\epsilon * (|t_4| + |t_7|) + 3\epsilon * |t_5|$.

Next, we further simplify the final error-bound expression by calculating the absolute value of each intermediate value or variable. We can avoid calculations of always-positive terms by referring to the Sign dictionary from step 2. In our example, $Sign(t_4) = 1$ and $Sign(t_5) = Sign(t_7) = 0$, so we only need to compute the absolute values of t_5 and t_7.

3.7   Step 7: Convert Reals into Floating-Points

To purpose of this step is to rigorously convert the error-bound expression over reals generated in the previous steps into an expression over floating-points. Let n be the total number of operations of the error-bound expression. Then, we turn the expression over reals into an expression over floating-points by simply converting all real operations into their floating-point counterparts, and then multiplying the final results with $1 + 8n\epsilon$. This ensures that the floating-point result is strictly greater than the real one, as we prove next.

Lemma 3. *For a positive floating-point number* $k, k(1+\epsilon) \leq k \otimes \theta$, *where* $\theta = 1+2\epsilon$.

Proof. Let p be the smallest power of 2 greater than k, and k' the next floating-point number after k. Then (i) $k(1 + \epsilon) \leq k + \epsilon p = k'$ and (ii) $p < 2k \simeq k' \leq k + 2k\epsilon \simeq rnd(k') \leq rnd(k(1+2\epsilon)) \simeq k' \leq k \otimes \theta$. From (i) and (ii) it follows that $k(1+\epsilon) \leq k \otimes \theta$.

Lemma 4. *For a positive floating-point number* k *and an integer* $n < \epsilon^{-1}/2, (1+\epsilon)^n k \leq (1 + 8n\epsilon) \otimes k$.

Proof. From Lemma 3 we infer $(1+\epsilon)^n k \leq ((k \otimes \theta) \otimes \theta) \otimes \dots$ [repeated n times] (i). Let p be the smallest power of 2 greater than k so that $k < p < 2k$. Let $H(k,t)$ be the t'th floating-point number after k, so that $H(k,1)$ is $k + \epsilon p$ and $H(k,2)$ is either $k + 2p\epsilon$ or $k + 3p\epsilon$. Then $(1 + 2\epsilon)k < k + 2p\epsilon \leq H(k,2) \simeq rnd((1 + 2\epsilon)k) \leq rnd(H(k,2)) \simeq k \otimes \theta \leq H(k,2) \simeq ((k \otimes \theta) \otimes \theta) \dots \leq H(k,2n)$ (ii). There are more than ϵ^{-1} floating-point numbers from k to $2p$. Hence, if $n < \epsilon^{-1}/2$, then

$H(k, 2n) < 2p \simeq \forall t \in [0, n] : H(k, t+1) - H(k, t) \leq 2\epsilon p \simeq H(k, 2n) \leq k + 4np\epsilon < k + 8nk\epsilon \simeq H(k, 2n) \leq rnd(k(1 + 8n\epsilon)) = (1 + 8n\epsilon) \otimes k$ (iii). From (i), (ii), and (iii) we can conclude that $(1 + \epsilon)^n k \leq (1 + 8n\epsilon) \otimes k$.

Lemma 5. *Let E be an expression of non-negative terms containing only additions and multiplications, and n be its total number of operations. Also, let $R(E)$ and $F(E)$ be its evaluation in real and floating-point arithmetic, respectively. Then $R(E) \leq (1 + \epsilon)^n F(E)$.*

Proof. We prove this lemma by induction. When $n = 1$, from Lemma 1 (Sect. 3.3) we conclude that $a + b \leq (1 + \epsilon)(a \oplus b)$ and and $a * b \leq (1 + \epsilon)(a \otimes b)$, where a and b are two floating-point numbers. As our hypothesis, we assume that $R(E) \leq (1 + \epsilon)^k F(E)$ holds for all $k < n$. Let E be a binary expression with operands E_1 and E_2. If n_1, n_2 are the numbers of operations in E_1, E_2, then $n_1 + n_2 = n - 1$, meaning that both n_1 and n_2 are less than n. Hence, based on our hypothesis, $R(E_1) \leq (1+\epsilon)^{n_1} F(E_1)$ and $R(E_2) \leq (1+\epsilon)^{n_2} F(E_2)$. We now have two cases for the operator of E:

1. If $E = E_1 + E_2$, then $R(E) = R(E_1) + R(E_2) < (1 + \epsilon)^{n-1}(F(E_1) + F(E_2)) \leq (1 + \epsilon)^n F(E)$.
2. If $E = E_1 * E_2$, then $R(E) = R(E_1) * R(E_2) < (1 + \epsilon)^{n-1} F(E_1) * F(E_2) \leq (1 + \epsilon)^n F(E)$.

Theorem 3. *Let $E, R(E), F(E)$, and n be defined as in Lemma 5. Then $R(E) \leq (1 + 8n\epsilon) \otimes F(E)$.*

Proof. Follows directly from Lemma 4 and Lemma 5.

Note that after we analyze each step of our algorithm, we can determine that the total number of operations of the generated error-bound computation cannot exceed 7 times the number of intermediate values in the input expression. Hence, we can compute a conservative $1 + 8n\epsilon$ constant ahead of time. In our implementation, we further simplify this by not counting the total number of operations by just using the constant $1 + 10^{-10}$ instead. This is conservative as long as the number of operations does not exceed a very large number of $\frac{10^{-10}}{8 \times 7 \times \epsilon}$. After this last step, the final error-bound expression for our example is $(1 + 10^{-10}) \otimes [9\epsilon \otimes (|t_4| \oplus |t_7|) \oplus 3\epsilon \otimes |t_5|]$.

3.8 Step 8: Remove Single-Use Intermediate Variables

After Step 7 above, we have the full synthesized program that calculates both the floating-point arithmetic result and its error-bound of the input expression. However, we observe that the generated computation often contains intermediate variables (introduced in Step 1) that are used only once. Therefore, we remove those intermediate variables and replace their usages with the subexpressions assigned to them in Step 1. Note that while this does not reduce the total number of operations, it often improves performance since it reduces the number of registers needed. In our example, t_1 and t_6 are only used once (in t_2 and *output*) and so we remove them to obtain $t_2 = t_0 \otimes (t_0 \otimes t_0)$ and *output* $= (t_4 \oplus t_5) \oplus t_7$.

4 Experiments

We implemented FPSyn in Python, and we heavily rely on the SymPy library [17] for expression manipulation. We made FPSyn and benchmarks publicly available at https://github.com/soarlab/fpsyn. FPSyn takes an expression as input, and outputs a synthesized C program that computes the input expression and its error-bound using floating-point arithmetic; FPSyn optimizes these computations using the steps we described in the previous section. In the current version, FPSyn supports expressions consisting of additions, subtractions, multiplications, and a single outer division. As our benchmarks, we collected 4 well-known geometric predicates (Orient2d, Orient3d, InCircle, InSphere) from Shewchuk [15] and added 4 more based on common calculations (ConvexHullArea, Intersection2D, Intersection3D, Polynomial). The benchmarks are diverse in size and structure, and only the Shewchuk's predicates include error-bound expressions manually derived by the expert author. Table 1 gives the description and the number of operations for each benchmark. We performed the experiments on an Intel Core i9-10900 system with 32 GB of memory. The runtimes of FPSyn (i.e., the predicate synthesis process) are always less than 8 h. This should not cause problems for a typical user—FPSyn is meant to be run as a batch job (overnight) since there is no need for immediate feedback.

Table 1. The number of variables and operations in our benchmarks.

Benchmark	Description	vars	add/sub	mul	div
Orient2d	Orientation of 3 2D-points	6	5	2	0
Orient3d	Orientation of 3 3D-points	9	14	9	0
InCircle	a 2D-point is inside/outside a circle	8	14	15	0
InSphere	a 3D-point is inside/outside a sphere	15	37	40	0
ConvexHullArea	Area of 10-vertex convex hull	20	33	17	0
Intersection2D	Intersection of two 2D-lines	8	8	8	1
Intersection3D	Intersection of three planes	27	64	45	1
Polynomial	10-degree single variable polynomial	1	10	18	0

Table 2. Number of operations in error-bound calculations produced by FPSyn, Shewchuk (manual), FPG, and Nanevski's tool.

	Orient2D			Orient3D			InSphere		
	$+$	$*$	$|x|$	$+$	$*$	$|x|$	$+$	$*$	$|x|$
FPSyn	1	2	2	6	6	10	21	19	20
Shewchuk	1	1	2	5	4	9	23	17	16
FPG	5	3	7	14	9	13	37	40	16
Nanevski	5	3	6	14	10	9	37	41	15

Table 3. Average runtimes (microseconds) of combined input and error-bound computations as well as full predicates.

	Comp&Error			Full Predicate		
	FPSyn	Manual	IA	FPSyn	Manual	IA
Orient2D	7	7	35	13	13	40
Orient3D	16	15	75	31	30	91
InCircle	16	14	98	116	112	198
InSphere	37	34	251	280	279	501
Polynomial	18	NA	108	21	NA	112
ConvexHullArea	43	NA	222	76	NA	256
Intersection2D	30	NA	72	44	NA	100
Intersection3D	159	NA	444	166	NA	456

In the first experiment, we compare the number of operations in the error-bound calculations generated by FPSyn with Schewchuk's manually-derived error-bounds [15] and two state-of-the-art automatic error-bound generators: FPG [8] and Nanevski's [11]. We do this over the three benchmarks that come with manually-derived error-bounds: Orient2D, Orient3D, and InSphere. The two automatic generators apply simple forward propagation techniques without any optimizations to reduce the number of operations in the error-bound calculation. For FPG, we obtain the number of operations required to calculate error-bounds for the three benchmarks from the respective publication [8]. For Nanevski's tool, according to the proposed forward propagation formulas, the number of absolute value operations, additions, and multiplications required to calculate error-bounds are correspondingly the number of variables, total number of additions and subtractions, and number of multiplications in the input expression (with an extra multiplication). Hence, based on this, we manually computed the number of operations needed. Table 2 shows the results. The number of operations in the error-bound calculations generated by FPSyn is very close to that of the Schewchuk's manually-derived error-bounds and significantly smaller than the two automatic error-bound generators.

In the second experiment, we compare the runtimes of the combined floating-point input expression and error-bound calculations as generated by FPSyn, manually (by an expert), and using interval arithmetic. For the first four benchmarks, as manually-derived implementations we use Schewchuk's state-of-the-art adaptive arithmetic calculations [15]. To precisely measure runtimes, we generate 100000 random inputs for each benchmark, and run each benchmark 1000 times on each input; we compute the average runtimes and standard deviations for each run. The values of the generated inputs are sampled uniformly over the set of floating-point numbers to exaggerate the f luctuation of the inputs' values, which leads to significantly greater round-off errors in computation. To ensure that overflows cannot happen, we set the range of sampling to be

Table 4. Result of our exact arithmetic frequency experiment. F stands for FPSyn, Man for Manual and IA for Interval Arithmetic.

Benchmark	F	Man	IA	F&Man	F\Man	Man\F	F&IA	F\IA	IA\F
Orient2D	553	521	550	521	12	0	533	0	17
Orient3D	1078	1078	1095	1078	0	0	1052	26	43
InCircle	7739	7739	7829	7739	0	0	7658	81	171
InSphere	7043	7219	7164	7036	7	183	7013	30	151
Polynomial	0	NA	0	NA	NA	NA	0	0	0
ConvexHullArea	897	NA	905	NA	NA	NA	892	5	13
Intersection2D	0	NA	0	NA	NA	NA	0	0	0
Intersection3D	0	NA	0	NA	NA	NA	0	0	0

$[-2^{15}, 2^{15}]$ for the Intersection3D predicate and $[-2^{63}, 2^{63}]$ for others. Table 3, under "Computation and Error-bound", shows the results. The average runtimes of FPSyn-synthesized computations are 0.0–14.3% greater than that of the manually-derived ones, but are also 2.4–4.5 times less than that of interval arithmetic.

In the third experiment, we compare the runtimes of the full predicate programs as generated by FPSyn, manually, and using interval arithmetic. Because in practice exact arithmetic does not support division and requires manual design for implementation, we replace it in the predicates' implementations by extended-precision arithmetic supported by the MPFR library [10] and set the number of precisions to be 1024. Table 3, under "Full Predicate", shows the results. Note that relative standard deviations for all runs are negligible and always smaller than 0.6%. The average runtimes of FPSyn-synthesized predicates are 0.0% to 3.6% greater than that of the Schewchuk's manually-derived ones, but are also 2.3 to 5.3 times less than that of interval arithmetic predicates. Our experiment's setup is similar to that of Nanevski et al.'s paper [11]. Nanevski et al.'s result shows that the performance of their generated predicates is close to that of Schewchuk's implementations for the first three benchmarks but is 2.4 times slower for InSphere predicate.

In the forth experiment, we evaluate whether the optimization techniques of FPSyn may lead to overly conservative error-bound calculations, which could potentially increase the frequency that extended-precision is triggered and hence affect the runtimes of the geometric predicates. We compare the frequency of triggering exact arithmetic when using FPSyn, manual, and interval arithmetic error-bound computations over 100000 random inputs, which are sampled in exactly the same way as the two previous experiments. Table 4 shows the results. The columns denoted with F, Man, and IA show the number of inputs (out of 100000) that trigger exact arithmetic in the FPSyn, manual, and interval arithmetic predicates, respectively. Other columns show the number of inputs that trigger exact arithmetic in both predicates (&) or in one but not the other (\). The results show that the frequency of triggering exact arithmetic is very low in all predicates, and we found no inputs that trigger exact arithmetic in the last two predicates. Moreover, the frequencies are similar for all 3 methods, including the typically very pessimistic interval arithmetic. This indicates that exploring even more aggressive optimizations in FPSyn could be beneficial in terms of improving the performance of the generated error-bound computations, while not having a significant impact on the frequency of exact arithmetic being triggered.

5 Related Work

Our work was greatly inspired by Shewchuk's manual adaptive arithmetic approach for geometric predicates [15]. The author improves the performance of geometric predicates by applying a floating-point filter technique that avoids exact arithmetic's calculation [4] whenever the error-bound of an approximation indicates that the approximation is good enough to achieve geometric exactness. Shewchuk's approach calculates multiple approximations of a geometric predicate's expression together with *manually-derived* error-bound expressions. In contrast, we synthesize error-bound expressions automatically.

There are several approaches for automatic generation of error-bound computations to replace the tedious task of deriving them manually. Pion [12] and Brönnimann et al. [2] suggest using interval arithmetic for this task. Their approach can be applied only for computing the sign of matrix determinant. In contrast, our synthesis method can be applied on a much wider class of expressions and achieves better performance as our experiments show. Nanevski et al. [11] developed an automatic code generator for geometric predicates. Like ours, their method generates the code to compute error-bounds at runtime. However, unlike us, they do not propose any optimizations to minimize the number of operation of the error-bound computations. Devillers et al. [6] propose an almost static filter technique for runtime error-bound estimation, which achieves better performance than straightforward interval arithmetic. Their computation method is similar to ours, but also without any optimizations. The error-bound is computed once for an input interval, and needs to be recomputed if an input falls outside of the interval. This approach performs well if inputs are close together such that they do not fall out of the prescribed range often. In contrast, we compute the error-bound for each input, and hence the performance is independent of the input distribution. Meyer et al. [8] develop a code generator for more geometric predicates, in which the error-bound is computed using the Devillers et al.'s method. Recently, Bartels et al. [1] devised a geometric predicate generator that supports most of the above automatic error-bound synthesis methods. They improve the performance of the generated predicates by leveraging C++ meta programming, which is an orthogonal optimization method to ours. Hence, our optimizations could potentially be combined with theirs to improve the performance even further.

References

1. Bartels, T., Fisikopoulos, V.: Fast robust arithmetics for geometric algorithms and applications to GIS. Int. Arch. Photogramm. Remote Sens. Spat. Inf. Sci. **46**, 1–8 (2021). https://doi.org/10.5194/isprs-archives-XLVI-4-W2-2021-1-2021
2. Brönnimann, H., Burnikel, C., Pion, S.: Interval arithmetic yields efficient dynamic filters for computational geometry. Discrete Appl. Math. **109**(1–2), 25–47 (2001). https://doi.org/10.1016/S0166-218X(00)00231-6
3. Darulova, E., Kuncak, V.: Sound compilation of reals. In: Proceedings of the 41st ACM SIGPLAN-SIGACT Symposium on Principles of Programming Languages (POPL), pp. 235–248. ACM, NY (2014)
4. Dekker, T.J.: A floating-point technique for extending the available precision. Numer. Math. **18**(3), 224–242 (1971). https://doi.org/10.1007/BF01397083
5. Delmas, D., Goubault, E., Putot, S., Souyris, J., Tekkal, K., Védrine, F.: Towards an industrial use of FLUCTUAT on safety-critical avionics software. In: Alpuente, M., Cook, B., Joubert, C. (eds.) FMICS 2009. LNCS, vol. 5825, pp. 53–69. Springer, Heidelberg (2009). https://doi.org/10.1007/978-3-642-04570-7_6
6. Devillers, O., Pion, S.: Efficient exact geometric predicates for Delaunay triangulations. Ph.D. thesis, INRIA (2002)
7. Glover, F.: Future paths for integer programming and links to artificial intelligence. Comput. Oper. Res. **13**(5), 533–549 (1986). https://doi.org/10.1016/0305-0548(86)90048-1
8. Meyer, A., Pion, S.: FPG: a code generator for fast and certified geometric predicates. In: Real Numbers and Computers, pp. 47–60 (2008)
9. Moore., R.E.: Interval Analysis. Prentice-Hall (1966)
10. The GNU MPFR library. https://www.mpfr.org
11. Nanevski, A., Blelloch, G., Harper, R.: Automatic generation of staged geometric predicates. In: Proceedings of the Sixth ACM SIGPLAN International Conference on Functional Programming, pp. 217–228 (2001). https://doi.org/10.1145/507669.507662
12. Pion, S.: Interval arithmetic: an efficient implementation and an application to computational geometry. In: Workshop on Applications of Interval Analysis to systems and Control (MISC) (1999)
13. Rubio-González, C., et al.: Precimonious: tuning assistant for floating-point precision. In: Gropp, W., Matsuoka, S. (eds.) SC, p. 27. ACM (2013). https://doi.org/10.1145/2503210.2503296
14. Sanchez-Stern, A., Panchekha, P., Lerner, S., Tatlock, Z.: Finding root causes of floating point error. In: Proceedings of the 39th ACM SIGPLAN Conference on Programming Language Design and Implementation, pp. 256–269 (2018). https://doi.org/10.1145/3192366.3192411
15. Shewchuk, J.R.: Adaptive precision floating-point arithmetic and fast robust geometric predicates. Discrete Comput. Geom. **18**(3), 305–363 (1997). https://doi.org/10.1007/PL00009321
16. Solovyev, A., Baranowski, M.S., Briggs, I., Jacobsen, C., Rakamarić, Z., Gopalakrishnan, G.: Rigorous estimation of floating-point round-off errors with symbolic Taylor expansions. ACM Trans. Program. Lang. Syst. **41**(1), 20 (2018). https://doi.org/10.1145/3230733
17. SymPy: A Python library for symbolic mathematics. https://www.sympy.org
18. Titolo, L., Feliú, M.A., Moscato, M., Muñoz, C.A.: An abstract interpretation framework for the round-off error analysis of floating-point programs. In: VMCAI 2018. LNCS, vol. 10747, pp. 516–537. Springer, Cham (2018). https://doi.org/10.1007/978-3-319-73721-8_24

Statistical Model Checking for Probabilistic Hyperproperties of Real-Valued Signals

Shiraj Arora[1] , René Rydhof Hansen[1] , Kim Guldstrand Larsen[1] ,
Axel Legay[2] , and Danny Bøgsted Poulsen[1(✉)]

[1] Department of Computer Science, Aalborg University, Aalborg, Denmark
dannybpoulsen@cs.aau.dk
[2] Department of Computer Science, Université catholique de Louvain,
Louvain-la-Neuve, Belgium

Abstract. Many security-related properties—such as non-interference—cannot be captured by traditional trace-based specification formalisms such as LTL. The reason is that they relate the events of two (or more) traces of the system, and LTL can only reason on one execution at a time. A number of hyper-property extensions of LTL have been proposed in the past few years, and case studies showing their ability to express interesting properties have also been shown. However, there has been less attention to hyper-properties for quantitative (timed) systems as well as very little work on developing a practically useful tool. Instead existing work focused on using ad-hoc implementations.

In this paper we present a probabilistic hyper-property logic HPSTL for stochastic hybrid and timed systems and we show how to integrate the logic into existing statistical model checking tools. To show the feasibility of our approach we integrate the technique into a prototype implementation inside UPPAAL SMC and apply it to the analysis of three side-channel attack examples. To our knowledge this is the first full implementation of a *hyper logic* inside a fully-fledged modelling environment.

1 Introduction

Hyperproperties are an extension of temporal properties that allows us to characterise not only single executions of a system but the relation between different independent executions of a system. Hyperproperties were first introduced by Clarkson and Schneider [9] as a way to formalise security properties such as non-interference. Clarkson et al. [8] proposed extending two well known temporal logics, LTL and CTL(*), by allowing quantification over multiple (execution)

Work partially sponsored by the ERC Advanced Grant LASSO, the Villum Investigator Grant S4OS, Danish National Research Center DIREC as well as the FNRS PDR/OL project T.0137.21.

O. Legunsen and G. Rosu (Eds.): SPIN 2022, LNCS 13255, pp. 61–78, 2022.
https://doi.org/10.1007/978-3-031-15077-7_4

paths and propositions, resulting in two *hyper logics* for specifying hyperproperties: HyperLTL and HyperCTL(*) respectively. Both have also seen dense-time extensions like HyperSTL [24] and HyperPSTL [26]. Several validation procedures have been proposed for HyperLTL, HyperCTL* and HyperSTL, e.g. based on testing [24] or encoding and model-counting for quantitative HyperLTL [17]. Further, monitoring algorithms have been proposed for HyperLTL [5,15]. The development of tools for validating hyper-properties on systems has also been actively explored. Firstly, model checking of (alternation-free) HyperLTL and HyperCTL* on hardware circuits has been implemented by the tool MCHyper [18] and secondly RVHyper [16] allows for runtime monitoring of HyperLTL properties. Another (very) recent effort in the model checking domain is Hyper-Qube [19]. It performs bounded model checking of NuSMV models and removes the alternation-free restriction of MCHyper.

In recent years, hyperproperties have been extended to the stochastic setting allowing us to express probabilistic relations between multiple executions of a system, e.g., HyperPCTL as an extension of the classical PCTL logic for Markov chains [2,14], later extended to Markov Decision Processes [1,13]. On the tool side, we have seen tools using adapting probabilistic model checking of Markov chains [2] and Markov Decision Processes [1,13] to hyper properties. Simulation based approaches have also been considered, e.g., for HyperPCTL* [25] and HyperPSTL [26], both of which are based on Statistical Model Checking [22].

Even though major contributions have been made in the area of using hyper logics to specify hyperproperties on stochastic cyber physical systems, little has been done on integrating this research in a functional and maintainable tool such as UPPAAL.

The present paper contributes to solving this problem. More precisely,

- We present the logic HPSTL–a hyperlogic and probabilistic extension of the real-time logic STL [23]. HPSTL enables quantitative reasoning on and relating several traces simultaneously through the use of probabilistic path quantifiers.
- The logic HPSTL is given stochastic dense-time semantics for stochastic timed transitions. In particular, the semantic of probabilistic path quantifiers is obtained using so-called self-composition.
- For efficient monitorability of properties we adapt the rewrite-technique of Bulychev et al. [6]
- Verification of HPSTL has been integrated in the UPPAAL SMC toolset [11] by extending the already existing MTL verification engine. Importantly, the full class of stochastic hybrid systems expressible in UPPAAL SMC is supported.
- Through a range of case studies, we show that HPSTL is expressive enough to capture many (most) interesting hyper-properties in security. In particular, we apply the hyper-property implementation in UPPAAL SMC to reveal the existence of timing attacks in RSA.

2   Stochastic Timed Transition Systems

In this work, we abstract from the high-level formalism used to describe systems, and instead consider a system component given as a transition system.

Definition 1. *A* timed transition system *(TTS) over actions Σ is a tuple $T = (S, s_0, \rightarrow, \mathsf{AP}, \mathcal{L})$ where*

- *S is a set of states*
- *s_0 is the initial state*
- *$\rightarrow \subseteq S \times (\Sigma \cup \mathbb{R}_{\geq 0}) \times S$ is the transition relation*
- *AP is a set of propositions and*
- *$\mathcal{L} : S \rightarrow 2^{\mathsf{AP}}$ is a labelling function that maps states to propositions.*

A run ρ over a timed transition system $T = (S, s_0, \rightarrow, \mathsf{AP}, \mathcal{L})$ is an alternating sequence of states, reals and actions, $\rho = s_0 d_0 a_0 s_1 d_1 a_1 \ldots$ such that $s_i \xrightarrow{d_i} \xrightarrow{a_i} s_{i+1}$. In all the following we only consider *deterministic* TTS: whenever $s \xrightarrow{\alpha} s_1$ and $s \xrightarrow{\alpha} s_2$, then $s_1 = s_2$ for $\alpha \in \Sigma \cup \mathbb{R}_{\geq 0}$. For a run $\rho = s_0 d_0 a_0 s_1 d_1 a_1 \ldots$ and $i \geq 0$, we denote by $\rho[i]$ the state s_i, by $\rho[i]^\delta$ the delay d_i, and by $\rho \dagger i$ the suffix $s_i d_i a_i s_{i+1} d_{i+1} a_{i+1} \ldots$. We will sometimes need to advance a run by time units rather than by a state index. To do so, we let $\rho \dagger_\delta \tau = s_i^\kappa (d_{i-k}) a_i s_{i+1} d_{i+1} a_{i+1} \ldots$ where $i = \min\{l \mid \sum_{j=0}^{l} d_j > \tau\}$, $\kappa = \tau - \sum_{j=0}^{i-1} d_j$, and $s_i \xrightarrow{\kappa} s^\kappa$. We denote by Ω_T the set of all infinite runs of T.

Example 1. To syntactically describe timed transition systems we use the extended timed automata [4] formalism of UPPAAL SMC [11]. As an example consider the automaton in Fig. 1 modelling a (fairly naive) login procedure. Initially the system randomly selects a password in `SetupPassword` by calling the function `initialisePassword`. Hereafter the user attempts to login by repeatedly entering randomly chosen characters – using the function `readkey`. Each character is read from the `WaitKey` location after at most one time unit (seen by the invariant `x ≤ 1`). In the `ValidateKey` location, the system checks whether a given character is correct with respect to the selected password:

- if it is, and there are more ciphers to be read, it goes back to `WaitKey`,
- if it is correct, and there no more ciphers to read, it goes to `Done` indicating the entered password attempt was correct,
- if the cipher was wrong, the system also goes to `Done` but indicates with `signinfailed` that the login was not successful.

For all cases, the check takes at most one time unit.

Signals. We shall assume a finite collection of *signals* Z which for each state $s \in S$ is assigned a real value, i.e. for $z \in Z$ the value of z in s is $s(z) \in \mathbb{R}$. Now let s^d (if it exists) denote the unique state reachable from s by a delay of d, i.e. $s \xrightarrow{d} s^d$. For any state s we shall assume that for any signal $z \in Z$ the real-valued function $\lambda d. s^d(z)$ is continuous. A particular group of signals is

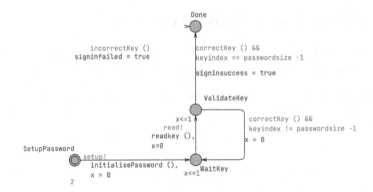

Fig. 1. Login procedure with a timing side-channel

the binary signals $Z_{\text{AP}} = \{z_{\text{p}} \mid \text{p} \in \text{AP}\}$ that attains the value 1 if its associated proposition is true and 0 if it is false i.e. $(z_{\text{p}}) = 1$ if $\text{p} \in \mathcal{L}(s)$ and 0 otherwise.

In a timed transition system, the delays and discrete actions are chosen non-deterministically. The notion of a stochastic timed transition system (STTS) refines these non-deterministic choices by stochastic choices.

Definition 2. *A stochastic timed transition system (STTS) is a triple $\mathcal{T} = (T, \omega)$, where*

- *$T = (S, s_0, \rightarrow, \text{AP}, \mathcal{L})$ is a timed transition system, and*
- *$\omega : S \rightarrow (\Sigma \times \mathbb{R}_{\geq 0} \rightarrow \mathbb{R}_{\geq 0})$ assigns a joint action-delay density to all states $s \in S$ requiring that:*

$$\sum_{a \in \Sigma} \left(\int_{t \in \mathbb{R}_{\geq 0}} \omega(s)(a, t) \, dt \right) = 1 \quad and \tag{1}$$

$$\omega(s)(a, t) \neq 0 \quad implies \quad s \xrightarrow{t} \xrightarrow{a} \tag{2}$$

The first condition captures that ω is a probability density, and the second condition demands that if ω assigns a non-zero density to a delay-action pair, then the underlying timed transition system should be able to perform that action with the given delay.

Example 2. Let us briefly consider how we can put a stochastic interpretation on the login model in Fig. 1 using the framework developed so far. Firstly let us consider the situation where the system is placed in SetupPassword with the clock $x = 0$ i.e. from the state $\langle \text{SetupPassword}, [x \mapsto 0] \rangle$. Since the automaton has no upper bound on how long it can wait in SetupPassword it draws its delay from an exponential distribution with rate parameter 2. The only action possible is setup! thus

$$\omega(\langle \text{SetupPassword}, [x \mapsto 0] \rangle, a, d) = \begin{cases} 2 \cdot e^{-2 \cdot d} & \text{if } a = \text{setup!} \\ 0 & \text{otherwise} \end{cases}$$

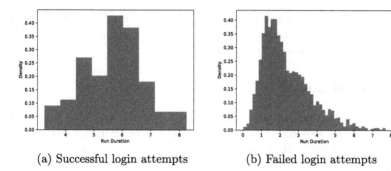

(a) Successful login attempts (b) Failed login attempts

Fig. 2. Time Distribution over successful and failed login attempts on Fig. 1. Plots obtained from UPPAAL SMC with the queries `Pr[<=100] (<> signinfailed)` and `Pr[<=100] (<> signinsuccess)`

From the state $\langle$WaitKey$, [\text{x} \mapsto 0]\rangle$ the **read!** must take place before 1 time-unit. Following the stochastic semantics of UPPAAL SMC this delay will be selected from a uniform distribution over $[0,1]$. Thus

$$\omega(\langle \text{WaitKey}, [\text{x} \mapsto 0]\rangle, a, d) = \begin{cases} 1 & \text{if } a = \text{read!} \wedge d \in [0,1] \\ 0 & \text{otherwise} \end{cases}$$

For an STTS $\mathcal{T}_i = (T_i, \omega_i)$ with $T_i = (S_i, s_0^i, \rightarrow_i, \text{AP}, \mathcal{L}_i)$ let $\delta_{\mathcal{T}_i}(s)(t)$ denote the probability that no action is performed from the state s before a delay of t, i.e.:

$$\delta_{\mathcal{T}_i}(s)(t) = 1 - \left(\sum_{a \in \Sigma} \int_{\tau < t} \omega_i(s)(a, \tau) d\tau \right)$$

Example 3. The naive login procedure in Fig. 1 is vulnerable to a timing attack. This is evident when looking at the time taken to successfully log in (Fig. 2a) and failing to log in (Fig. 2b). From these plots, it is clear that failed logins generally take shorter time than successful logins—this is caused by the fact the login procedure terminates immediately when a character is wrong.

Definition 3 (Composition). *For $i = 1, 2$ let $\mathcal{T}_i = (T_i, \omega_i)$ be an STTS over an alphabet Σ_i with $\Sigma_1 \cap \Sigma_2 = \emptyset$ and $T_i = (S_i, s_0^i, \rightarrow_i, \text{AP}, \mathcal{L}_i)$. The parallel composition $\mathcal{T} = (T_1 \otimes T_2, \omega_1 \otimes \omega_2)$ is the stochastic labelled transition system with $T_1 \otimes T_2 = (S_1 \times S_2, (s_0^1, s_0^2), \rightarrow, \text{AP}, \mathcal{L})$ and $\omega = \omega_1 \otimes \omega_2$ where:*

1. $(s_1, s_2) \xrightarrow{a} (s_1', s_2)$ *whenever* $s_1 \xrightarrow{a}_1 s_1'$ *and* $a \in \Sigma_1$,
2. $(s_1, s_2) \xrightarrow{a} (s_1, s_2')$ *whenever* $s_2 \xrightarrow{a}_2 s_2'$ *and* $a \in \Sigma_2$,
3. $(s_1, s_2) \xrightarrow{d} (s_1^d, s_2^d)$,
4. $\mathcal{L}(s_1, s_2) = \mathcal{L}_1(s_1) \cup \mathcal{L}_2(s_2)$,
5. $\omega((s_1, s_2))(a, t) = \omega_1(s_1)(a, t) \cdot \delta_{\mathcal{T}_2}(s_2)(t)$ *whenever* $a \in \Sigma_1$,
6. $\omega((s_1, s_2))(a, t) = \omega_2(s_2)(a, t) \cdot \delta_{\mathcal{T}_1}(s_1)(t)$ *whenever* $a \in \Sigma_2$.

The above definition of parallel composition extends readily to STTS over disjoint signals Z_1 and Z_2, with the composition having signals $Z_1 \cup Z_2$ and with $(s_1, s_2)(z) = s_i(z)$ whenever $z \in Z_i$ $(i = 1, 2)$.

3   Temporal Logics

Statistical Model Checking has generally been focused on properties that can be determined by looking at just one run. However, it turns out that many interesting properties such as *non-interference* cannot be determined by looking at a single run. The realization that a single-run view is not enough to capture security properties has led to defining logics that allow reasoning on several runs simultaneously. The logic we consider in this paper is HPSTL which is built on top of Signal Temporal Logic (STL) [23].

3.1   Signal Temporal Logic

Before defining HPSTL let us briefly review the syntax and semantics of STL. Signal Temporal Logic (STL) [23] is a temporal logic that deals with time-constrained path operators. It consists of the same path operators as LTL but has a time interval attached to the temporal operators. Let Z be a set of signals then the set of STL formulas is generated by the syntax:

$$\psi ::= \text{tt} \mid z > 0 \mid \neg\psi \mid \psi_1 \wedge \psi_2 \mid \psi_1 \, \mathsf{U}^I \, \psi_2$$

where $z \in Z$, and $I = [t_1, t_2]$ is an interval such that $t_1, t_2 \in \mathbb{Q}_+$ and $t_1 \leq t_2$. We let $\Psi(Z)$ denote the set of all STL formulas over Z.

Remark 1. Since we have seen that a proposition p can easily be transformed into a $0, 1$ signal z_{p}, we will for notational convenience allow just writing p in lieu of $z_{\mathsf{p}} > 0$.

Given a TTS T, an STL property ψ and a run $\rho = s_0 d_0 a_0 s_1 d_1 a_1 \ldots$, we define $\rho \models_T \psi$ – denoting that ρ satisfies ψ – inductively in ψ as follows:

$$
\begin{aligned}
\rho \models_T \text{tt iff} \quad & \text{always} \\
\rho \models_T z > 0 \text{ iff} \quad & \rho[0](z) > 0 \\
\rho \models_T \neg\psi \text{ iff} \quad & \rho \not\models_T \psi \\
\rho \models_T \psi_1 \wedge \psi_2 \text{ iff} \quad & \rho \models_T \psi_1 \text{ and } \rho \models_T \psi_2 \\
\rho \models_T \psi_1 \mathsf{U}^I \psi_2 \text{ iff} \quad & \exists d \in I. \left(\rho \dagger_\delta d \models_T \psi_2 \text{ and } \forall j < d. \rho \dagger_\delta j \models_T \psi_1 \right)
\end{aligned}
$$

Definition 4. *Given an STTS $T = (T, \omega)$ with $T = (S, s_0, \rightarrow, \text{AP}, \mathcal{L})$, an STL property ψ and a state s, we denote by $\mathbb{P}_s^T(\psi)$ the probability that a random run ρ starting in s satisfies ψ, i.e.:*

$$\mathbb{P}_s^T(\psi) = \mathbb{P}^T \left(\{ \rho \mid \rho \models_T \psi \wedge \rho[0] = s \} \right)$$

Here $\mathbb{P}^T$ is the unique probability measure on the σ-algebra on the sets of runs Ω_T generated from cylinders of the form $C_s = \Delta_1 Z_1 \Delta_2 Z_2 \ldots \Delta_k Z_k$, where Δ_i are intervals of the reals, and $Z_i = \zeta_i^1 \times \cdots \times \zeta_i^l$ with ζ_i^j also being intervals of the reals. Now the cylinder C_s describes all runs $\rho = sd_1 a_1 s_1 d_2 a_2 \ldots d_k a_k$ such that $d_i \in \Delta_i$ and $s_i \in Z_i$ $(i = 1 \ldots k)$[1]. The probability $\Pi(C_s)$ assigned to the cylinder C_s is defined inductively as:

$$\Pi(C_s) = \int_{t \in \Delta_1} \sum_{a \in \Sigma : s^{t,a} \in Z_1} \left(\omega(s)(a,t) \cdot \Pi(C'_{s^{t,a}}) \right) dt$$

where $C' = \Delta_2 Z_2 \ldots \Delta_k Z_k$.

3.2   HPSTL

HPSTL is a logic built to reason about *hyperproperties* i.e. properties specified across two or more traces of a system. It adds to STL the possibility of observing multiple runs simultaneously, and allows specifying what atomic propositions has to hold for different simulations. To quantify over different runs, we assume the existence of a finite set of run variables Π. For a set of signals Z and a vector of run variables $\vec{\pi} = [\pi_1, \pi_2, \ldots, \pi_n]$ we let $Z^{\vec{\Pi}} = \{z^\pi | z \in Z \wedge \pi \in \{\pi_1, \ldots \pi_n\}\}$. For a set of signals Z we generate all valid HPSTL formulas by the syntax

$$\Theta :: = \neg\Theta \,|\, \Theta_1 \wedge \Theta_2 \,|\, \Phi_1 \geq \Phi_2$$

$$\Phi :: = \mathbf{P}^{\vec{\pi}}(\psi^{\vec{\pi}}) \,|\, \mathbf{P}^{\vec{\pi}}(\psi_1^{\vec{\pi}} \,|\, \psi_2^{\vec{\pi}}) \, - \, C$$

where $\vec{\pi}$ is a vector of run variables, $\vec{\pi} = [\pi_1, \pi_2, ..., \pi_k]$, $\psi_1^{\vec{\pi}}, \psi_2^{\vec{\pi}} \in \Psi(Z^{\vec{\Pi}})$ are STL formulas over $Z^{\vec{\Pi}}$ and $C \in \mathbb{Q}$.

HPSTL has two parts: a quantitative fragment covered by the Φ part of the syntax, and a qualitative fragment covered by the Θ part. Intuitively, the qualitative fragment Θ is a Boolean formula over comparisons of the quantities of Φ. Here, Φ is either a constant C, the probability, $\mathbf{P}^{\vec{\pi}}(\psi)$, that independent sampled runs of the variables in $\vec{\pi}$ will satisfy the formula, or a conditional probability, $\mathbf{P}^{\vec{\pi}}(\psi_1^{\vec{\pi}} \,|\, \psi_2^{\vec{\pi}})$. Finally, a run formula ψ is constructed using the classical STL operators, but with constraints referring to specific run variables $\pi \in \Pi$. We emphasize that, due to the presence of conditional probability formulas, HPSTL allows to express in a single formula any arbitrary Bayesian Networks over a collection of events $\{\psi_i \,|\, i \in I\}$ expressed as STL formula. This may be useful for run-time monitoring as shown in [20].

Remark 2. HPSTL can be seen as a fragment of HyperPSTL [26] as it does not allow nesting of path quantifiers. It makes HPSTL less expressive than Hyper-PSTL. This is a deliberate choice as it allows the logic to be monitorable, as needed for Statistical Model Checking in later sections.

---

[1] Here $s_i \in Z_i$ is a shorthand for $s_i(z_o) \in \zeta_i^o$ for any $o = 1 \ldots l$.

Semantics. Let $\mathcal{T} = (T, \omega)$ be an STTS over action set Σ, where $T = (S, s_0, \rightarrow, AP, \mathcal{L})$. For a run variable $\pi \in \Pi$, we denote by $\mathcal{T}^\pi$ the STTS over the action set $\Sigma \times \{\pi\}$ which is isomorphic to $\mathcal{T}$ except that all actions $a \in \Sigma$ have been renamed to (a, π), and all propositions **a** have been renamed to **a**$^\pi$. We denote by $\mathcal{T}^\Pi$ the following $|\Pi|$-fold self-composition of $\mathcal{T}$:

$$\mathcal{T}^\Pi = \bigotimes_{\pi \in \Pi} \mathcal{T}^\pi \qquad (3)$$

Note that the set of runs $\Omega_{\mathcal{T}^\Pi}$ is isomorphic to the set of run assignments $[\Pi \rightarrow \Omega_{\mathcal{T}}]$. Here the map from $\Omega_{\mathcal{T}^\Pi}$ to $[\Pi \rightarrow \Omega_{\mathcal{T}}]$ is given by projections, and the map from $[\Pi \rightarrow \Omega_{\mathcal{T}}]$ to $\Omega_{\mathcal{T}^\Pi}$ is obtained by merging. Let $v : [\Pi \rightarrow \Omega_{\mathcal{T}}]$ be a run assignment. Using the above isomorphism we may define the i'th state assignment $v[i]$ as well as the suffix run assignment $v \dagger i$ for $i \geq 0$.

Now, let Φ be a quantitative formula. We define the corresponding real value $[\![\Phi]\!]_{\mathcal{T}}$ inductively as follows:

$$[\![\mathbf{P}^{\bar{\pi}}(\psi)]\!]_{\mathcal{T}} = \mathbb{P}^{\mathcal{T}^\Pi}_{\mathbf{s_0}}(\psi), \quad \text{where } \forall \pi. \, \mathbf{s_0}(\pi) = s_0.$$

$$[\![\mathbf{P}^{\bar{\pi}}(\psi_1 | \psi_2)]\!]_{\mathcal{T}} = \frac{\mathbb{P}^{\mathcal{T}^\Pi}_{\mathbf{s_0}}(\psi_1 \wedge \psi_2)}{\mathbb{P}^{\mathcal{T}^\Pi}_{\mathbf{s_0}}(\psi_2)}, \quad \text{where } \forall \pi. \, \mathbf{s_0}(\pi) = s_0.$$

Finally, let Θ be a (qualitative) HPSTL formula. We define $\mathcal{T} \models \Theta$ – that $\mathcal{T}$ satisfies Θ – inductively as follows:

$$\mathcal{T} \models \neg\Theta \quad \text{iff} \quad \mathcal{T} \not\models \Theta$$
$$\mathcal{T} \models \Theta_1 \wedge \Theta_2 \quad \text{iff} \quad \mathcal{T} \models \Theta_1 \text{ and } \mathcal{T} \models \Theta_2$$
$$\mathcal{T} \models \Phi_1 \bowtie \Phi_2 \quad \text{iff} \quad [\![\Phi_1]\!]_{\mathcal{T}} \bowtie [\![\Phi_2]\!]_{\mathcal{T}}$$

Example 4. As already discussed, the login procedure in Fig. 1 is vulnerable to a timing attack i.e. by observing the timing of login attempts an attacker might deduce how many characters were correct in his guess. To avoid such attacks, the run-time of the login procedure should be independent of the typed password. In particular, the run-time of two independent runs of our model should be the same—or at least a δ close to each other. In HPSTL we can express the probability of having this property as

$$\mathbf{P}^{\pi_0, \pi_1}\left((\neg\mathsf{Done}^{\pi_0} \wedge \neg\mathsf{Done}^{\pi_1}) \, \mathsf{U}^{[0, \Delta]}\left(\bigvee_{i=0,1}\left(\mathsf{Done}^{\pi_i} \wedge \Diamond^{[0, \delta]}\mathsf{Done}^{\pi_j}\right)\right)\right), \quad (4)$$

where $j = (i + 1) \bmod 2$, and Δ is a time-bound large enough for all login-attempts to finish. In our implementation of HPSTL in UPPAAL SMC we have assessed this probability for varying values of δ (Table 1a).

Example 5. The conditional probability operator of HPSTL is useful to gather information about a model given another property. As an example, consider again our login procedure and compare the probability that the sign-in fails within some limit δ given it terminates before the same time limit (Eq. 5) against the probability that the sign-in succeeds within δ time units given it terminates within δ time units (Eq. 6). We have estimated these probabilities for various deltas in Table 1b.

$$\psi ::= \mathbf{P}^{\pi_0} \left((\lozenge^{[0,\delta]} \mathtt{signinfailed}^{\pi_0}) | (\lozenge^{[0,\delta]} \mathtt{Done}^{\pi_0}) \right), \qquad (5)$$

$$\upsilon ::= \mathbf{P}^{\pi_0} \left((\lozenge^{[0,\delta]} \mathtt{signinsuccess}^{\pi_0}) | (\lozenge^{[0,\delta]} \mathtt{Done}^{\pi_0}) \right), \qquad (6)$$

4   Statistical Model Checking of Hyperproperties

We use *Statistical Model Checking* (SMC) [27] to test if a STTS satisfies a HPSTL formula. Statistical model checking is a simulation-based verification technique for which we need 1. a *generator* creating a new random run of a self-composed STTS, 2. a *monitor* that determines whether a run satisfies an STL property, and 3. *statistical core algorithms* per HPSTL construct used for determining how many samples are needed. To apply statistical model checking to HPSTL we thus need to implement the generator for the self-composed system, a monitoring technique, and the core algorithm. In practice we monitor runs while generating them.

Generation/Monitoring. UPPAAL already has built-in support for monitoring MTL [21] properties using *rewrite* technique [6] where a MTL formula ψ to be monitored is repeatedly rewritten and evaluated during run-generation. We adopt this technique to the setting of HPSTL through the construction of self-composition. The strategy for estimating a quantitative property $\mathbf{P}^{\vec{\pi}}(\psi)$, where $\vec{\pi} = \langle \pi_1, \pi_2 \ldots, \pi_n \rangle$, is simply to make n copies of the transition systems, rename signals appropriately (as discussed in Subsect. 3.2) and monitor the property as if it was an ordinary MTL-formula. We adapt the work of Bulychev et al. [6] to dense-time HPSTL through discretization using a user-defined granularity. In this way, we can approximate the dense-time semantics arbitrarily closely.

Table 1. Probability estimates for the running example

δ	Probability	Confidence
1	$[0.45, 0.46]$	0.95
2	$[0.69, 0.71]$	0.95
3	$[0.84, 0.86]$	0.95
4	$[0.92, 0.94]$	0.95

(a) Probability of satisfying Equation 4

δ	ψ	υ	Confidence
2	$[0.990, 1.000]$	$[0.000, 0.000]$	0.99
4	$[0.987, 0.999]$	$[0.000, 0.000]$	0.99
8	$[0.961, 0.979]$	$[0.022, 0.040]$	0.99
16	$[0.953, 0.972]$	$[0.026, 0.044]$	0.99

(b) Probability of satisfying Equation 5 (ψ) and Equation 6 (υ)

Core Algorithms. Depending on the syntactical structure of HPSTL we use a different core algorithm for each of its operators (to be discussed in the following). For every operator, the algorithms draw samples from a Bernoulli random variable $\mathcal{X}_T^{\psi,\vec{\pi}}$ attaining the values $\{0,1\}$ by using the discussed monitoring technique.

$\mathbf{P}^{\vec{\pi}}(\psi^{\vec{\pi}}) \geq C$ where C is a constant. In this setting we wish to determine whether $\mathbb{P}_{\mathbf{s}_0}^{\mathcal{T}^{II}}(\psi)$ is greater than the constant C. This can be statistically determined using hypothesis testing. In essence, we wish to test the hypothesis $\mathrm{H} : \mathbb{P}_{\mathbf{s}_0}^{\mathcal{T}^{II}}(\psi) \geq C$ against the alternative $\mathrm{K}:\mathbb{P}_{\mathbf{s}_0}^{\mathcal{T}^{II}}(\psi) < C$. However, in practice we soften the hypotheses to test $\mathrm{H}_1 : \mathbb{P}_{\mathbf{s}_0}^{\mathcal{T}^{II}}(\psi) \geq C + \delta_0$ against $\mathrm{K}_1 : \mathbb{P}_{\mathbf{s}_0}^{\mathcal{T}^{II}}(\psi) < C - \delta_1$ for $\delta_0, \delta_1 \in [0,1]$. The hypothesis test has two strength parameters α and β. The parameter α (*significance*) is the probability our test rejects H_1 when H_1 holds, while β (*power*) is the probability of accepting H_1 when K_1 holds.
The algorithm we use for performing the above hypothesis test is Wald's SPRT algorithm.

$\mathbf{P}^{\vec{\pi}_1}(\psi_1^{\vec{\pi}_1}) \geq \mathbf{P}^{\vec{\pi}_2}(\psi_2^{\vec{\pi}_2})$ For comparing probabilities we use a modified SPRT algorithm as detailed by [12].

$\Theta_1 \wedge \Theta_2$ We determine this property by doing a hypothesis test of $\mathrm{H} : \Theta_1 \wedge \Theta_2$ against $\mathrm{K} : \neg\Theta_1 \vee \neg\Theta_2$ in the following way. Assume we have tests for determining whether Θ_1 and Θ_2 are true with significance α_1 (resp. α_2) and power β_1 (resp. β_2). Then we conclude that $\Theta_1 \wedge \Theta_2$ is true (H holds) if the tests say that Θ_1 and Θ_2 are true, and it is false if one of them is false (K holds). We now investigate what is the significance and power of this test. In order to reject H when it holds, one of the tests has to reject when it should accept. The probability of this happening is $1 - (1 - \alpha_1) \cdot (1 - \alpha_2)$. Thus, we conclude our test has significance $\alpha = 1 - (1 - \alpha_1) \cdot (1 - \alpha_2)$. In order to accept H when K then either
- both Θ_1 and Θ_2 are false, but determined to be true. The probability of this is $\beta_1 \cdot \beta_2$.
- $\Theta_i, i \in \{1,2\}$ is false, but determined to be true. The probability of accepting H now depends on the result of the test for Θ_j, $j \neq i$. Let $\gamma \leq 1$ be the probability that Θ_j is determined to be true. Then the probability of accepting $\Theta_1 \wedge \Theta_2$ is $\beta_i \cdot \gamma \leq \beta_i$. Thus our test has power $\beta \leq \beta_i$

In either case we notice that our power β must be less than or equal to $\max(\beta_1, \beta_2)$.

$\neg\Theta$ Assume we have a test for determining with significance α_1 and power β_1 whether Θ holds. Then we determine $\neg\Theta$ by simply testing Θ and negating the result. The resulting test of $\neg\Theta$ has significance β_1 and power α_1.

$\mathbf{P}^{\vec{\pi}}(\psi)$ The algorithm we employ for estimating probabilities is a sequential algorithm based around the *Clopper-Pearson exact* confidence interval [10] for binomial distributions. The algorithm constructs a confidence interval and takes two parameters: the desired confidence level α and the desired confidence interval width $2 \cdot \epsilon$. The algorithm proceeds in the following way: a sample is generated, and it is determined if it satisfies the property of interest. Afterwards, the algorithm constructs an α-confidence interval based on the result of previous samples. If the confidence interval has a width of $2 \cdot \epsilon$ the algorithm terminates and returns the confidence interval. Otherwise, it asks for another sample.

$\mathbf{P}^{\vec{\pi}}(\psi_1|\psi_2)$ A naive strategy for calculating conditional probabilities could be first estimate $\alpha \approx \mathbf{P}^{\vec{\pi}}(\psi_1 \wedge \psi_2)$ and $\beta \approx \mathbf{P}^{\vec{\pi}}(\psi_2)$ and then calculate $\frac{\alpha}{\beta}$. This follows trivially from the definition, and all we need to do is combine the confidence interval of α and β. This strategy however performs two sets of simulations which is unnecessary. We instead estimate conditional probabilities by implementing a generator/monitor that monitors both ψ_1 and ψ_2 simultaneously: if during generation ψ_2 is false at any point, the run is discarded and a new run is created instead. If ψ_2 is determined to be satisfied then the result of monitoring $\psi_1|\psi_2$ (for that particular run) is the result of monitoring ψ_1. This means that the monitor effectively only generates a sample that satisfies ψ_2. It thus generates samples of the Bernoulli random variable $\mathcal{X}_T^{\psi_1|\psi_2,\vec{\pi}}$ and we can "just" reuse the Clopper-Pearson algorithm discussed for $\mathbf{P}^{\vec{\pi}}(\psi)$.

5   Experiments

We have extended the UPPAAL SMC tool suite with support for verifying HPSTL properties. The extension supports all modelling features of UPPAAL SMC and is to our knowledge the first fully-fledged modelling tool with support for verification of probabilistic hyperproperties. Figure 3 shows the overall structure of the implementation. On the left of the figure, we have an HPSTL formula, Θ, and the stochastic timed automaton model to be verified. The model is created using the classic UPPAAL SMC GUI and Θ is likewise typed in as a verification query. Users experience no major difference between verifying hyperproperties or classic SMC properties . The engine is the middle part of Fig. 3. At the bottom, the engine consists of a *hyper-trace* generator generating traces of the self-composed system. This generator produces traces for a monitor of the path formula, ψ^2. The monitor decides if the trace satisfies ψ. In the figure, there is a loop between the monitor and generator two since they continuously exchange hyper-states to determine satisfaction/violation early. The monitor is invoked by *SMC Core Algorithm* that asks for as many samples as it needs. The *SMC Core Algorithm* is of course selected depending on Θ is. The user has full control of the strength parameters $(\alpha, \beta, \epsilon)$ the SMC core algorithms needs. The result of qualitative properties is satisfied (✔) or not satisfied (➖), and for quantitative properties it is a probability. In the following we analyse two case-studies using our implementation.[3]

---

[2] For formulas involving multiple path formulas there are multiple monitors as well.

[3] The UPPAAL models and scripts for reproducing the results in the paper is available from https://github.com/dannybpoulsen/HyperPropertiesModels.

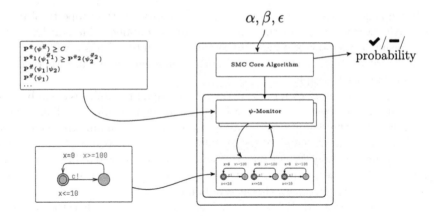

Fig. 3. Architectural overview of the UPPAAL implementation

5.1   Dining Cryptographers

Several cryptographers from a company are gathered to have dinner at a restaurant. The bill for the meal is either paid anonymously by one of the cryptographers or is paid by the owner of the company. If the bill is paid by a cryptographer, it is necessary to maintain the privacy of the same. However, it is also necessary to communicate between the cryptographers whether the owner has paid. Thus, to maintain both privacy and communication, each cryptographer can share information with only the neighbour on the right side based on the following rules: 1. Each cryptographer tosses an unbiased coin and shares the information (either true or false) with the neighbour on the right side. 2. Each cryptographer then compares the shared information with the one of their own coin. 3. If a cryptographer has not paid for the meal and both coins show the same, then the cryptographer broadcasts an "agree" to all other cryptographers and a "disagree" otherwise. 4. A cryptographer that has paid the bill broadcasts a "disagree" if the two coins show the same and an "agree" if the two coins are different. These rules ensure that if there are N cryptographers with N being even, an even number of "agrees" indicates that the owner has paid whereas an odd number of "agrees" indicates that one of the cryptographers has paid. Conversely, if N is odd, the mapping is reversed. This problem was first discussed in [7]. In the following, we reconsider the Dining Cryptographers' problem in a timed setting using the statistical model checking engine of UPPAAL SMC. In Fig. 4 the Dining Cryptographers Problem is modelled using stochastic timed automata. The model consists of an automaton (on the right side) for randomly (uniformly) choosing the payer among the N cryptographers (indices $0 \ldots N - 1$) and the owner (index N). In addition the model contains N instances of the C automaton template (on the left side) parameterised with an id. Here the cryptographer C(id) first randomly tosses her coin, coin[id], followed by the appropriate announcement of agreement in agree[id] according to the rules above.

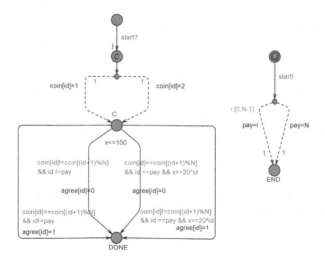

Fig. 4. Dining cryptographer Problem in UPPAAL SMC

Correctness of the untimed protocol has already been established [7,26], so here we focus on the timed behaviour as shown in Fig. 4: Once the cryptographers have tossed their coins, the announcement of an agreement by the cryptographer C(id) will be subject to some time delay as expressed by the constraints on the clock x. The invariant x <= 100 in location C guarantees that the agreement will be announced before 100 time units. However the constraint x >= 20 * id in the guards on the two right-most transitions out

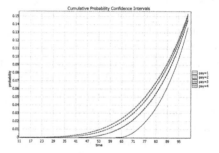

Fig. 5. Probabilities $\mathbb{P}^\pi \left(\Diamond_{\leq T} (\bigwedge_{i=0}^{N-1} \mathtt{C(i)}.\right.$ $\left.\mathtt{DONE}) \wedge \mathtt{pay} = j \right)$ for $j \in \{1,2,3,4\}$ and $T \in [0,100]$ obtained using UPPAAL SMC.

of C reflects that a cryptographer has some hesitation in announcing the agreement in the case she actually paid the bill. The delay before the announcement will be chosen uniformly in the interval $[\ell, 100]$, where $\ell = 20 * \mathtt{id}$ if the cryptographer paid and $\ell = 0$ otherwise. Now preservation of privacy in this timed setting may be expressed by the HPSTL formula below, expressing that for any completion time T, the probabilities that any two cryptographers j and k paid are the same:

$$\mathbf{P}^{\pi_1} \left(\Diamond_{\leq T} (\bigwedge_{i=0}^{N-1} \mathtt{C(i)}.\mathtt{DONE}) \wedge \mathtt{pay} = j \right) = \mathbf{P}^{\pi_2} \left(\Diamond_{\leq T} (\bigwedge_{i=0}^{N-1} \mathtt{C(i)}.\mathtt{DONE}) \wedge \mathtt{pay} = k \right)$$

However, as can be seen by Fig. 5 (with $N = 4$) the properties above do not hold. In fact, if the protocol completes before $T = 100$ with the agreement-

```
s = 1; i = 0;
while(i < w) {
   if(k[i])
      r = (s * x) mod n
   else {
      r = s;

   }
   s = r * r; i = i + 1;
}
```

```
s = 1; i = 0;
while(i < w) {
   if(k[i])
      r = (s * x) mod n
   else {
      r = s;
      ChooseDelay(...);
   }
   s = r * r; i = i + 1;
}
```

Listing 1.1. RSA Exponentiation Algorithm (adapted from [3])

Listing 1.2. RSA Exponentiation Algorithm with added random delay

parity indicating that a cryptographer has paid, then it is most likely that the cryptographer C(1) has paid. Thus the protocol is vulnerable to timing attacks.

5.2 RSA

As shown by the login example above, an attacker may use the timing properties of a system to learn about sensitive information such as passwords. Timing-channels are also a major challenge when implementing cryptographic algorithms. Consider for example the RSA cryptographic algorithm where both encryption and decryption operations are defined essentially by exponentiation of the message to be de-/en-crypted using the private/public key as an exponent. However, a naive implementation of the exponentiation operation, as seen in Listing 1.1, may leak information through timing. Here 'k' is a Boolean array containing the binary representation of the *private* key of an RSA public/private key pair, 'w' is the width (in bits) of the private key, 'x' is the value to be exponentiated, and 'n' is the so-called modulus of the public and private keys, while 's' and 'i' are temporary variables. Finally, 'r' stores the end result of the exponentiation. In order to optimise performance, the above code follows different code paths depending on the (bit-)value of each position of the secret key: for zero bit positions in the private key, no update of the (current) exponent is necessary, leading to a significantly faster computation than for the key positions with a one bit. This optimisation is exactly what leads to a timing channel: if an attacker can observe the timing behaviour of the above code, i.e., can observe how long each iteration through the while-loop takes, then it is possible to reconstruct the private key.

One way to counter such an attack is to require that *any two runs of the algorithm on two different keys must result in observable execution times that are δ-close* where δ is a constant describing the timing granularity of observations an attacker can make. Thus, in our probabilistic setting we want to ensure that the probability of loop iterations finishing within δ time units of each other in two different execution paths (π_1 and π_2) is greater than a certain threshold of *acceptable risk* (ϵ):

$$\mathbf{P}^{\{\pi_1,\pi_2\}}\,\Big[\,\bigwedge_{i=0}^{w-1}\big((\neg(z_i^{\pi_1}>0)\wedge\neg(z_i^{\pi_2}>0))\;\mathsf{U}$$
$$((z_i^{\pi_1}>0\wedge(\mathsf{tt}\,\mathsf{U}^{[0,\delta]}z_i^{\pi_2}>0))\vee(z_i^{\pi_2}>0\wedge(\mathsf{tt}\,\mathsf{U}^{[0,\delta]}z_i^{\pi_1}>0))))\,\Big]\geq 1-\epsilon$$
$$\tag{7}$$

where the set of signals, $Z_{\text{Iteration}}=[z_1,\dots,z_w]$, encodes the timing of loop iterations such that $z_i^\pi>0$ signals that the ith loop iteration in trace π_i has completed. Note the use of the $\mathsf{U}^{[0,\delta]}$ operator, to encode that loop iterations in the two traces finish within δ time units of each other.

One way to obtain time-sensitive non-interference in our example program, as demonstrated in [3], is to add pseudo-instructions in such a way that both branches of the conditional takes exactly the same amount of time to execute. However, this also "guarantees" that the program will exhibit the worst case execution time in every execution. In our probabilistic setting, we can explore a different approach: adding random delay (in the fast branch, see below) allowing us to investigate whether that is (sufficiently) secure and if so, to find a suitable trade-off between performance and security as defined by the granularity of the attacker's observations (δ).

We first add a delay in the shorter branch (represented by the function `ChooseDelay(...)`) in Listing 1.2. For our initial exploration, we pick the random delays from an exponential distribution with an expected value equal to the worst case running time of the algorithm. Next we construct a UPPAAL encoding of the exponentiation algorithm (shown in Fig. 6). In this model the length of the key is held in the variable W and the actual key held in the array s.key. The local variables i, s, r, and n are kept in the UPPAAL struct s.

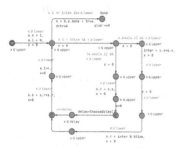

Fig. 6. UPPAAL timed automaton for the RSA exponentiation algorithm.

Finally, we perform a range of experiments: we consider different values of δ (1–5) representing attackers able to make observations of the time-channel with varying degrees of granularity. For each of these values, we then perform experiments to determine the probability of loop iterations finishing within δ time units of each other for any two runs of the algorithm, i.e., Property 7 without the final filtering on acceptable risk (ϵ) to better illustrate the differing results for varying values of δ.

From a security point of view, Fig. 7a shows that for $2\leq\delta\leq 4$ the probability of two loop iterations being indistinguishable to an attacker is significantly higher than without the added delay[4]. However, for $\delta=1$ and $\delta=5$ the added random

---

[4] Note that to highlight the differences, we have elided the graph for the "worst case" running time (which always has probability = 1, since both branches take the same amount of time).

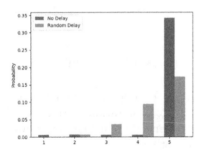
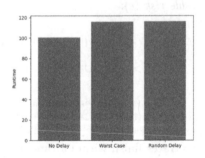

(a) Probability of satisfying Property 7 for (b) Execution times for: no delay, worst case,
$1 \leq \delta \leq 5$ and added random delay

Fig. 7. Results for the performance vs security trade-off comparison for RSA crypto-graphic algorithm

delay does not improve security, quite the contrary. Nevertheless, this seems to indicate that by careful choice of distribution for the random delay, it is possible to reduce the capacity of the timing channel and thus improve security. This will of course require significant further exploration and verification efforts which is facilitated by our tool. Turning to running times, we see in Fig. 7b that, for our chosen distribution of random delays, the running time is *not* improved over the worst case running time, thus obviating the (potential) security benefits derived from adding random delays. We conjecture that, again, a better choice of random distribution for the random delay may enable gains in execution times. This will also require significant further exploration which is again facilitated by our tool.

6   Conclusion

In this paper, we proposed a hyper temporal logic HPSTL: a hyper and proba-bilistic extension of the real-time logic Signal Temporal Logic. We used HPSTL to observe and reason several traces simultaneously for stochastic timed transi-tion systems. The statistical model checking algorithm for verification of HPSTL is adapted from self-composition and rewrite based monitoring techniques and has been implemented in UPPAAL SMC tool set. This implementation supports the full class of stochastic hybrid systems expressible in UPPAAL SMC. We then also exhibit the expressiveness of the logic to capture many important hyper-properties using case studies, in the domain of security, in particular vulnerability of systems to timing attacks.

References

1. Ábrahám, E., Bartocci, E., Bonakdarpour, B., Dobe, O.: Probabilistic hyperproperties with nondeterminism. In: Hung, D.V., Sokolsky, O. (eds.) ATVA 2020. LNCS, vol. 12302, pp. 518–534. Springer, Cham (2020). https://doi.org/10.1007/978-3-030-59152-6_29
2. Ábrahám, E., Bonakdarpour, B.: HyperPCTL: a temporal logic for probabilistic hyperproperties. In: McIver, A., Horvath, A. (eds.) QEST 2018. LNCS, vol. 11024, pp. 20–35. Springer, Cham (2018). https://doi.org/10.1007/978-3-319-99154-2_2
3. Agat, J.: Transforming out timing leaks. In: Proceedings of the Annual ACM Symposium on Principles of Programming Languages (POPL 2000), pp. 40–53 (2000)
4. Alur, R., Dill, D.L.: A theory of timed automata. Theor. Comput. Sci. 126(2), 183–235 (1994). https://doi.org/10.1016/0304-3975(94)90010-8
5. Bonakdarpour, B., Sanchez, C., Schneider, G.: Monitoring hyperproperties by combining static analysis and runtime verification. In: Margaria, T., Steffen, B. (eds.) ISoLA 2018. LNCS, vol. 11245, pp. 8–27. Springer, Cham (2018). https://doi.org/10.1007/978-3-030-03421-4_2
6. Bulychev, P., David, A., Larsen, K.G., Legay, A., Li, G., Poulsen, D.B.: Rewrite-based statistical model checking of WMTL. In: Qadeer, S., Tasiran, S. (eds.) RV 2012. LNCS, vol. 7687, pp. 260–275. Springer, Heidelberg (2013). https://doi.org/10.1007/978-3-642-35632-2_25
7. Chaum, D.: The dining cryptographers problem: Unconditional sender and recipient untraceability. J. Cryptology 1, 65–75 (1988)
8. Clarkson, M.R., Finkbeiner, B., Koleini, M., Micinski, K.K., Rabe, M.N., Sánchez, C.: Temporal logics for hyperproperties. In: Abadi, M., Kremer, S. (eds.) POST 2014. LNCS, vol. 8414, pp. 265–284. Springer, Heidelberg (2014). https://doi.org/10.1007/978-3-642-54792-8_15
9. Clarkson, M.R., Schneider, F.B.: Hyperproperties. J. Comput. Secur. 18(6), 1157–1210 (2010)
10. Clopper, C.J., Pearson, E.S.: The use of confidence or fiducial limits illustrated in the case of the binomial. Biometrika 26(4), 404–413 (1934). http://www.jstor.org/stable/2331986
11. David, A., Larsen, K.G., Legay, A., Mikucionis, M., Poulsen, D.B.: Uppaal SMC tutorial. Int. J. Softw. Tools Technol. Transf. 17(4), 397–415 (2015), https://doi.org/10.1007/s10009-014-0361-y
12. David, A., Larsen, K.G., Legay, A., Mikučionis, M., Poulsen, D.B., van Vliet, J., Wang, Z.: Statistical model checking for networks of priced timed automata. In: Fahrenberg, U., Tripakis, S. (eds.) FORMATS 2011. LNCS, vol. 6919, pp. 80–96. Springer, Heidelberg (2011). https://doi.org/10.1007/978-3-642-24310-3_7
13. Dimitrova, R., Finkbeiner, B., Torfah, H.: Probabilistic hyperproperties of markov decision processes. In: Hung, D.V., Sokolsky, O. (eds.) ATVA 2020. LNCS, vol. 12302, pp. 484–500. Springer, Cham (2020). https://doi.org/10.1007/978-3-030-59152-6_27
14. Dobe, O., Ábrahám, E., Bartocci, E., Bonakdarpour, B.: HYPERPROB: a model checker for probabilistic hyperproperties. In: Huisman, M., Păsăreanu, C., Zhan, N. (eds.) FM 2021. LNCS, vol. 13047, pp. 657–666. Springer, Cham (2021). https://doi.org/10.1007/978-3-030-90870-6_35
15. Finkbeiner, B., Hahn, C., Stenger, M., Tentrup, L.: Monitoring hyperproperties. In: Lahiri, S., Reger, G. (eds.) RV 2017. LNCS, vol. 10548, pp. 190–207. Springer, Cham (2017). https://doi.org/10.1007/978-3-319-67531-2_12

16. Finkbeiner, B., Hahn, C., Stenger, M., Tentrup, L.: Rvhyper: A runtime verification tool for temporal hyperproperties. CoRR abs/1906.00798 (2019). http://arxiv.org/abs/1906.00798
17. Finkbeiner, B., Hahn, C., Torfah, H.: Model checking quantitative hyperproperties. In: Chockler, H., Weissenbacher, G. (eds.) CAV 2018. LNCS, vol. 10981, pp. 144–163. Springer, Cham (2018). https://doi.org/10.1007/978-3-319-96145-3_8
18. Finkbeiner, B., Rabe, M.N., Sánchez, C.: Algorithms for model checking Hyper-LTL and HyperCTL*. In: Kroening, D., Păsăreanu, C.S. (eds.) CAV 2015. LNCS, vol. 9206, pp. 30–48. Springer, Cham (2015). https://doi.org/10.1007/978-3-319-21690-4_3
19. Hsu, T.H., Bonakdarpour, B., Sánchez, C.: Hyperqube: A qbf-based bounded model checker for hyperproperties (2021). https://arxiv.org/abs/2109.12989
20. Jaeger, M., Larsen, K.G., Tibo, A.: From statistical model checking to run-time monitoring using a bayesian network approach. In: Deshmukh, J., Ničković, D. (eds.) RV 2020. LNCS, vol. 12399, pp. 517–535. Springer, Cham (2020). https://doi.org/10.1007/978-3-030-60508-7_30
21. Koymans, R.: Specifying real-time properties with metric temporal logic. Real Time Syst. **2**(4), 255–299 (1990). https://doi.org/10.1007/BF01995674
22. Legay, A., Lukina, A., Traonouez, L.M., Yang, J., Smolka, S.A., Grosu, R.: Statistical model checking. In: Steffen, B., Woeginger, G. (eds.) Computing and Software Science. LNCS, vol. 10000, pp. 478–504. Springer, Cham (2019). https://doi.org/10.1007/978-3-319-91908-9_23
23. Maler, O., Nickovic, D.: Monitoring temporal properties of continuous signals. In: Lakhnech, Y., Yovine, S. (eds.) FORMATS/FTRTFT -2004. LNCS, vol. 3253, pp. 152–166. Springer, Heidelberg (2004). https://doi.org/10.1007/978-3-540-30206-3_12
24. Nguyen, L.V., Kapinski, J., Jin, X., Deshmukh, J.V., Johnson, T.T.: Hyperproperties of real-valued signals. In: Proceedings of the 15th ACM-IEEE International Conference on Formal Methods and Models for System Design, pp. 104–113 (2017)
25. Wang, Y., Nalluri, S., Bonakdarpour, B., Pajic, M.: Statistical model checking for hyperproperties. In: 2021 IEEE 34th Computer Security Foundations Symposium (CSF), pp. 1–16. IEEE (2021)
26. Wang, Y., Zarei, M., Bonakdarpour, B., Pajic, M.: Statistical verification of hyperproperties for cyber-physical systems. ACM Trans. Embed. Comput. Syst. **18**(5s), 92:1–92:23 (2019). https://doi.org/10.1145/3358232
27. Younes, H.L.S., Simmons, R.G.: Probabilistic verification of discrete event systems using acceptance sampling. In: Brinksma, E., Larsen, K.G. (eds.) CAV 2002. LNCS, vol. 2404, pp. 223–235. Springer, Heidelberg (2002). https://doi.org/10.1007/3-540-45657-0_17

SpecRepair: Counter-Example Guided Safety Repair of Deep Neural Networks

Fabian Bauer-Marquart[1]([✉]) [iD], David Boetius[1] [iD], Stefan Leue[1] [iD], and Christian Schilling[2] [iD]

[1] University of Konstanz, Konstanz, Germany
fabian.marquart@uni-konstanz.de
[2] Aalborg University, Aalborg, Denmark

Abstract. Deep neural networks (DNNs) are increasingly applied in safety-critical domains, such as self-driving cars, unmanned aircraft, and medical diagnosis. It is of fundamental importance to certify the safety of these DNNs, i.e. that they comply with a formal safety specification. While safety certification tools exactly answer this question, they are of no help in debugging unsafe DNNs, requiring the developer to iteratively verify and modify the DNN until safety is eventually achieved. Hence, a repair technique needs to be developed that can produce a safe DNN automatically. To address this need, we present SpecRepair, a tool that efficiently eliminates counter-examples from a DNN and produces a provably safe DNN without harming its classification accuracy. SpecRepair combines specification-based counter-example search and resumes training of the DNN, penalizing counter-examples and certifying the resulting DNN. We evaluate SpecRepair's effectiveness on the ACAS Xu benchmark, a DNN-based controller for unmanned aircraft, and two image classification benchmarks. The results show that SpecRepair is more successful in producing safe DNNs than comparable methods, has a shorter runtime, and produces safe DNNs while preserving their classification accuracy.

Keywords: Neural networks · Safety repair · Safety specification

1 Introduction

Autonomous systems are increasingly steered by machine-learned controllers. The moment these controllers are integrated into self-driving cars [28], unmanned drones [15], or software for medical diagnosis [4], they become safety-critical. Machine learning models, such as *deep neural networks* (DNNs), have been shown to not be robust against small modifications to the input [32]. These inputs, which we call *counter-examples*, can radically change the classification outcome, thus leading to safety hazards. Consequently, various safety certification tools have been proposed to show the absence of counter-examples [14]. However, if the controller is not safe, using these tools results in a tedious process of iteratively verifying and modifying the controller until a safe version, free

© The Author(s), under exclusive license to Springer Nature Switzerland AG 2022
O. Legunsen and G. Rosu (Eds.): SPIN 2022, LNCS 13255, pp. 79–96, 2022.
https://doi.org/10.1007/978-3-031-15077-7_5

of any counter-examples, is eventually obtained. While several methods have addressed this problem by focusing only on classification robustness [9,25], it is essential to target the more general *formal safety properties* [20] instead. Such logic properties are crucial when analyzing and verifying these safety-critical systems.

To address the issues mentioned above, we introduce *SpecRepair*, a safety repair tool for DNNs that renders manual iterative modification obsolete. This is achieved by a counter-example search algorithm tailored to formal safety properties, a repair procedure that balances accuracy and counter-example elimination, and a final safety certification.

Related Work. We summarize three threads of work towards counter-example search and repair of DNNs in the context of formal safety specifications:

Certification. The verification community has developed techniques that provably determine a DNN's safety [23]: either giving a formal guarantee that the specification is satisfied or finding a counter-example. This problem is NP-hard, and approaches such as [13,17] solve the problem precisely and thus are only suitable for relatively small DNNs. ERAN [29] uses an abstract interpretation to make verification more scalable. To find a counter-example, all the above approaches require a logic encoding of the DNN to use SMT or MILP solvers, which limits their scalability, whereas we found that our way to obtain counter-examples even scales to large DNNs.

Adversarial Attacks and Adversarial Search. The machine-learning community has designed several algorithms to find counter-examples. Most algorithms only consider *classification robustness*, which expresses that a classifier assigns the same label to similar inputs. Goodfellow et al. [9] proposed the fast-gradient sign method (FGSM), one of the first such attack algorithms. Moon et al. [27] accelerate search via an optimization procedure for image classifiers that perturbs only parts of the input image, and Chen et al. [2] generate counter-examples optimized for the ℓ_2 and ℓ_∞ norms. DL2 by Fischer et al. [7] can express specifications beyond robustness and send queries to a basin-hopping optimizer. Its repair capabilities are discussed in the next paragraph. Some works monitor a DNN for adversarial attacks but do not target other safety properties [3,12,24].

Formal Safety Repair of Neural Networks. Verification and adversarial attacks alone only analyze DNNs statically. The ultimate goal, however, is to repair the DNNs such that they become *provably safe* and at the same time *maintain high classification accuracy* (the ratio of correct classifications amongst all inputs). We explicitly distinguish the concept of formal safety repair from 'repairs' that mainly target improving a model's test accuracy, as done in [33]. We also need to distinguish formal safety repair from adversarial defence techniques, such as [11,25], as these do not lead to any guarantees. DL2 by Fischer et al. [7] integrates logic constraints into the DNN training procedure, but does not give formal guarantees that the resulting DNN ultimately satisfies these logic constraints. Goldberger et al. [8] (minimal modification) use the verifier Marabou

[17] to directly modify network weight parameters to satisfy a given specification; the technique is based on SMT solving and hence suffers from limited scalability. Also, the modification of such parameters may harm the DNN's accuracy. The approach nRepair by Dong et al. [5] iteratively generates counter-examples using a verifier. Instead of modifying the DNN directly, violating inputs are sent to a copy of the original DNN with modified parameters. Then, the combined model is verified again until no counter-example is found. The method only handles fully-connected feed-forward DNNs and does not support convolutional neural networks (CNNs). In the evaluation, we show that our approach is more efficient. Finally, Sotoudeh and Thakur [31], similarly to [8], aim to minimally modify a given DNN according to a formal specification using an LP solver. However, the specifications that the method supports are limited: for ACAS Xu-sized DNNs, only two-dimensional input regions are supported.

In conclusion, existing repair procedures mainly consider robustness, without giving any safety guarantees. Only four methods are concerned with safety specifications: however, these either have scalability issues [5,8,31], or do not give any formal guarantee for the resulting network [7].

Contributions. To address the lack of scalable and performance-preserving neural network repair methods, we propose *SpecRepair*, an efficient and effective technique for specification-based counter-example guided repair of DNNs.

First, we define the *satisfaction function*, an objective function that combines the function represented by the original DNN with the formal safety specification. This facilitates the search for counter-examples, i.e. inputs that lead to unsafe behavior due to violating the specification. **Second**, we propose an approach to find these counter-examples. For that, we turn the counter-example generation problem into an optimization [18] problem. A global optimizer then carries out the specification-based counter-example search. **Third**, we introduce an automated repair mechanism that uses the original DNN's loss function and the counter-examples from the second step to create a penalized training loss function. Additional training iterations are performed on the DNN and eliminate the counter-examples in the process while preserving high accuracy. A verifier then checks specification compliance of the repaired network. Crucially, the verifier is typically used only once. **Finally**, we demonstrate the performance of SpecRepair compared to several state-of-the-art approaches. The experimental results show that SpecRepair efficiently finds counter-examples in the DNNs and successfully repairs more DNNs while also achieving better classification accuracy for the repaired DNNs.

2 Background

In this work, we study deep neural networks (DNNs). While our approach is independent of the particular application, to simplify the presentation, we restrict our attention to classification tasks. A *deep neural network* $N : \mathbb{R}^n \rightarrow \mathbb{R}^m$ assigns a given input $\mathbf{x} \in \mathbb{R}^n$ to confidence values $\mathbf{y} \in \mathbb{R}^m$ for m class labels. A DNN comprises k layers that are sequentially composed such that $N = f_k \circ \cdots \circ f_1$. Each layer i is assigned an activation function σ_i and learnable parameters θ, consisting of a weight matrix W and a bias vector $\mathbf{b}$, such that the output of the ith layer is a function $f_i : \mathbb{R}^{k_{i-1}} \to \mathbb{R}^{k_i}$ with $f_i(\mathbf{z}) = \sigma_i(W_i \mathbf{z} + \mathbf{b}_i)$.

We consider *formal specifications* $\Phi = \{\varphi_1, \ldots, \varphi_s\}$ composed of s input-output properties. Such a property $\varphi = (X_\varphi, Y_\varphi)$ specifies that for all points in an input set X_φ, the network needs to predict outputs that lie in an output set Y_φ. For simplicity, we consider interval input sets X_φ and assume that Y_φ is a Boolean combination of constraints given in conjunctive normal form (CNF).

$$X_\varphi = \left\{ \prod_{i=1}^n [l_i, u_i] \,\middle|\, l_i, u_i \in \mathbb{R}, l_i \le u_i \right\}, \tag{1}$$

$$Y_\varphi = \left\{ \mathbf{y} \in \mathbb{R}^m \,\middle|\, \mathbf{y} \models \bigwedge_{j_1=1}^{a_\varphi} \bigvee_{j_2=1}^{b_\varphi} B_{j_1,j_2} \right\}, \tag{2}$$

where $a_\varphi, b_\varphi \in \mathbb{N}$ are the total number of logical conjunctions and disjunctions, respectively. The atomic constraints B_{j_1,j_2} are of the form

$$B_{j_1,j_2} \equiv g_{j_1,j_2}(\mathbf{y}) \ge 0 \tag{3}$$

where the $g_{j_1,j_2} : \mathbb{R}^m \to \mathbb{R}$ are computable functions of the output values $\mathbf{y}$. Common examples of output constraints include linear constraints (such as comparing two outputs $y_1 \le y_2$; see Table 1 for constraints used in the running example).

An ℓ_∞ *robustness property* φ_ϵ is a special case of the above class of specifications. Such a property specifies stable classification for all inputs from a hypercubic neighborhood around a given input $\mathbf{x}$ with radius ϵ and is defined for the desired class c (i.e., the value of the corresponding output neuron is y_c):

$$X_{\varphi_\epsilon} = \left\{ \prod_{i=1}^n [x_i - \epsilon, x_i + \epsilon] \right\}, \qquad Y_{\varphi_\epsilon} = \left\{ \mathbf{y} \in \mathbb{R}^m \,\middle|\, y_c = \max_j y_j \right\}. \tag{4}$$

A DNN N satisfies a property φ, resp. a specification Φ, if the following holds:

$$\begin{aligned} N \models \varphi &\iff \forall \mathbf{x} \in X_\varphi : N(\mathbf{x}) \in Y_\varphi \\ N \models \Phi &\iff \forall \varphi \in \Phi : N \models \varphi. \end{aligned} \tag{5}$$

2.1   Running Example

ACAS Xu [15] is a system for collision avoidance of two aircraft, consisting of 45 fully connected DNNs. Five inputs describe the relative position and speed of the two aircraft, while the outputs are five advisories, shown in Fig. 1. Two additional parameters, the time until loss of vertical separation τ and the previous advisory a_{prev}, are used to index which of the 45 DNNs applies to the specific scenario. The advisory that is suggested corresponds to the DNN output with the minimum value.

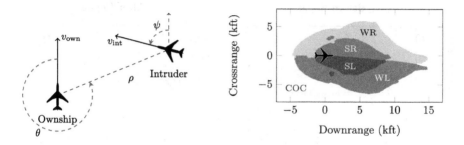

Fig. 1. Running example description. *Left*: Input variables for the ACAS Xu DNNs [15]: Distance from ownship to intruder ρ, angle to intruder relative to ownship heading direction θ, heading angle of intruder relative to ownship heading direction ψ, speed of ownship v_{own}, and speed of intruder v_{int}. *Right*: Output advisories: Clear-of-conflict (COC), weak left (WL), weak right (WR), strong left (SL), and strong right (SR). Both aircraft are in the same horizontal plane. Crossrange is perpendicular to the flight direction, while downrange is horizontal to the flight direction.

Table 1. Running example properties. ACAS Xu safety properties; If the intruder is distant and is significantly slower than the ownship, φ_1 "Clear-of-conflict (COC, y_1) is always below 1500" and φ_2 "Clear-of-conflict is never the maximum output", taken from [16].

Spec	X_φ	Y_φ
φ_1	$[55947.691, \infty] \times \mathbb{R}^2 \times [1145, \infty] \times [-\infty, 60]$	$\{\mathbf{y} \mid y_1 \leq 1500\}$
φ_2	$[55947.691, \infty] \times \mathbb{R}^2 \times [1145, \infty] \times [-\infty, 60]$	$\{\mathbf{y} \mid y_1 \leq \max_{i \neq 1} y_i\}$

To specify the safe behavior of the system, 10 safety properties have been formulated [16] (see Sect. A of the supplementary material [1]). Two example properties are given in Table 1.

Figure 2 illustrates the goal of our paper using the ACAS Xu example: eliminate counter-examples from a given DNN by performing an automated specification-based repair. In the figure we see that the original network (left) gives an unsafe advisory in the red region, while the repaired network (right) only gives safe advisories.

3   SpecRepair Overview

In this section, we give a high-level overview of our approach called *SpecRepair*. A detailed explanation follows in the later sections. The general structure of SpecRepair is depicted in Fig. 3. SpecRepair iterates back and forth between the two main components *counter-example generation* and *repair* until it terminates after a fixed number of repair steps.

The counter-example generation component takes a formal specification $\Phi = \{\varphi_1, \ldots, \varphi_s\}$ and a DNN N and produces s counter-examples $\mathbf{x}_1^c, \ldots, \mathbf{x}_s^c$. Subse-

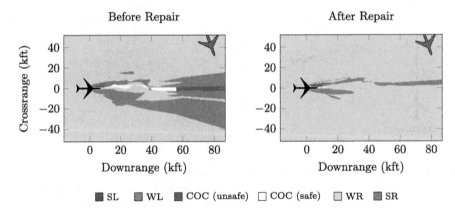

Fig. 2. *Least* **advised actions of ACAS Xu network $N_{2,1}$ before (left) and after repair (right).** The advised actions are described in Fig. 1. Both aircraft are in the same horizontal plane. Crossrange is perpendicular to the flight direction, while downrange is horizontal to the flight direction. This figure visualizes property φ_2 before and after repair. Here, $\tau = 0$, a_{prev} = weak left, $\psi = -70°$, $v_{own} = 1185.0$, and $v_{int} = 7.5$. The **red area** shows unsafe behavior according to φ_2 and thus constitutes counter-examples.

quently, the repair component retrains the DNN, for which it uses the original data set (X, Y) that N was trained with, the counter-examples obtained in the last step, and a penalty weight μ_i, which steers counter-example removal, starting with the original parameters θ. This strategy balances counter-example removal from the DNN and classification accuracy. After re-training has taken place, the counter-example generation component is executed again. If no counter-example is detected, as a final step, we attempt to verify the DNN using a formal verification method. Since the previous counter-example search is fast but incomplete (i.e., may miss counter-examples), the verifier may still find a counter-example, in which case SpecRepair goes back to the repair component. Otherwise, the repaired DNN N is verified and returned by SpecRepair.

In Sect. 4 we describe how counter-example generation for a DNN N with respect to a formal specification Φ is performed. In Sect. 5 we explain the counter-example guided repair approach.

4   Finding Violations of Safety Specifications

In this section, we show how the existence of a counter-example can be cast as an optimization problem. This allows us to use an optimization procedure to find counter-examples.

4.1   An Optimization View on Safety Specifications

Here we show how to map a specification to an objective function, which we call the *satisfaction function* f_{sat}.

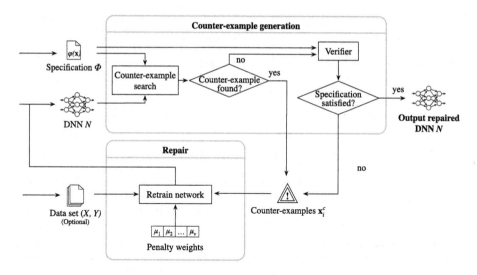

Fig. 3. SpecRepair architecture.

Definition 1. *The satisfaction function for an atomic constraint B_{j_1,j_2} of the form $g_{j_1,j_2}(\mathbf{y}) \geq 0$ from (3) is defined as*

$$f_{\mathrm{sat}\,B_{j_1,j_2}}(\mathbf{y}) = g_{j_1,j_2}(\mathbf{y}). \tag{6}$$

The satisfaction function for a given specification, i.e., set of input-output properties $\varphi = (X_\varphi, Y_\varphi)$ of the form (1) and (2), is defined as

$$f_{\mathrm{sat}}(\mathbf{x}) := \min_{\varphi \in \Phi} \min_{j_1 \in \{1...a_\varphi\}} \max_{j_2 \in \{1...b_\varphi\}} f_{\mathrm{sat}\,B_{j_1,j_2}}(N(\mathbf{x})). \tag{7}$$

In the following we focus on a single property φ. Given a property φ, the satisfaction function is negative if and only if φ is violated, which is summarized in the following theorem.

Theorem 1. *Given a satisfaction function f_{sat} obtained from a network N and an input-output property $\varphi = (X_\varphi, Y_\varphi)$, we have*

$$N \not\models \varphi \iff \exists \mathbf{x} \in X_\varphi : f_{\mathrm{sat}}(\mathbf{x}) < 0.$$

Proof. Fix a network N and a property $\varphi = (X_\varphi, Y_\varphi)$. Clearly, we have

$$f_{\mathrm{sat}\,B_{j_1,j_2}}(\mathbf{y}) \text{ is negative if and only if } B_{j_1,j_2} \text{ is violated for } \mathbf{y}. \quad (*)$$

First suppose that $N \not\models \varphi$. According to (5), there exists an input $\mathbf{x} \in X_\varphi$ such that $N(\mathbf{x}) \notin Y_\varphi$. Since the output constraints Y_φ in (2) are given in conjunctive normal form, one of the disjunctions and hence all corresponding disjuncts must be violated. By $(*)$ we have that $f_{\mathrm{sat}\,B}$ is negative for all these disjuncts. Thus the max in (7) and hence the image of f_{sat} itself is negative too.

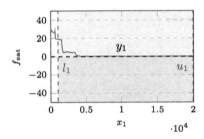
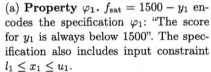
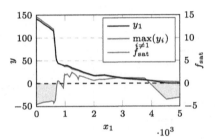

(a) **Property** φ_1. $f_{\text{sat}} = 1500 - y_1$ encodes the specification φ_1: "The score for y_1 is always below 1500". The specification also includes input constraint $l_1 \le x_1 \le u_1$.

(b) **Property** φ_2. $f_{\text{sat}} = -y_1 + \max_{i \ne 1}(y_i)$ encodes specification φ_2: "y_1 is never the maximum value". The red curve has been scaled by a factor of 10 for better visibility.

Fig. 4. Running example. Safety properties on the ACAS Xu DNNs are mapped to satisfaction functions f_{sat}, which map counter-examples (safety violations) to negative values, shaded in red. The two examples illustrate the properties φ_1 and φ_2 from Table 1.

Now suppose that $N \models \varphi$. Then for each input $\mathbf{x} \in X_\varphi$ we have that $N(\mathbf{x}) \in Y_\varphi$. By a similar argument as above, in each disjunction there is at least one disjunct that is satisfied. Using (*), we know that $f_{\text{sat}\,B}$ is non-negative for this disjunct. Finally, from (7) we get that $f_{\text{sat}}(\mathbf{x})$ is non-negative. $\square$

4.2   Using Optimization to Find Counter-examples

Using Theorem 1, for detecting *counter-examples* we can now equivalently minimize the function f_{sat} in search of values below zero. The examples in Fig. 4 show this for the topology of the DNN outputs, compared to the satisfaction function for the properties φ_1 and φ_2 from the running example in Table 1.

The satisfaction function f_{sat} enables us to turn the problem of finding counter-examples witnessing a specification violation of a DNN into a multivariate optimization problem. Note that both the DNN and the specification are fully captured by f_{sat} and hence we can call any off-the-shelf black-box optimization algorithm with X_φ as the input bounds and f_{sat} as the objective function to be minimized. The optimization procedure used here [6] was chosen experimentally. For details refer to Sect. B of the supplementary material [1]. Optimization tools are efficient in driving a function, here f_{sat}, toward its minimum; hence our approach often finds counter-examples much faster than other approaches.

5   Repair Framework

In the previous section, we have seen how to find counter-examples that violate the specification of a DNN. In this section, we build a framework around that algorithm to *repair* the DNN. By "repair" we mean to modify the network parameters such that the new DNN satisfies the specification. However, modifying the network parameters generally changes the accuracy of the DNN as well. Thus, as a second goal, we intend to preserve the accuracy of the DNN as much as possible. Our repair technique can be summarized as follows: *minimize the loss in accuracy of the DNN such that the DNN satisfies the given specification.*

DNN training uses unconstrained optimization of a *loss function* [10]. In contrast, *constrained* optimization problems can be stated as follows:

$$\text{minimize } f(\theta) \text{ such that } c_i(\theta) \geq 0 \text{ for all } i \in \{1, \ldots, v\}.$$

Here, f is a loss function and the c_i are constraints under which a point θ is admissible to the problem.

We introduce constraints into the training procedure by incorporating penalty functions [30] into the loss function. We want to minimize this loss function such that it satisfies the additional constraints c_i, which are assigned a positive penalty weight μ_i, defining the penalized objective function problem as

$$\underset{\theta}{\arg\min} \ f(\theta) + \sum_{i=1}^{v} \mu_i \cdot c_i^+(\theta) \tag{8}$$

where penalty function c_i^+ is defined as $c_i^+(\theta) = \max(0, -c_i(\theta))$. Intuitively, the penalty function forces the unconstrained optimization algorithm, which is used to solve Equation (8), to minimize the constraint violation: If a constraint is violated, it adds a large positive term to the objective function.

By enhancing the training procedure using the penalized loss function defined in Equation (8), training both incorporates model accuracy (since the old loss function is part of the new loss function) and decreases the violation of the counter-examples $\mathbf{x}_1^c, \ldots, \mathbf{x}_v^c$. After each training iteration, the penalty weights μ are updated, and the current model parameters are used as starting points for subsequent iterations.

Algorithm 1 gives a detailed view of one repair step. As inputs, the algorithm takes a DNN N to repair with weights θ, the original data set to train N (if not available, a uniform sampling of N can be used), a set of counter-examples $\mathbf{x}_i^c$ for the set of safety properties φ_i that have been found during the counter-example generation step, and the training loss function λ originally used to train N.

The algorithm first iterates over all the counter-example/property pairs that it was given, assigning each counter-example $\mathbf{x}_i^c$ an initial penalty weight $\mu_i = 1$. Then, we build the constraint function c_i by using the f_{sat} function and applying it to the counter-example and current network weights (Line 3).

In the second loop, the DNN N is iteratively trained. In Line 6, each counter-example is converted into a penalized constraint. Each unsatisfied constraint adds a positive term to the loss function's objective value. Therefore, the loss function is likely not minimal when there are any unsatisfied constraints. This updated loss function is then used to re-train the DNN. After training, we check if the counter-examples still occur in the re-trained DNN. If so, the penalty

---

Algorithm 1: Penalty function repair.

Input: DNN $N : \mathbb{R}^n \to \mathbb{R}^m$ with parameters θ, data set (X, Y),
counter-examples and properties $(\mathbf{x}_1^c, \varphi_1), (\mathbf{x}_2^c, \varphi_2), \ldots, (\mathbf{x}_v^c, \varphi_v)$, loss
function $\lambda : \mathbb{R}^{\dim(\theta)} \to \mathbb{R}$.

Data: Penalty weights $\mu_1, \mu_2, \ldots, \mu_v$, constraint functions $c_i : \mathbb{R}^{\dim(\theta)} \to \mathbb{R}$ for
$i \in \{1, \ldots, v\}$, penalized loss function $\lambda' : \mathbb{R}^{\dim(\theta)} \to \mathbb{R}$.

Output: Repaired DNN N with new parameters θ'.

1 **foreach** $i \in \{1, \ldots, v\}$ **do**
2 | $\mu_i \leftarrow 1$;   // default initial penalty weight
3 | $c_i(\theta') \leftarrow f_{\text{sat}_{\varphi_i}}(N_{\theta'}(\mathbf{x}_i^c))$;
4 **end**
5 **while** $\exists j \in \{1, \ldots, v\} : N(\mathbf{x}_j^c) \notin Y_{\varphi_j}$ **do**
6 | $\lambda'(\theta') \leftarrow \lambda(\theta') + \sum_{i=1}^{v} \mu_i \cdot c_i^+(\theta')$;
7 | $\text{train}(N, (X, Y), \lambda')$;
8 | **foreach** $i \in \{1, \ldots, v\}$ **do**
9 | | **if** $N(\mathbf{x}_i^c) \notin Y_{\varphi_i}$ **then**
10 | | | $\mu_i \leftarrow 2\mu_i$;   // default penalty increase strategy
11 | | **end**
12 | **end**
13 **end**

---

weight is doubled; otherwise, the successfully repaired DNN with new weights θ' is returned.

The *counter-example generation* component outputs counter-examples and hands them over to the *repair* component. This process is repeated iteratively. As outlined in Sect. 4, the satisfaction function f_{sat} is input to a global optimization algorithm. Intuitively, it would be possible to exit the optimization routine early when any negative value is detected. However, in our experiments we found that taking the counter-examples at the minimum, expressing a higher violation severity, ultimately results in more successful repairs.

6   Evaluation

This section presents our experimental evaluation, demonstrating the algorithm's effectiveness in repairing a neural network subject to a safety specification. Our implementation of SpecRepair uses PyTorch for DNN interactions. We conduct the experiments on an Intel Xeon E5-2680 CPU with 2.4 GhZ and 170 GB of memory. For the final verification step, our implementation uses the verifier ERAN [29]. We note that ERAN uses an internal timeout and may hence return UNKNOWN. This can be circumvented by increasing the timeout, but in the evaluation we use the default settings of ERAN and give up with the result UNKNOWN instead.

6.1   Experimental Setup

Our experiments use 36 networks for the tasks of aircraft collision avoidance and image classification, where we replicate the benchmark networks from [29] for the latter. In detail:

- The collision avoidance system *ACAS Xu* [15] consists of 45 fully connected DNNs, $N_{1,1}$ to $N_{5,9}$. The inputs and outputs are described in Sect. A of the supplementary material [1]. Each of the 45 networks has 6 hidden layers with 50 ReLU nodes. We use the 34 networks that were shown to violate at least one of the safety properties from [16] to evaluate our method. Because the training data is not openly available, we resort to a uniform sampling of the original model and compare the repaired model to it in terms of classification accuracy (reminder: the percentage of correct classifications) and mean average error (MAE) between the classification scores of the original and repaired models.
- *MNIST* [21] contains 70k grayscale images, showing a handwritten digit from 0 to 9, with 28×28 pixels. We use a fully connected DNN trained to a test accuracy of 97.8% using DiffAI-defended training [26], with five hidden dense layers of 100 units each.
- *CIFAR10* [19] contains 60k color images, showing an object from one of ten possible classes, with 32×32 pixels. We use the benchmark CNN from [29], which was trained to an accuracy of 58.6%. It has two convolutional layers [22] and a max-pooling layer, repeated once with 24 and 32 channels, respectively, followed by two dense layers with 100 units each.

6.2   Counter-Example-Based Repair

We compare SpecRepair against three state-of-the-art repair techniques that we described in Sect. 1: minimal modification (MM) by Goldberger et al. [8], nRepair (NR) by Dong et al. [5], and DL2 by Fischer et al. [7]. We do not compare against [31] because its specification encoding is only applicable to two dimensions for small-scale networks and thus neither supports the ACAS Xu [16] nor any image classification robustness properties. We run DL2 with 5 different values for the DL2 weight parameter: 0.01, 0.05, 0.1, 0.2, and 0.5 (for more details see [7]). We analyze all final repair outcomes with ERAN to assess whether the repairs produced by the tools are genuinely safe.

For the *collision avoidance task*, we repair different problem instances: 34 DNNs subject to three different properties. As an additional challenge, we also create a combined specification $\Phi = \{\varphi_1, \varphi_2, \varphi_3, \varphi_4, \varphi_8\}$ consisting of five properties. We evaluate the classification accuracy (percentage of correct classifications) and mean average error (MAE) after repair to measure the level of correct functionality. Because we have no access to the original training and test data sets, we use a uniform sampling from the original network as test data for calculating accuracy and MAE. We set a timeout of three hours for all techniques.

For the *image classification task*, we repair a total of 100 cases for an ℓ_∞ robustness specification, with a robustness parameter $\epsilon = 0.03$, replicating the

Table 2. Safety repair results of the ACAS Xu DNNs: SpecRepair (this work), DL2 [7], nRepair (NR) [5], and minimal modification (MM) [8]. We compare the cumulative repair outcome for all 35 instances, test accuracy and mean average error (MAE) after repair, and the median runtime. '✓' indicates successful repairs, '×' indicates failed repairs, '✦' indicates a timeout, and '?' marks cases where the verifier returned UNKNOWN.

	Repair Outcome				Accuracy[%]	MAE	Runtime [s]
Tool	SUCCESS	FAIL	UNKNOWN	TIMEOUT	median	median	median
SpecRepair	28	0	2	6	**99.5**	**0.1**	573.2
NR	**29**	0	1	6	87.6	1996.1	**10.0**
DL2	3	33	0	0	93.4	6.03	10840.7
MM	0	0	0	35	–	–	10832.1

robustness experiment by Dong et al. [5]. Additionally, for MNIST, we compare batch repair of 10 and 25 counter-examples at the same time. This, however, is only applicable to SpecRepair and nRepair (NR), because MM and DL2 do not have this functionality. We do not compare against minimal modification (MM) [8] because of problems that let the internally used Marabou solver [17] fail to generate any counter-examples. We have reported this error to the Marabou developers[1]. Also, the authors of MM themselves already described their technique to perform sub-optimally for CNF properties because it relies on the exact encoding needed by Marabou. Furthermore, because nRepair (NR) does not support convolutional layers, we cannot evaluate it on the network for CIFAR10.

We compare the number of successful repairs, test accuracy (to measure preservation of the model's functionality), and runtime.

Results. Table 2 shows the aggregated repair results for the collision avoidance task, counting the number of successful repairs, failures, unknown outcomes, and timeouts. Additionally, it shows the accuracy and mean average error (MAE) of the DNNs after they have been repaired by the respective method. Results per benchmark instance are given in Table 3.

SpecRepair successfully repairs 28 of the 36 instances. The DNNs that have been repaired by SpecRepair achieve the highest classification accuracy with 99.5 and lowest mean average error with 0.1. Two times ERAN (and hence SpecRepair) terminates with a result of UNKNOWN. Six times, SpecRepair could not repair the DNN within the time limit.

nRepair (NR) repairs one more instance than SpecRepair, but at the cost of yielding the lowest test accuracy of the three successful tools. Also, the mean average error (MAE) is extremely high: NR does not consider the classification scores but instead is only concerned with maintaining the correct class, leading to large deviations from the original policy.

---

[1] https://github.com/NeuralNetworkVerification/Marabou/issues/494.

Table 3. Safety repair results of the ACAS Xu DNNs: SpecRepair (this work), nRepair (NR) [5], and DL2 [7]. Each row shows the results for one benchmark instance with the property/specification in the first column (see Sect. A of the supplementary material [1]) and the DNN in the second column (names taken from [15]). '✓' indicates successful repairs, '×' indicates failed repairs, '▲' indicates a timeout, and '?' marks cases where the verifier returned UNKNOWN.

Spec	Model	Repair Outcome			Accuracy [%]			MAE		
		SpecRepair	NR	DL2	SpecRepair	NR	DL2	SpecRepair	NR	DL2
φ_2	$N_{2,1}$	✓	✓	×	**99.1**	83.9	–	**0.22**	2242.6	–
φ_2	$N_{2,2}$	✓	✓	✓	**98.7**	85.1	93.4	**0.23**	2279.3	6.29
φ_2	$N_{2,3}$	✓	✓	×	**99.3**	83.5	–	**0.13**	2420.6	–
φ_2	$N_{2,4}$	✓	▲	×	**99.5**	–	–	**0.09**	–	–
φ_2	$N_{2,5}$	▲	✓	×	–	84.1	–	–	**2433.8**	–
φ_2	$N_{2,6}$	▲	✓	×	–	85.6	–	–	**2303.7**	–
φ_2	$N_{2,7}$	✓	✓	✓	14.5	**87.0**	89.5	**0.15**	1644.8	5.97
φ_2	$N_{2,8}$	✓	✓	×	**99.6**	87.3	–	**0.14**	663.6	–
φ_2	$N_{2,9}$	✓	✓	×	**99.8**	88.6	–	**0.13**	2405.1	–
φ_2	$N_{3,1}$	✓	✓	×	**98.6**	77.5	–	**0.27**	6.1	–
φ_2	$N_{3,2}$	✓	▲	×	**99.9**	–	–	**0.10**	–	–
φ_2	$N_{3,4}$	✓	▲	×	**99.5**	–	–	**0.10**	–	–
φ_2	$N_{3,5}$	✓	✓	×	**99.5**	84.2	–	**0.09**	2384.2	–
φ_2	$N_{3,6}$	?	✓	×	–	81.8	–	–	**2387.0**	–
φ_2	$N_{3,7}$	✓	✓	×	**99.7**	87.0	–	**0.11**	2251.7	–
φ_2	$N_{3,8}$	✓	✓	×	**99.7**	87.9	–	**0.09**	1311.1	–
φ_2	$N_{3,9}$	▲	✓	×	–	87.2	–	–	**2442.5**	–
φ_2	$N_{4,1}$	✓	✓	×	**99.8**	87.7	–	**0.11**	1939.3	–
φ_2	$N_{4,3}$	✓	✓	✓	**99.4**	87.8	96.0	**0.13**	2419.4	6.03
φ_2	$N_{4,4}$	✓	✓	×	**99.5**	87.9	–	**0.10**	1090.5	–
φ_2	$N_{4,5}$	✓	✓	×	**99.4**	87.5	–	**0.08**	2.7	–
φ_2	$N_{4,6}$	✓	✓	×	**99.6**	89.8	–	**0.07**	1329.1	–
φ_2	$N_{4,7}$	✓	✓	×	**98.3**	88.9	–	**0.14**	1996.1	–
φ_2	$N_{4,8}$	✓	✓	×	**99.1**	88.6	–	**0.16**	584.3	–
φ_2	$N_{4,9}$	✓	✓	×	**99.5**	88.8	–	**0.06**	2292.2	–
φ_2	$N_{5,1}$	✓	✓	×	**99.5**	87.5	–	**0.11**	2227.2	–
φ_2	$N_{5,2}$	✓	✓	×	**99.7**	87.6	–	**0.10**	2438.8	–
φ_2	$N_{5,4}$	✓	✓	×	**99.6**	87.8	–	**0.09**	405.1	–
φ_2	$N_{5,5}$	▲	✓	×	–	87.9	–	–	**749.8**	–
φ_2	$N_{5,6}$	✓	▲	×	**99.5**	–	–	**0.12**	–	–
φ_2	$N_{5,7}$	✓	✓	×	**98.4**	88.0	–	**0.16**	957.7	–
φ_2	$N_{5,8}$	✓	✓	×	**99.4**	87.7	–	**0.11**	382.5	–
φ_2	$N_{5,9}$	✓	✓	×	**98.1**	87.9	–	**0.13**	181.2	–
φ_7	$N_{1,9}$	?	▲	×	–	–	–	–	–	–
φ_8	$N_{2,9}$	▲	?	×	–	–	–	–	–	–
Φ_1	$N_{2,9}$	▲	▲	×	–	–	–	–	–	–
		28	29	3	**99.5**	87.6	93.4	**0.1**	1996.1	6.03
		SUCCESS frequency			median			median		

While DL2's repair accuracy is still reasonably high, with a median value of 93.4 and MAE of 6.03, it only delivers three successful repairs and fails to repair the other 33 instances. This is likely due to DL2's algorithm design, which includes a hard-coded cross-entropy loss function and no termination criteria beyond performing a large number of iterations. Experiments using DL2 with a task loss function did not result in any successful repair.

Minimal modification (MM) times out for every instance. We explain this with the high computational cost using the SMT-based method Marabou [17] to modify network parameters directly.

Table 4. Robustness repair results of the DiffAI-defended [26] MNIST DNN: SpecRepair (this work), nRepair (NR) [5], and DL2 [7]. We compare the cumulative repair outcome for all 100 instances, the test accuracy (minimum, median, and maximum) after repair, and the median runtime.

	Repair Outcome				Accuracy [%]	Runtime [s]
Tool	SUCCESS	FAIL	UNKNOWN	TIMEOUT	median	median
SpecRepair	**100**	0	0	0	96.0	163.6
NR	84	16	0	0	**97.3**	**36.0**
DL2	10	82	0	8	91.9	18839.2

Table 5. Collective robustness repair results of the DiffAI-defended [26] MNIST DNN: SpecRepair (this work), and nRepair (NR) [5]. We compare the cumulative repair outcome for all 100 instances, supplemented by two partitions into groups of 10 and 25 points per instance, and the test accuracy (minimum, median, and maximum) after repair.

			Repair Outcome				Accuracy [%]
Tool	Points	Inst.	SUCCESS	FAIL	UNKNOWN	TIMEOUT	median
SpecRepair	1	100	**100**	0	0	0	96.0
	10	10	**10**	0	0	0	93.1
	25	4	**3**	0	1	1	93.5
NR	1	100	84	16	0	0	**97.3**
	10	10	0	10	0	0	–
	25	4	0	4	0	0	–

For repairing the DiffAI-defended [26] MNIST DNNs, the results are presented in Table 4. The non-aggregated data is provided in Sect. C of the supplementary material [1]. SpecRepair successfully repairs all 100 instances, with a

Table 6. Robustness repair results of the CIFAR10 CNN: SpecRepair (this work), minimal modification (MM) [8], and DL2 [7]. We compare the cumulative repair outcome for all 100 instances, the test accuracy (minimum, median, and maximum) after repair, and the median runtime.

		Repair Outcome			Accuracy [%]	Runtime [s]
Tool	SUCCESS	FAIL	UNKNOWN	TIMEOUT	median	median
SpecRepair	88	5	1	6	**69.6**	**4269.7**
DL2	**100**	0	0	0	61.8	26724.1

median test accuracy after repair of 96%. Table 5 shows collective repair results, with SpecRepair successfully repairing 10 counter-examples at once, and for three out of four instances, it repairs 25 counter-examples in one run. nRepair repairs only 84 instances, with a slightly higher accuracy of 97.3%, and better runtime. Yet, it fails when tasked to collectively repair more than one counter-example in one execution. DL2 only repairs ten instances, failing to repair 82, and timing out on eight. Also, it achieves the lowest median repair accuracy of 91.9% for the successfully repaired cases. This indicates that DL2's counter-example generation cannot handle the DiffAI defense mechanism particularly well. Also, its runtime is two orders of magnitude slower than SpecRepair and nRepair (NR).

For the CIFAR10 CNN, we present the results in Table 6, with non-aggregated data given in Sect. C of the supplementary material [1]. SpecRepair and DL2 are successful for 88 and 100 instances, respectively. SpecRepair maintains the highest mean test accuracy after repair with a value of 69.6%, with DL2 sacrificing quantity over accuracy, only achieving 61.6%. Also, DL2 is six times slower than SpecRepair. We observe a lower test accuracy than for the collision avoidance task and the MNIST network for all approaches. These results suggest that the higher input dimension of CIFAR10 ($32 \times 32 \times 3$ versus 28×28 with MNIST) is a limiting factor not only for SpecRepair but all the repair methods that we have evaluated.

7 Discussion

In Sect. 3 we gave an overview of our procedure. Maintaining the correct functionality of the repaired DNN is a fundamental challenge: a successful repair is worthless if we compromise accuracy for it. We have demonstrated that SpecRepair consistently achieves high performance on several types of networks, often outperforming state-of-the-art repair methods. The performance of SpecRepair for the collision avoidance and image classification tasks is the best among the methods compared in the evaluation in terms of successful repairs, accuracy, or scalability, while still providing formal safety guarantees. This demonstrates that SpecRepair is highly suitable for safety-critical applications.

The quality and success of our repair technique stems from its algorithmic design. Instead of relying on accurate yet computationally expensive encodings backed by SMT or linear programming, we use heuristics based on global optimization to produce counter-examples fast.

The insights gained in our experiments also support the hypothesis that using a task loss function that integrates into standard DNN training procedures, as in our approach or in [7], is not only more efficient, but also better in preserving the DNN's accuracy. Although the approaches in [8,31] try to keep the modifications of DNN parameters minimal, original training data is not considered, and the experiments demonstrate that there may still be a significant negative impact on the model's test accuracy.

One limitation of our repair approach is that, for image classification tasks, it does not always return with a successfully repaired DNN within the specified time limit. Future research may seek the combination of SpecRepair with different penalty functions during re-training to gain insights into the quality of repair results when applied to other network architectures.

8   Conclusion

We presented SpecRepair, an efficient technique for generating counter-examples and repairing deep neural networks (DNNs) such that they comply with a formal specification. Due to its black-box nature, SpecRepair supports arbitrary DNNs and specifications. Our technique consists of two main components. The first component (counter-example generation) translates the specification into an objective function, which becomes negative for all network inputs that violate the specification, and then detects counter-examples using a global optimization method. The second component (repair) utilizes these counter-examples to make the DNN safe via penalized re-training. SpecRepair finally gives a safety guarantee for the resulting DNN using a verifier. Experimental results demonstrate that SpecRepair can be used effectively for both counter-example generation and repair of DNNs, generating useful counter-examples, achieving a high quality of repair, and outperforming existing approaches.

Acknowledgments. This research was partly supported by DIREC - Digital Research Centre Denmark and the Villum Investigator Grant S4OS.

References

1. Bauer-Marquart, F., Boetius, D., Leue, S., Schilling, C.: SpecRepair: counter-example guided safety repair of deep neural networks - supplementary material (2022)
2. Chen, J., Jordan, M.I., Wainwright, M.J.: HopSkipJumpAttack: a query-efficient decision-based attack. In: IEEE Symposium on Security and Privacy, pp. 1277–1294. IEEE (2020). https://doi.org/10.1109/SP40000.2020.00045

3. Cheng, C.: Provably-robust runtime monitoring of neuron activation patterns. In: DATE, pp. 1310–1313. IEEE (2021). https://doi.org/10.23919/DATE51398.2021. 9473957
4. Djavanshir, G.R., Chen, X., Yang, W.: A review of artificial intelligence's neural networks (deep learning) applications in medical diagnosis and prediction. IT Prof. **23**(3), 58–62 (2021)
5. Dong, G., Sun, J., Wang, X., Wang, X., Dai, T.: Towards repairing neural networks correctly. In: QRS, pp. 714–725. IEEE (2021)
6. Endres, S.C., Sandrock, C., Focke, W.W.: A simplicial homology algorithm for Lipschitz optimisation. J. Global Optim. **72**(2), 181–217 (2018). https://doi.org/ 10.1007/s10898-018-0645-y
7. Fischer, M., Balunovic, M., Drachsler-Cohen, D., Gehr, T., Zhang, C., Vechev, M.T.: DL2: training and querying neural networks with logic. In: ICML, Proceedings of Machine Learning Research, vol. 97, pp. 1931–1941. PMLR (2019)
8. Goldberger, B., Katz, G., Adi, Y., Keshet, J.: Minimal modifications of deep neural networks using verification. In: LPAR, EPiC Series in Computing, vol. 73, pp. 260–278. EasyChair (2020)
9. Goodfellow, I.J., Shlens, J., Szegedy, C.: Explaining and harnessing adversarial examples. In: ICLR (Poster) (2015)
10. Goodfellow, I.J., Bengio, Y., Courville, A.C.: Deep learning. In: Adaptive Computation and Machine Learning. MIT Press (2016). ISBN 978-0-262-03561-3. http:// www.deeplearningbook.org/
11. Goodfellow, I.J., et al.: Generative adversarial networks. Commun. ACM **63**(11), 139–144 (2020)
12. Henzinger, T.A., Lukina, A., Schilling, C.: Outside the box: abstraction-based monitoring of neural networks. In: ECAI, FAIA, vol. 325, pp. 2433–2440. IOS Press (2020). https://doi.org/10.3233/FAIA200375
13. Huang, X., Kwiatkowska, M., Wang, S., Wu, M.: Safety verification of deep neural networks. In: Majumdar, R., Kunčak, V. (eds.) CAV 2017. LNCS, vol. 10426, pp. 3–29. Springer, Cham (2017). https://doi.org/10.1007/978-3-319-63387-9_1
14. Huang, X., et al.: A survey of safety and trustworthiness of deep neural networks: verification, testing, adversarial attack and defence, and interpretability. Comput. Sci. Rev. **37**, 100270 (2020)
15. Julian, K.D., Lopez, J., Brush, J.S., Owen, M.P., Kochenderfer, M.J.: Policy compression for aircraft collision avoidance systems. In: 2016 IEEE/AIAA 35th Digital Avionics Systems Conference (DASC), pp. 1–10. IEEE (2016)
16. Katz, G., Barrett, C., Dill, D.L., Julian, K., Kochenderfer, M.J.: Reluplex: an efficient SMT solver for verifying deep neural networks. In: Majumdar, R., Kunčak, V. (eds.) CAV 2017. LNCS, vol. 10426, pp. 97–117. Springer, Cham (2017). https:// doi.org/10.1007/978-3-319-63387-9_5
17. Katz, G., et al.: The Marabou framework for verification and analysis of deep neural networks. In: Dillig, I., Tasiran, S. (eds.) CAV 2019. LNCS, vol. 11561, pp. 443–452. Springer, Cham (2019). https://doi.org/10.1007/978-3-030-25540-4_26
18. Kochenderfer, M.J., Wheeler, T.A.: Algorithms for Optimization. MIT Press, Cambridge (2019)
19. Krizhevsky, A., Hinton, G., et al.: Learning multiple layers of features from tiny images (2009)
20. Lamport, L.: Proving the correctness of multiprocess programs. IEEE Trans. Software Eng. **3**(2), 125–143 (1977)
21. LeCun, Y., Cortes, C.: MNIST handwritten digit database (2010). http://yann. lecun.com/exdb/mnist/

22. LeCun, Y., et al.: Backpropagation applied to handwritten zip code recognition. Neural Comput. **1**(4), 541–551 (1989)
23. Liu, C., Arnon, T., Lazarus, C., Strong, C.A., Barrett, C.W., Kochenderfer, M.J.: Algorithms for verifying deep neural networks. Found. Trends Optim. **4**(3–4), 244–404 (2021)
24. Lukina, A., Schilling, C., Henzinger, T.A.: Into the unknown: active monitoring of neural networks. In: Feng, L., Fisman, D. (eds.) RV 2021. LNCS, vol. 12974, pp. 42–61. Springer, Cham (2021). https://doi.org/10.1007/978-3-030-88494-9_3
25. Madry, A., Makelov, A., Schmidt, L., Tsipras, D., Vladu, A.: Towards deep learning models resistant to adversarial attacks. In: ICLR (Poster) (2018). OpenReview.net
26. Mirman, M., Gehr, T., Vechev, M.: Differentiable abstract interpretation for provably robust neural networks. In: International Conference on Machine Learning (ICML) (2018). https://www.icml.cc/Conferences/2018/Schedule?showEvent=2477
27. Moon, S., An, G., Song, H.O.: Parsimonious black-box adversarial attacks via efficient combinatorial optimization. In: ICML, PMLR, vol. 97, pp. 4636–4645 (2019). http://proceedings.mlr.press/v97/moon19a.html
28. Onishi, T., Motoyoshi, T., Suga, Y., Mori, H., Ogata, T.: End-to-end learning method for self-driving cars with trajectory recovery using a path-following function. In: IJCNN, pp. 1–8. IEEE (2019)
29. Singh, G., Gehr, T., Püschel, M., Vechev, M.T.: An abstract domain for certifying neural networks. In: POPL, vol. 3, pp. 41:1–41:30 (2019). https://doi.org/10.1145/3290354
30. Smith, A.E., Coit, D.W., Baeck, T., Fogel, D., Michalewicz, Z.: Penalty functions. In: Handbook of Evolutionary Computation, vol. 97, no. (1), C5 (1997)
31. Sotoudeh, M., Thakur, A.V.: Provable repair of deep neural networks. In: PLDI, pp. 588–603. ACM (2021)
32. Szegedy, C., et al.: Intriguing properties of neural networks. In: ICLR (2014). http://arxiv.org/abs/1312.6199
33. Usman, M., Gopinath, D., Sun, Y., Noller, Y., Păsăreanu, C.S.: NNREPAIR: constraint-based repair of neural network classifiers. In: Silva, A., Leino, K.R.M. (eds.) CAV 2021. LNCS, vol. 12759, pp. 3–25. Springer, Cham (2021). https://doi.org/10.1007/978-3-030-81685-8_1

Verifying the SHA-3 Implementation from OpenSSL with the Software Analysis Workbench

Parker Hanson[(✉)], Benjamin Winters, Eric Mercer, and Brett Decker

Brigham Young University, Provo, UT 84602, USA
phanson46@gmail.com

Abstract. This paper discusses a proof of SHA-3 in OpenSSL. SHA-3 is the new standard from NIST for computing digests. OpenSSL is one of the most widely used implementations of cryptographic protocols. Cryptol and the Software Analysis Workbench (SAW) are a language and verification engine to specify cryptographic primitives and prove equivalence to implementations. As digests are the basis for all cryptographic protocols, the research in this paper is an automated SAW proof of equivalence between the SHA-3 standard and its OpenSSL implementation in C. The research contributes Cryptol specifications for the standard. The equivalence proof shows the importance of overrides in SAW that replace models from C code with those from Cryptol to reduce the complexity of the proof obligations that must be accomplished relative to the implementation in C. The research establishes the viability of verifying modern cryptographic primitives and the importance of modularity in their definitions, and implementations, for overrides to manage complexity.

Keywords: Formal verification · Cryptography · SHA-3 · Cryptol · SAW

1 Introduction

This paper discusses an automated proof of the *Secure Hash Algorithm 3* (SHA-3) in OpenSSL using the *Software Analysis Workbench* (SAW) by Galois. SHA-3 is the latest algorithm for computing *digests*, or hashes, from data to be published by the *National Institute of Standards and Technology* (NIST). The algorithm is the successor to SHA-2. Its intent is to address weaknesses in SHA-2, and it departs from its predecessors in that it is based on the KECCAK family of cryptographic primitives [12].

OpenSSL is a commercial grade free cryptographic library [20]. Its implementation of the *Secure Sockets Layer* (SSL) and *Transport Layer Security* protocols are widely deployed on internet facing applications. Computing digests is a critical operation in these protocols and is the basis to the security guarantees provided by these protocols. Widely deployed implementations, such as OpenSSL, are especially important to be correct because of the available attack

© The Author(s), under exclusive license to Springer Nature Switzerland AG 2022
O. Legunsen and G. Rosu (Eds.): SPIN 2022, LNCS 13255, pp. 97–113, 2022.
https://doi.org/10.1007/978-3-031-15077-7_6

surface to hackers if a vulnerability were discovered in such implementations. The seriousness of getting these implementations correct is recently seen in the Apache log4j vulnerability affecting virtually all internet facing servers [19].

SAW is a formal verification tool to prove equivalence between SAWCore models. SAWCore models are defined in the Cryptol functional language or extracted from C or Java with *symbolic execution*. Cryptol itself is designed to specify cryptographic primitives at the bit level. SAW has been shown capable in proving implementations of cryptographic primitives equivalent to hardware and software implementations [5,11,18]. Recent work emphasizes not just the utility of SAW, but the importance of modular decomposition of cryptographic primitives in their definition as that decomposition lends itself to efficient verification in SAW [8].

This paper details another example of SAW verification only this time it is a proof showing the OpenSSL C implementation of SHA-3 matches a Cryptol specification derived from the published FIPS 202 standard by NIST [12]. The Cryptol specifications, SAW scripts, and extracted SAWCore model from the OpenSSL C implementation are documented, and available, in a public GitHub repository for independent verification [25]. The proof relies on two specifications, both created as part of this research, of the SHA-3 algorithm: one that closely matches the published standard and another incorporating features in the C implementation. SAW shows an input to output equivalence between these two specifications for the 256 bit digest over a fixed set of message sizes. The proof takes around 60 h of computation time.

The proof then turns to the inner KECCAK function that computes the actual bits for the digest. Here it shows that the C implementation exactly matches the Cryptol specification on any input. The proof requires the use of *overrides* in SAW to simplify the extracted model from C after symbolic execution. The proof of equivalence between the KECCAK in C and Cryptol takes around 15 min of computation time.

The proof, with its artifacts in the published repository, make the following contributions:

- Cryptol for SHA-3 that passes the test vectors and correlates with FIPS 202.
- Cryptol for SHA-3 that uses a reordered memory layout and precomputed tables that correlate with C implementations.
- A SAW proof showing the two specifications equivalent for the 256 bit digest over a series of message sizes.
- A SAW proof that the KECCAK specification in Cryptol is equivalent to the OpenSSL C implementation of the same function for all inputs.

The proof shows that SAW is capable of proving equivalence to C implementations of modern cryptographic primitives. It also shows that the modular definition of SHA-3 naturally lends itself to formal verification in SAW. The work in its entirety argues the importance of using formal languages such as Cryptol for the specification of cryptographic primitives rather than English prose and math. It also argues the necessity, and viability, of proving at the intermediate representation level equivalence between cryptographic specifications and actual C implementations.

2   Background

Cryptol and SAW are used to prove properties of OpenSSL's implementation of SHA-3 relative to the NIST FIPS 202 publication [12]. What the proofs actually say, and an understanding of their limitations, relies on (1) a basic knowledge of how SAW works and what Cryptol does relative to SAW [9], and (2) how the SHA-3 algorithm computes a digest [12]. This section provides that basic knowledge of the tools and a general overview of the SHA-3 algorithm.

2.1   Cryptol and SAW

Cryptol is a domain specific functional language for describing cryptographic primitives, such as algorithms to compute digests, at the bit-level. Cryptographic primitives are the building blocks for complex cryptographic protocols, such as the *Secure Sockets Layer* (SSL) and *Transport Layer Security* (TLS) protocols, that provide a broad range of security guarantees. Cryptol is executable, being able to run test vectors to validate specifications, and more importantly, it compiles directly to SAWCore, which is the language for formal models in SAW.

SAW is a tool to extract formal models from programs with support for C, Java, and Cryptol input. These formal models are expressed in the SAWCore language that supports formal reasoning. As mentioned previously, Cryptol compiles directly to SAWCore, but that is not the case for C and Java. SAW uses *symbolic execution* to extract SAWCore models from C and Java inputs.

Symbolic execution reasons about all computation paths in the C or Java input. It must unroll all loops a static number of times to create the model in SAWCore. As such, the number of iterations in any loop must be statically known at compile time or the symbolic execution fails to terminate. SAWCore models from symbolic execution tend to be more complex than those from Cryptol.

SAW's function, among other things, is to prove input to output equivalence between SAWCore models. It accomplishes such proofs with equivalence preserving rewrites on the SAWCore and with automated reasoning. The rewrites simplify the SAWCore for a model to reduce the cost of automated reasoning. The rewrites also try to structurally reduce one model to the other thus avoiding automated reasoning altogether. When rewriting is not sufficient, the equivalence between two models is reduced to a satisfiability problem and dispatched to external backend solvers.

SAW supports hierarchical reasoning with *overrides*. An override replaces one SAWCore model with another in the formal analysis. As an example, consider a C function a() that itself calls another C function as part of its implementation: T a() {... b() ...}. The SAWCore generated from symbolic executions for a() of necessity inlines and executes the code for b(), and as a result, yields a model in SAWCore that is too big and complex to accomplish the equivalence

---

Algorithm 1. SHA-3 sponge construction with KECCAK

Require: $n \geq 0$ and $(d, r) \in \{(224, 1152) \ (256, 1088) \ (384, 832) \ (512, 576)\}$
Ensure: $D = $ SHA-3(N,d,r)
1: $p_0, \ldots, p_m = $ pad(N, r)
2: $A = 0_0, \ldots, 0_{1599}$
3: **for** $p_i = p_0, \ldots, p_m$ **do**
4:    $A = A$ **xor** zeroExtend$(p_i, a - r)$
5:    $A = $ KECCAK(A)
6: **end for**
7: $D = $ squeeze(A, d)

---

proof between a() and the Cryptol specification of a(). Now suppose that b() is specified in Cryptol. If SAW is able to prove that the specification for b() and its C implementation are equivalent, then after symbolic execution an override is able to replace b() in a() with the SAWCore from the Cryptol for b().

As mentioned previously, SAWCore from Cryptol is less complex than equivalent models created by symbolic execution from C or Java; thereby, the overrides reduce the overall complexity of the final extracted SAWCore from C or Java. In the example, the equivalence of a() and its specification using the override for b() now proves out quickly. As such, proving a property about a complex C function or Java method generally requires the use of overrides from Cryptol in order for the equivalence proof to be successful, and that is regardless of how that proof is accomplished. Overrides improve the likelihood of the rewrites showing equivalence and the likelihood of the backend solver being able to show equivalence if the rewrites fail. Indeed, the use of overrides are key to the SAW proof in this paper showing equivalence between the SHA-3 specification and the OpenSSL C implementation.

2.2   SHA-3 Overview

SHA-3 uses *sponge construction* to generate hashes as shown in Algorithm 1 (see NIST FIPS 202 [12]). Sponge construction *absorbs* data into an internal state A at a rate of r bits per cycle (Line 4 and Line 5), transforming the state on each cycle, and once all the data is absorbed, then it *squeezes* out a final d-bit digest (Line 7). The transformation function, KECCAK-f[1600], simply KECCAK in the rest of this presentation, defines the size of the state A to be $a = 1600$ bits, which is initialized to 0 (Line 2).

The state itself consists of r bits that are written or read plus a capacity of $c = s - r$ bits that are untouched by input or output. The NIST standard defines pairs of allowed hash sizes and rates. These are defined in the requires statement in Algorithm 1. The input N is padded such that its final size is a multiple of r bits, and it is partitioned into r-bit size blocks (Line 1) for the absorption phase. The padding is defined by the regular expression 10*1. Padding is always added to N even if adding it creates an extra block.

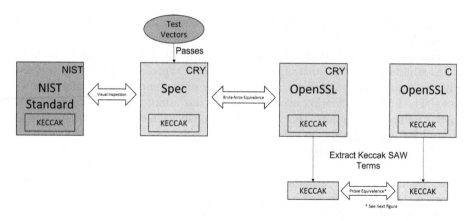

Fig. 1. Equivalence proof for the SHA-3 standard and the OpenSSL C implementation.

The KECCAK transformation function takes place over twenty-four rounds with each round consisting of five steps: θ, ρ, π, χ, and ι. The state A itself is viewed as a 5×5 array of 64-bit words (e.g. $5 * 5 * 64 = 1600$) in each of the steps. θ computes a parity over the columns in the state. ρ is a bitwise rotate over the state. π is a permutation on the state. χ is a non-linear operation that combines along the rows in the state. And ι mixes in twenty-four different constants, one for each iteration, into portions of the state.

3   Proof Outline and Results

The goal of the work presented in this paper is to prove the OpenSSL implementation of SHA-3 matches the FIPS 202 specification by NIST. Figure 1 illustrates the proof strategy. The proof begins on the left of the figure with the box labeled *NIST Standard*. This box represents the FIPS 202 specification that defines the SHA-3 algorithm with English prose and math. The specification also provides several test inputs with the corresponding expected digests. The first step of the proof reproduces the FIPS 202 SHA-3 description in Cryptol. That is the box to the right of the *NIST Standard* box labeled *Spec*.

3.1   Visual Inspection and Test Vectors

The equivalence between the FIPS 202 standard and the Cryptol specification is argued by visual inspection along with tests over the published test vectors with their expected digests. SHA-3 is described algorithmically in the standard making use of universal quantifiers and other looping structures in the definition. Cryptol is functional in that it uses list comprehensions for iteration, and it does not have quantifiers. Visually certifying a specification of SHA-3 that uses list comprehensions is less direct. The list comprehensions can be complex, and at times, they obscure the algorithmic, and mathematic, structure in the published standard.

The syntactic disconnect between the quantification and looping in the published standard and the functional nature of the Cryptol specification is bridged with a library that hides list comprehensions with appropriately named functions. The final specification using the library has a more direct correspondence to the published standard that is more obviously visually certified. Its size is around 200 *lines of code* (LOC) in Cryptol.

The specification is further validated by tests in Cryptol over the published test vectors. The digests computed from the Cryptol specification exactly match those published in the standard on each given input. The equivalence arrow between the *NIST Standard* box and the *Spec* box represents the visual certification and test vector results. Section 4 details the library using examples from the specification.

3.2   Memory Layout and Optimized Computation

The extracted SAWCore from the OpenSSL C implementation of SHA-3 is too big and complex for SAW to reason about directly. Adding to the complexity of the equivalence proof is that the OpenSSL implementation changes the meaning of the state S in the algorithm so that it no longer directly matches the meaning defined in the published standard. It also changes the computation of the inner KECCAK functions. These changes effectively reorder the matrix definition of the state to be more amenable to memory and optimize the different functions in KECCAK to be more efficient when operating on the state. This includes using pre-computed constants for ι. The changes are significant enough to make it extremely difficult to argue manually that the computation implemented in OpenSSL matches that defined in the standard.

The next step of the equivalence proof creates a Cryptol specification that matches the state reordering in the OpenSSL implementation, but still follows the bit-level updates in the FIPS 202 standard in an effort to show an equivalence between it and the Cryptol specification for the standard. It also adds the computation of the constants to the specification. This new specification is the box in the right middle of Fig. 1 labeled *OpenSSL* with the *CRY* annotation in the upper right corner and is around 221 LOC. SAW is not able to reason symbolically about input and digest sizes to construct a general proof of equivalence between the published standard and the OpenSSL Cryptol specification with the state reordering, but it is able to prove equivalence between the two specifications given specific sizes for the input and digest.

A series of SAW proofs over a range of input sizes with the digest size fixed at 256 bits is used to prove the equivalence between the published standard and the OpenSSL Cryptol specifications. The series of proofs varies the input size from zero bits to 1,088 bits, in one byte increments, to reflect the 1,088 bit rate required for a 256 bit digest. The proofs establish the correctness of the input padding and cover the situation where the padding adds an additional 1,088 bit block to the input. The total running time for these proofs is around

60 h. As such, the meaning of the equivalence arrow between the *Spec* box and the *OpenSSL* box in the middle of the figure is that the two specifications have equivalent computation for a 256 bit digest for message sizes from 0 bits to $1,088$ bits.

Fig. 2. Inner function contracts

3.3 Overrides and KECCAK

The rest of the equivalence proof between the standard and the OpenSSL implementation centers on the KECCAK algorithm as shown in the bottom right of Fig. 1. The meaning of the equivalence arrow between the KECCAK definition in the Cryptol specification based on the OpenSSL implementation and the actual implemented KECCAK algorithm in the OpenSSL C implementation is that their computation exactly matches for any input state. That proof cannot be constructed directly by SAW since the extracted SAWCore from the C implementation is too big for automated reasoning when considering all twenty-four rounds required by KECCAK. The disconnect is largely a result of the C implementation operating in 64-bit words at a time where the specification is bit level. The full proof requires overrides.

The proof of equivalence between the specification of KECCAK and the C implementation of KECCAK in OpenSSL relies on overrides in SAW as shown in Fig. 2. Here, SAW proves equivalence between the bit-level Cryptol specifications and the word level C implementations for each of the five functions that comprise one round of KECCAK given some arbitrary input state. That is the meaning of the left hand side of Fig. 2. These are equivalent on any state S.

The implementations for each of the five KECCAK functions in the C implementation are replaced by the corresponding equivalent Cryptol specifications in the extracted model from C. SAW is then able to prove the C implementation of KECCAK equivalent to the Cryptol specification of the OpenSSL implementation of KECCAK over all twenty-four rounds for any arbitrary input state. The equivalence is independent of the digest size, message size, or state. As a minor note, the OpenSSL code for the ι function was modified in one place to remove an assert-statement safe-guarding an index into a table of constants since the assert-statement is not supported by SAW's symbolic execution engine. The proof takes less than 15 min including the proofs for the overrides.

3.4   Results and Summary

Table 1 is a summary of the cost of the verification in running time and LOCs. These are from fairly banal hardware seen in any laptop. The Cryptol specification of the FIPS 202 standard relies on visual inspection and test vectors for equivalence having to look at around 200 LOC. The equivalence between the Cryptol specification of the standard and the Cryptol specification of the OpenSSL specification that reorders the state array is limited to the 256 bit digest on input sizes from 0 bits to 1,088 bits and takes around 60 h of computation time. That is a proof that considers all of Algorithm 1. The equivalence between the OpenSSL Cryptol specification that reorders the state array and the actual C implementation is limited to the KECCAK algorithm only. That is a proof that only considers Line 5 in Algorithm 1 but holds for any state and is independent of the digest size and rate. The cost of proving the equivalence for each of the overrides is trivial with the exception of ι. ι is more costly because it uses a lookup table in the C code so every entry in the table had to be proved out (see Sect. 5). The final cost of proving the equivalence in KECCAK with the overrides is less than 15 min with the yices solver.

Table 1. Proof runtimes and code sizes where OV means overrides.

Function	yices	abc	Cry LOC	C LOC
π	0.8951595 s	0.4171096 s	7 lines	35 lines
ρ	4.5090218 s	5.879199 s	19 lines	41 lines
θ	25.9416942 s	14.8692876 s	17 lines	55 lines
χ	5.0592874 s	1.3271656 s	7 lines	18 lines
ι	11.0476514 s	612.4968917 s	37 lines	31 lines
Keccak (With OV's)	745.205611 s	2910.5493025 s	93 lines	129 lines

4   FIPS 202 Specification in Cryptol

This section illustrates with a few examples how the FIPS 202 specification is captured in Cryptol. Cryptol's list comprehensions do not directly align with the quantification and iteration in the specification. This misalignment makes the Cryptol specification more difficult to read and to manually argue its equivalence relative to the published specification. The two specifications are better aligned through a library of two methods in Cryptol that hide the list comprehensions so that the Cryptol specification reads more like the FIPS 202 specification. The two library methods are the *for-method* and the *while-method* discussed in this section.

4.1   The for-method

A common idiom in the FIPS 202 publication is using quantification over a finite
domain defined by linear constraints to define input for some computation. The
definition of the π function for KECCAK shown in Fig. 3(a) is one such example.
Here the quantification is used to define the set of indices that are part of the π
computation that transforms the state array. The intent is that of a *parallel-for*
where order does not matter since the new state array A' only depends on the
old state array A.

1. For all triples (x,y,z) such that
   $0 <= x < 5,\ 0 <= y < 5,$ and $0 <= z < w,$
   let $A'[x,\ y,\ z] = A[(x + 3y) \bmod 5,\ x,\ z]$.
2. Return A'.

(a)

```
1    type STATE_ARR = [5][5][64]
2    pi : STATE_ARR -> STATE_ARR
3    pi a = [ [ [a @x @((x + 3*y) % 5) @z
4               | z <- [0..63]]
5             | y <- [0..4]]
6           | x <- [0..4]]
```

(b)

```
for : {n, a, b} [n]a -> (a -> b) -> [n]b
for vals f = [f i | i <- vals]
```

(c)

```
pi a = for [0..4] (\x ->
         for [0..4] (\y ->
           for [0..63] (\z ->
             a @x @((x + 3*y) % 5) @z)))
```

(d)

Fig. 3. The π function. (a) The FIPS 202 specification. (b) The Cryptol with comprehensions. (c) The for-method definition. (d) The Cryptol with the for-method.

The Cryptol definition using list comprehensions is given in Fig. 3(b). Line 1
defines the state as a 5×5 array of 64-bit words. Line 3 starts the definition of
π. Here the comprehensions are nested with the list indices appearing in reverse
order to follow the nesting. Line 4 gives the domain for z as a list with values
from 0 to 63. The domains for x and y are given similarly. The domains for x, y,
and z all match the domains defined in the quantification in Fig. 3(a). Although
the list comprehensions are not unreadable, the Cryptol can be improved by
creating a for-method to hide some of the details.

Figure 3(c) is the Cryptol definition of the for-method. It takes two arguments: a list, *vals*, for the comprehension, and a function, f, to apply to each element of the list. Its definition is as expected: it creates a new list that is the result of applying f to each element in *vals*.

Figure 3(d) is the rewritten Cryptol using the for-method. It still requires the indices lists for the list comprehensions, but it has a more obvious correspondence to the original definition in Fig. 3(a). The for-method reorders and structures the arguments in a very elegant way. It hides the list comprehensions to simplify the task of visual inspection for equivalence.

> 1. If t mod 255 = 0, return 1.
> 2. Let R = 10000000.
> 3. For i from 1 to t mod 255, let:
>   a. R = 0 || R;
>   b. R[0] = R[0] ^ R[8];
>   c. R[4] = R[4] ^ R[8];
>   d. R[5] = R[5] ^ R[8];
>   e. R[6] = R[6] ^ R[8];
>   f. R = Trunc8[R].
> 4. Return R[0].

Fig. 4. The FIPS 202 specification for *rc*.

4.2 The while-method

Another common idiom in the FIPS 202 standard is to iteratively transform some state a fixed number of times to arrive at a final state. The definition of the *round constant*, *rc*, function in Fig. 4 is one such example. The *rc* function is a support function for the ι function in KECCAK and is used to build a mask.

The *rc* function checks the value of the input integer t, and returns the bit 0 if it is a multiple of 255. If not, then Line 2 defines R as the 8-bit value 128, and Line 3 iteratively transforms R a fixed number of times: t **mod** 255. The transform is defined on Line 3a through Line 3f. Line 3a prepends a 0 bit to R so that it is now a 9-bit value. The array indexing refers to bit positions from left to right so $R[0]$ is the prepended left-most bit and $R[8]$ is the right-most bit. Each transform on R prepends the 0 (Line 3a), does an exclusive-or with specific bit positions (Line 3b through Line 3e), and then takes the left-most 8 bits for the next round effectively dropping the right-most bit (Line 3f). It returns the $R[0]$ bit at the end.

The Cryptol equivalent for *rc* in Fig. 5(a) is considerably more complex with the list comprehensions. Returning 1 when the input is a multiple of 255 is straightforward. It is when that is not the case that it is less obvious. The list comprehension builds a list of 255 8-bit values. Line 3 returns the bit at index 0

```
1        rc  :  [64] -> Bit
2        rc t =   if (t % 255) == 0 then 1
3                 else rs !0 @0 where
4                     rs = [0b10000000] #
5                          [if i <= t % 255 then
6                               ((nextR r) where r = [0] # (rs @(i - 1)))
7                           else rs @(i - 1)
8                           | i <- [1..254]]
```

(a)

```
while : {a} a -> (a -> Bit) -> (a -> a) -> a
while state cond f =
    if (cond state) then (while (f state) cond f)
    else state
```

(b)

```
1        rc  :  [64] -> Bit
2        rc t =   if (t % 255) == 0 then 1
3                 else (while {i = 1, R = 0b10000000}
4                          (\state -> state.i <= t % 255)
5                          (\state -> {
6                              i = state.i + 1,
7                              R = (nextR r) where r = [0] # state.R})
8                      ).R @0
```

(c)

Fig. 5. The *rc* function in Cryptol where *nextR* elides steps 3b to 3f of Fig. 4. (a) The Cryptol with list comprehensions. (b) The recursive while-method definition. (c) The Cryptol with the while-method.

(@0) from the last 8-bit value in the array (!0). The computation of the list of 8-bit values follows.

Line 4 is the first entry in the list and it is the initial value of R. The following entries depend on the value of the input t and the value of i that comes from the list used in the list comprehension on Line 8. Line 5 checks if i is within the number of iterations, and if it is, then the new entry in the list is computed from the previous entry as defined by the transform in Fig. 4. Line 7 is the case for when i is not within the number of iterations. Here the previous value in the list is copied to stutter the last value of R. The Cryptol specification creates all 255 entries in the list regardless of the input value t except for the case when t is a multiple of 255. As before, Fig. 5(a) is not altogether unreadable, but it can be improved considerably.

Figure 5(b) is a recursive definition of a *while-loop*. It takes as input a state, a predicate on the state, *cond*, that is true when it should loop and false otherwise, and a function, f, that computes a new state from the old state on each iteration. The definition makes recursive calls to the while-method until the state predicate is false at which point it returns the current value of *state*.

Figure 5(c) is the definition of *rc* using the while-method in Fig. 5(b). Line 3 defines the state for the while loop to be both an integer i for a counter and the

8-bit value R. Line 4 is the looping condition defined on the state. The body of the loop not only computes the new value of R but Line 6 increments i to track the loop iteration. The return value is given on Line 8 as the 0th bit from the last value of R. Here, R is computed only the number of times required by t. This change differs significantly from the definition without the while-method. As with the for-method, the while-method reduces the gap between how things are defined in FIPS 202 and how they are defined in Cryptol.

5   OpenSSL Differences

This section details the key differences between the OpenSSL implementation of SHA-3 and the FIPS 202 specification that prevented a direct proof of equivalence between the Cryptol and C code. These differences are expressed in a second Cryptol model derived from the FIPS 202 model discussed in the previous section. SAW proves these two models equivalent for the 256-bit digest size as discussed in Sect. 3. This equivalence considers the whole of the sponge construction algorithm proving that the digest is the same from each of them. That said, and as a reminder, the equivalence between the KECCAK description in Cryptol and the C implementation in OpenSSL holds for any input message and any digest size. That proof uses the Cryptol definition for the model discussed in this section that includes all the differences seen in OpenSSL, and the overrides used in that proof also come from the Cryptol discussed in this section.

5.1   State Array Structure and Computation

The first set of differences in the OpenSSL SHA-3 implementation is in the structure of the state array and how it operates on that state array. The difference in structure is an artifact of how C maps arrays to memory. The FIPS 202 structures the state array as a 5×5 grid of 64-bit words with each 64-bit word being a *lane*. It assumes the layout of the data follows a normal cartesian three dimensional coordinate system with x being the horizontal axis, y being the vertical axis, and z being the depth on a lane to access an individual bit. For a state A, $A[x, y, z]$ accesses the zth bit from the 64-bit word on the xth column and the yth row.

OpenSSL declares the state as follows: uint64_t A[5][5]. The C standard stores multidimensional arrays in contiguous memory in *row-major* order meaning that each row of five 64-bit values appear consecutively in memory. Indexing the multidimensional array follows the standard mathematical definition for indexing matrices: $A[x, y]$ is the element at the xth row and y^{th} column. This meaning is just opposite of that in the standard.

Adding to the complexity is that the C standard does not provide array indexing to get a bit from a value. For the $A[x, y, z]$ example, there is no array bracket notation to get the zth bit in a 64-bit word, so notation in the FIPS 202 standard such as that seen in the definition of the rc function in Fig. 4(a) has no direct analogue in C. The consequence is that the OpenSSL implementation does

```
pi a = for [0..4] (\y ->
          for [0..4] (\x ->
            for [0..63] (\z ->
              a @x @((x + 3*y) % 5) @z)))
```

Fig. 6. The OpenSSL implementation of π that reverses indexes.

```
iota a i =  for LIST4 (\y ->
              for LIST4 (\x ->
                for LIST63 (\z ->
                  if ((x == 0) \\ (y == 0))
                    then (a @0 @0 @z) ^ (LISTIOTAS @i @z)
                    else a @y @x @z)))
LISTIOTAS = [reverse (
   (while {RC = 0:[W], j = 0}
      (\state -> state.j <= `L)
      (\state -> {
         RC = for [0..63]
            (\z -> if z == index then rc (state.j + 7*i)
               else state.RC @z)
         where index = ((1:[8]) << state.j) - 1,
                  j = state.j + 1})
   ).RC) | i <- LISTROUNDS: [_][64]]
```

Fig. 7. The computed rc table with the lookup in ι.

everything at the level of the lanes, operating on each lane as a 64-bit entity, and it never refers to an individual bit in a lane. Finally, the bit ordering in the lanes in the FIPS 202 standard is just opposite the ordering in C meaning that the direction of shifting in the standard is opposite the direction used in the C implementation.

The Cryptol for the FIPS 202 model is rewritten to reflect the memory layout differences but leaves in place the bit-level operations. The x and y indexing is swapped, and the shifts are reversed. For reference, Fig. 6 is the rewritten π function in Cryptol than matches the swapping of the indices in OpenSSL (compare to Fig. 3(d)).

5.2   Constant Lookup Tables

The second difference is in hardcoding lookup Tables for constants rather than computing the constants along the way. The FIPS 202 Cryptol specification computes each constant on-the-fly as needed in each round. This redundant computation is seen with the rounding constants, rc, for ι, and the rotate constants for ρ. The OpenSSL implementation hardcodes these constants in tables without the provenance of the computation and looks up the constants in the tables. The new Cryptol specification for the OpenSSL uses the same lookup tables, but it differs from the OpenSSL implementation in that it computes the lookup tables once so that the values in the table now have provenance. This provenance is sufficient for the equivalence proof with the C code. Figure 7 shows the ι function that uses the computed lookup table.

The change to the state array structure and the added provenance giving the computation for lookup constants are the only changes to the Cryptol from the FIPS 202. These changes are sufficient for SAW to prove the input to output equivalence between the two Cryptol specifications for a fixed set of message sizes. And they are sufficient to prove the equivalence to the actual C code in OpenSSL in the KECCAK function for any arbitrary state. The result adds more evidence to the ability to prove out implementations of cryptographic primitives when given specifications.

6 Related Work

Almeida et al. give a formal specification of SHA-3 in Jasmin [1]. They then prove that SHA-3 is resistant to collisions, correctly implemented by Jasmin in vectorized x86, and that implementation is resistant to side-channel attacks. The proofs are mechanized and carried out by the EasyCrypt proof assistant [10]. The vectorized implementation is performant and efficient.

EverCrypt from Protzenko *et al.* is a library of verified cryptographic primitives including several state of art algorithms for computing digests [21]. Here the algorithms are specified in F* [13]. Automated proofs of properties of the crypto-primitives are done with a weakest-precondition calculus. As subset of F* is compilable to C the library is compiled to different target backends. The resulting library is performant and efficient.

The work is this paper differs from the these related efforts in that this work does not prove properties of SHA-3 itself but rather proves an existing implementation of SHA-3 is correct relative to the published standard. Here the verification effort is to prove OpenSSL correct in its implementation of SHA-3. OpenSSL being a widely deployed implementation written for performance not thinking of verification makes it an interesting target for formal verification and an interesting case study for SAW.

Cryptol has been used to formally verify several cryptographic algorithms in the past. As a demonstration of Cryptol, Lewis *et al.* provided portions of the *Advanced Encryption Standard* (AES) implemented in the language [18]. The language has also been used to verify equivalence between Skein Hash algorithm implementations [11]. Cryptol is not limited to software, as Browning and Weaver [5] have shown that the language can be tuned to provide an abstraction of hardware. They later provided a proof of equivalence between the FIPS AES specification and various optimized Cryptol implementations. For certain tables, they initially demonstrated equivalence through mathematical principles. These tables were also proven equivalent to less time-intensive statically defined tables used for the rest of their proofs. As the OpenSSL implementation was highly optimized with similar static values, this paper mirrored the method Browning and Weaver outlined. The language was also used to verify equivalence between the specification and hardware of the Verilog RTL's pseudorandom number generator [24].

Decker et al.'s verification of OpenSSL's SHA-2 256 bit digest implementation served as a direct predecessor to this work [8]. While SHA-2 is also part of the NIST Secure Hash Algorithms, its internal structure differs vastly from the more complex and resistant SHA-3. The SHA-2 proof, in turn, expanded the methodology by which Amazon's s2n HMAC was verified [6,23]. While SHA-3 is not implemented in s2n, the HMAC verification provided utilized both a high-level and low-level Cryptol specification in a similar manner to this work. Both works compared equivalent C and Cryptol specification through SAW. Decker's work is inspired by the OpenSSL verification of HMAC from Beringer [3].

Other tools have been used on a wide variety of cryptographic algorithms. STP [14], a SAT-based procedure, has been used to verify implementation of AES, DES, SHA-1, and other block cipher functions [26]. Isabelle has aided in formal verification of networking protocols [15,17]. The Coq proof assistant was used to prove equivalence between the OpenSSL, mbedTLS, and NIST implementations of HMAC-DRBG [7,28]. Using Jasmin [16], Barthe *et al.* showed that implementations of the ChaCha20 and Poly1305 were equivalent to their specifications [2]. Vale has been used to verify the SHA-2 256 bit digest and AES implementations [4]. Also of interest, the VeriHash framework demonstrated a bug in the RHash implementation of SHA-3 with the 256 bit digest [22,27].

7   Conclusion

This paper presents the proof of the SHA-3 implementation in OpenSSL using the SAW tool. The proof is accomplished by writing a Cryptol specification for the NIST FIPS 202 specification that defines the SHA-3 algorithm. The Cryptol specification is aided with two additional Cryptol library functions, the for-method and while-method, to hide the functional list comprehensions. The for-method is a parallel-for operating on each element in a list, and the while-method is a list iteration. The Cryptol is shown equivalent to the FIPS 202 standard through visual inspection and input to output matching on published test vectors.

The proof uses a second Cryptol specification based on the actual OpenSSL C implementation of SHA-3. This specification reorders arrays in the specification to match the C standard following row major order. It also includes table lookups for constant values in the computation but it computes those tables to show the provenance of the constants. That provenance is needed later for the proof of equivalence with the C code. SAW proves the input to output relationship equivalent between the FIPS 202 specification and this revised specification for the 256-bit digest on any message of size 0 to $1,088$ bits.

The final SAW proof shows the KECCAK function in the revised specification is equivalent to the KECCAK function in the actual C implementation. KECCAK is the core of the SHA-3 algorithm and the most complex part. The proof relies of the use of overrides. SAW proves the Cryptol specifications of the five inner KECCAK functions equivalent to their C counterparts and replaces them in the C code with the SAWCore from the Cryptol. With the overrides, SAW proves the equivalence for KECCAK in Cryptol and C over any input.

Future work is to prove out the equivalence of the input padding and the squeeze part of the SHA-3 computation. These proofs are complicated by the typing in Cryptol and the layout of bytes in C. There is also some effort to show the equivalence for the other digest sizes. Other work looks to accomplish a proof of a Dafny implementation of SHA-3. Dafny synthesizes to several different backend languages making a proven SHA-3 implementation very interesting.

References

1. Almeida, J.B., et al.: Machine-checked proofs for cryptographic standards: indifferentiability of sponge and secure high-assurance implementations of SHA-3. In: Proceedings of the 2019 ACM SIGSAC Conference on Computer and Communications Security, CCS 2019, pp. 1607–1622. Association for Computing Machinery, New York (2019). https://doi.org/10.1145/3319535.3363211
2. Barthe, G., et al.: High-assurance cryptography in the spectre era. In: 2021 IEEE Symposium on Security and Privacy (SP), pp. 1884–1901 (2021). https://doi.org/10.1109/SP40001.2021.00046
3. Beringer, L., Petcher, A., Ye, K.Q., Appel, A.W.: Verified correctness and security of OpenSSL HMAC. In: 24th USENIX Security Symposium (USENIX Security 15), pp. 207–221. USENIX Association, Washington, D.C., August 2015. https://www.usenix.org/conference/usenixsecurity15/technical-sessions/presentation/beringer
4. Bond, B., et al.: Vale: verifying high-performance cryptographic assembly code. In: 26th USENIX Security Symposium (USENIX Security 2017), pp. 917–934. USENIX Association, Vancouver, August 2017. https://www.usenix.org/conference/usenixsecurity17/technical-sessions/presentation/bond
5. Browning, S., Weaver, P.: Designing tunable, verifiable cryptographic hardware using Cryptol. In: Hardin, D. (ed.) Design and Verification of Microprocessor Systems for High-Assurance Applications, pp. 89–143. Springer, Boston (2010). https://doi.org/10.1007/978-1-4419-1539-9_4
6. Chudnov, A., et al.: Continuous formal verification of Amazon s2n. In: Chockler, H., Weissenbacher, G. (eds.) CAV 2018. LNCS, vol. 10982, pp. 430–446. Springer, Cham (2018). https://doi.org/10.1007/978-3-319-96142-2_26
7. The Coq proof assistant. https://coq.inria.fr/
8. Decker, B., Winters, B., Mercer, E.: Towards verifying SHA256 in OpenSSL with the software analysis workbench. In: Dutle, A., Moscato, M.M., Titolo, L., Muñoz, C.A., Perez, I. (eds.) NFM 2021. LNCS, vol. 12673, pp. 72–78. Springer, Cham (2021). https://doi.org/10.1007/978-3-030-76384-8_5
9. Dockins, R., Foltzer, A., Hendrix, J., Huffman, B., McNamee, D., Tomb, A.: Constructing semantic models of programs with the software analysis workbench. In: Blazy, S., Chechik, M. (eds.) VSTTE 2016. LNCS, vol. 9971, pp. 56–72. Springer, Cham (2016). https://doi.org/10.1007/978-3-319-48869-1_5
10. Easycrypt: Computer-aided cryptographic proofs. https://github.com/EasyCrypt/easycrypt
11. Erkök, L., Carlsson, M., Wick, A.: Hardware/software co-verification of cryptographic algorithms using Cryptol. In: 2009 Formal Methods in Computer-Aided Design, pp. 188–191 (2009). https://doi.org/10.1109/FMCAD.2009.5351121
12. SHA-3 standard: permutation-based hash and extendable-output functions (2015). https://csrc.nist.gov/publications/detail/fips/202/final. Accessed Jan 2020
13. F* programming language. https://www.fstar-lang.org/
14. Ganesh, V., Dill, D.L.: A decision procedure for bit-vectors and arrays. In: Damm, W., Hermanns, H. (eds.) CAV 2007. LNCS, vol. 4590, pp. 519–531. Springer, Heidelberg (2007). https://doi.org/10.1007/978-3-540-73368-3_52

15. Isabelle. https://isabelle.in.tum.de/
16. Jasmin. https://github.com/jasmin-lang/jasmin
17. Klenze, T., Sprenger, C., Basin, D.: Formal verification of secure forwarding protocols. In: 2021 IEEE 34th Computer Security Foundations Symposium (CSF), pp. 1–16 (2021). https://doi.org/10.1109/CSF51468.2021.00018
18. Lewis, J., Martin, B.: Cryptol: high assurance, retargetable crypto development and validation. In: IEEE Military Communications Conference 2003, MILCOM 2003, vol. 2, pp. 820–825 (2003). https://doi.org/10.1109/MILCOM.2003.1290218
19. Apache log4j vulnerability guidance. https://www.cisa.gov/uscert/apache-log4j-vulnerability-guidance
20. OpenSSL. https://openssl.org
21. Protzenko, J., et al.: Evercrypt: a fast, verified, cross-platform cryptographic provider. In: 2020 IEEE Symposium on Security and Privacy (SP), pp. 983–1002 (2020). https://doi.org/10.1109/SP40000.2020.00114
22. RHash. https://github.com/rhash/RHash
23. Verifying s2n HMAC with SAW. https://galois.com/blog/2016/09/verifying-s2n-hmac-with-saw/
24. Selvakumar, D., Mervin, J., Pattanshetty, S., Vivian, D.: Formal verification and analysis of a pseudo random number generator. In: 2021 25th International Symposium on VLSI Design and Test (VDAT), pp. 1–6 (2021). https://doi.org/10.1109/VDAT53777.2021.9601109
25. SHA-3 verification. https://github.com/ericmercer/sha3-verification
26. Smith, E., Dill, D.L.: Automatic formal verification of block cipher implementations. In: 2008 Formal Methods in Computer-Aided Design, pp. 1–7 (2008). https://doi.org/10.1109/FMCAD.2008.ECP.10
27. Wang, D., Jiang, Y., Song, H., He, F., Gu, M., Sun, J.: Verification of implementations of cryptographic hash functions. IEEE Access 5, 7816–7825 (2017). https://doi.org/10.1109/ACCESS.2017.2697918
28. Ye, K.Q., Green, M., Sanguansin, N., Beringer, L., Petcher, A., Appel, A.W.: Verified correctness and security of MbedTLS HMAC-DRBG. In: Proceedings of the 2017 ACM SIGSAC Conference on Computer and Communications Security, CCS 2017, pp. 2007–2020. Association for Computing Machinery, New York (2017). https://doi.org/10.1145/3133956.3133974

Bounded-Memory Runtime Enforcement

Saumya Shankar[1]([✉]), Antoine Rollet[2], Srinivas Pinisetty[1], and Yliès Falcone[3]

[1] Indian Institute of Technology, Bhubaneswar, India
{ss117,spinisetty}@iitbbs.ac.in
[2] Univ. Bordeaux, CNRS, Bordeaux INP, LaBRI, UMR 5800,
33400 Talence, France
antoine.rollet@labri.fr
[3] Univ. Grenoble Alpes, CNRS, Inria, Grenoble INP, LIG,
38000 Grenoble, France
ylies.falcone@univ-grenoble-alpes.fr

Abstract. Runtime Enforcement (RE) is a monitoring technique to ensure that a system obeys a set of formal requirements (properties). RE employs an enforcer (a safety wrapper for the system) which modifies the (untrustworthy) output by performing actions such as delaying (by storing/buffering) and suppressing events, when needed. In this paper, to handle practical applications with memory constraints, we propose a new RE paradigm where the memory of the enforcer is bounded/finite. Besides the property to be enforced, the user specifies a bound on the enforcer memory. Bounding the memory poses various challenges such as how to handle the situation when the memory is full, how to optimally discard events from the buffer to accommodate new events and let the enforcer continue operating. We define the bounded-memory RE problem and develop a framework for any regular property. The proposed framework is implemented and its performance evaluated via some examples from application scenarios indicates that the enforcer has reasonable execution time overhead.

Keywords: Formal methods · Runtime enforcement · Automata

1 Introduction

Runtime Enforcement (RE) [3, 4, 6, 8, 9, 12, 20] is a monitoring technique to ensure that a system complies with a set of formal requirements (properties) at runtime. An enforcer can be considered as a safety wrapper for the system, which modifies an (untrustworthy) input (in the form of a sequence of events) into an output

This work has been partially supported by IIT Bhubaneswar Seed Grant (SP093). Y. Falcone acknowledges the support from the H2020-ECSEL-2018-IA call -Grant Agreement number 826276 (CPS4EU), from the French ANR project ANR-20- CE39-0009 (SEVERITAS), the Auvergne-Rhône-Alpes research project MOAP, and LabEx PERSYVAL-Lab (ANR-11-LABX-0025-01) funded by the French program Investissement d'avenir.

The original version of this chapter was revised: the Figure 3 was incorrect. The correction to this chapter is available at https://doi.org/10.1007/978-3-031-15077-7_9

O. Legunsen and G. Rosu (Eds.): SPIN 2022, LNCS 13255, pp. 114–133, 2022.
https://doi.org/10.1007/978-3-031-15077-7_7

Fig. 1. Enforcement mechanism

sequence that complies with the specified property. RE usually aims at ensuring the so-called *soundness* (the output must satisfy the property) and *transparency* (a correct input should remain unchanged).

We focus on the online enforcement of regular properties meaning that enforcement of property φ is done on the fly. The general schema is depicted in Fig. 1, where an enforcer is placed between an event emitter and an event receiver that executes asynchronously. The enforcer takes a sequence of events σ as input and transforms it into a sequence of events o that is correct with respect to φ. The enforcer is equipped with an internal memory (*buffer*) to store some events that are received as input which would be released as output only when the satisfaction of the property is ensured. We will use the word *buffer* for referring to the internal memory of the enforcer throughout the paper.

In usual RE mechanisms such as [9,12], the buffer of the enforcer is considered to be infinite. But this assumption is obviously not realistic in the case of a real implementation of the enforcer: an internal buffer is necessarily bounded [10,22]. Then an important question arises: what should be done when the bound of the buffer is reached? To illustrate the problem, consider for instance an enforcement mechanism protecting a critical system by filtering dangerous requests in a network, i.e., inputs that are ill-formatted or suspicious. The situation where the buffer of this protecting mechanism is full is also a critical situation which has to be considered carefully. Naive reactions may lead to dangerous inputs being transmitted to the system and then make the enforcement mechanism useless.

In this work, we study RE with a bounded buffer, i.e., we will see how our enforcer tackles the situation when the buffer is finite. We allow an enforcer to continue operating even when its buffer is full. To handle the situation where the buffer of the enforcer is full, a simple possibility would be to discard the received event, or to remove the oldest one. However, these approaches do not guarantee compliance with the specified property or minimal deviation from an "ideal" enforcer (i.e., an enforcer without memory limitation). Thus, cleaning the buffer when it is full in an optimal way (minimal dropping of events, minimal deviation) in order to continue enforcement becomes the major challenge of a bounded-memory enforcement problem.

Formally speaking, given a regular property φ, and maximum size of buffer k, we aim to synthesize an enforcer that takes as input a word σ and outputs a word o that (i) satisfies φ (soundness), and (ii) is a prefix, or subword of input σ (transparency). In addition, (iii) the output should be as long as possible (optimality) and equivalent to one produced by an enforcer with unbounded memory (∞-compatible), as explained in Sect. 4. We refer to this problem as *Bounded-Memory Runtime Enforcement*.

Context and Objectives. We tackle the problem of obtaining an enforcer given a regular property specified as a Deterministic Finite-state Automaton (DFA). The enforcer intervenes when an execution is about to violate the property being enforced by catching events. The synthesized enforcers have the following abilities: storing events in a buffer, releasing them when the property is finally satisfied, and suppressing events, but only if there is no other way to avoid a buffer overflow. At the point of filtering them out, the filtered/suppressed events should be invariant with respect to the property (DFA's) language. The number of events suppressed in the buffer must be minimal. As illustrated in the abstract architecture in Fig. 1, we consider that the emitter and receiver run in an asynchronous manner, thus delaying an event from the emitter does not have any impact on its successive events. These are reasonable assumptions for many practical applications such as networks and components in systems like autonomous vehicles.

Contributions. We introduce the first formal framework for bounded-memory runtime enforcement. The notions of soundness and monotonicity are similar to the ones used in the standard RE frameworks [11]. However, transparency is modified to take into account the possibility of suppressing/dropping events when needed. In addition, we propose a new notion of optimality. At an abstract level, we model enforcers as functions that transform words. We define the constraints that an enforcement function (for some φ) should satisfy. We present algorithms describing how the proposed enforcement functions can be implemented. All our results are formalized. The proposed algorithms are implemented in Python and are evaluated using some example properties, and also using properties based on application scenarios related to concurrency and autonomous vehicles. The overhead of enforcers is observed to be reasonable.

2   Preliminaries and Notations

Languages: A (finite) word w over a finite alphabet Σ is a finite sequence of elements of Σ. The length of w, denoted as $|w|$, is the number of elements in w. The empty word over Σ is denoted by ϵ. The sets of all words and all non-empty words are denoted by Σ^* and Σ^+ respectively. A language or a property over Σ is any subset of Σ^* and is denoted by φ.

The concatenation of two words w and w' is denoted by $w \cdot w'$. A word w' is a prefix of word w, denoted $w' \preccurlyeq w$, whenever there exists a word w'' such that $w = w' \cdot w''$, and $w' \prec w$ if additionally $w' \neq w$; conversely w is said to be an extension of w'. The set $\mathrm{pref}(w)$ denotes the *set of prefixes* of w and subsequently, $\mathrm{pref}(\mathcal{L}) \overset{\text{def}}{=} \bigcup_{w \in \mathcal{L}} \mathrm{pref}(w)$ is the set of prefixes of words in $\mathcal{L}$. A language $\mathcal{L}$ is *prefix-closed* if $\mathrm{pref}(\mathcal{L}) = \mathcal{L}$ and *extension-closed* if $\mathcal{L} \cdot \Sigma^* = \mathcal{L}$.

A word $w' = a_1...a_n$ is a subword of w, denoted $w' \triangleleft w$, if w' can be obtained by deleting letters from w or, equivalently, $w = w_0 a_1 w_1...a_n w_n$ for some $w_0, ..., w_n \in \Sigma^*$. Given a n-tuple of symbols $e = (e_1, ..., e_n)$, for $i \in [1, n]$, $\Pi_i(e)$ is the projection of e on its i-th element ($\Pi_i(e) = e_i$).

For a word w and $i \in [1, |w|]$, the i-th letter of w is denoted by $w_{[i]}$. Given a word w and integers i, j, s.t. $1 \leq i \leq j \leq |w|$, the *subword* from index i to j is denoted by $w_{[i...j]}$ and the suffix of word w starting from index i by $w_{[i...]}$.

Deterministic and complete automata: A deterministic and complete automaton A is a tuple $A = (Q, q_0, \Sigma, \delta, F,)$ where, Q is the set of states, $q_0 \in Q$ is the initial state, Σ is the finite alphabet, $\delta : Q \times \Sigma \to Q$ is the (total) transition function and $F \subseteq Q$ is the set of accepting states. A dead state of an automaton is a state from where there is no way for the automaton to reach an accepting state[1]. The transition function δ is extended to words by setting $\delta(q, \epsilon) = q$, and $\delta(q, a \cdot \sigma) = \delta(\delta(q, a), \sigma)$, for any $q \in Q, a \in \Sigma, \sigma \in \Sigma^*$.

Languages of automata: A word σ is accepted by A starting from state q if $\delta(q, \sigma) \in F$, and σ is accepted by A if σ is accepted starting from the initial state q_0. The language of A starting from state q is denoted $L(A, q)$ and is the set of all accepted words from $q : L(A, q) = \{\sigma \in \Sigma^* | \delta(q, \sigma) \in F\}$. The language of A, denoted $L(A)$, is $L(A, q_0)$, i.e., the language of A from the initial state q_0. A word w satisfying φ is denoted by $w \models \varphi$, meaning w belongs to the language accepted by the automaton defining φ. The next lemma relates accepted words and the states reached by their prefixes in an automaton.

Lemma 1. $\forall \sigma, \sigma' \in \Sigma^* : \sigma \cdot \sigma' \in L(A) \Longleftrightarrow (\sigma' \in L(A, \delta(q_0, \sigma)))$

Lemma 1 states that given any two words $\sigma, \sigma' \in \Sigma^*$, the word obtained by concatenating them $(\sigma \cdot \sigma')$ belongs to the language of A if and only if the word σ' belongs to the language accepted by A starting from the state reached by reading σ in A (i.e., from $\delta(q_0, \sigma)$).

Minimal automata: An automaton A is minimal, if there does not exist an automaton A' with states Q' such that $L(A) = L(A')$ and $|Q'| < |Q|$.

Any non-deterministic, incomplete and non-minimal automaton can be determinized, completed and minimized. Hence, in this paper we consider only deterministic, complete and minimal automata and the term *"automaton"* refers to a *"deterministic, complete and minimal automaton"*.

Equivalence of two words: Two words σ and σ' are φ-equivalent, noted $\sigma \sim_\varphi \sigma'$ if all their continuations evaluate equivalently with respect to φ. Formally: $\sigma \sim_\varphi \sigma'$ iff $\forall \sigma'', \sigma.\sigma'' \models \varphi \Leftrightarrow \sigma'.\sigma'' \models \varphi$.

Lemma 2. *If φ is defined by a deterministic and minimal automaton with transition function δ and initial state q_0:* $\sigma \sim_\varphi \sigma' \Leftrightarrow \delta(q_0, \sigma) = \delta(q_0, \sigma')$.

3 Runtime Enforcement with Unbounded Buffer

We adapt an RE framework based on [9,15] where enforcers are synthesized from regular properties modeled as automata. The input-output behaviour of an enforcer is specified by an enforcement function. The enforcement function E^φ transforms some input word σ which is possibly incorrect w.r.t. φ into a

---

[1] A dead state is represented by a square throughout the paper.

word satisfying φ. Enforcement mechanisms in [9,15] cannot change the order of events, cannot suppress/insert events and have only the ability of blocking and delaying events (by storing them internally in a buffer) when a violation is detected. Thus, when considering the mechanisms in [9,15], the output produced by the enforcer $E^\varphi(\sigma)$ is a prefix of the input word σ. In this work, in addition to buffering events, we also consider suppressing events when there is no possible continuation (future) of the current observation that can lead to the satisfaction of the desired property φ in the future.

Definition 1 (Enforcer). *Given property $\varphi \subseteq \Sigma^*$, a runtime enforcer for φ is a function, $E^\varphi : \Sigma^* \to \Sigma^*$, satisfying the constraints in Table 1.*

Table 1. Constraints on an enforcer.

Soundness	(Snd)	$\forall \sigma \in \Sigma^* : E^\varphi(\sigma) \neq \epsilon \implies E^\varphi(\sigma) \in \varphi$
Monotonicity	(Mo)	$\forall \sigma, \sigma' \in \Sigma^* : \sigma \preccurlyeq \sigma' \implies E^\varphi(\sigma) \preccurlyeq E^\varphi(\sigma')$
Transparency	(Tr1)	$\forall \sigma \in \Sigma^* \setminus \mathrm{pref}(\varphi) : E^\varphi(\sigma) \vartriangleleft \sigma$
	(Tr2)	$\forall \sigma \in \mathrm{pref}(\varphi) : E^\varphi(\sigma) \preccurlyeq \sigma$
Optimal suppression	(Opt)	$\forall \sigma \in \Sigma^*, \forall a \in \Sigma : \sigma \in \mathrm{pref}(\varphi) \land \sigma \cdot a \notin \mathrm{pref}(\varphi)$
		$\implies \forall \sigma_{\mathrm{con}} \in \Sigma^* : E^\varphi(\sigma \cdot a \cdot \sigma_{\mathrm{con}}) = E^\varphi(\sigma \cdot \sigma_{\mathrm{con}})$

Soundness means that for any input word σ, if the output $E^\varphi(\sigma)$ is not empty ($\neq \epsilon$), then it must satisfy φ. *Monotonicity* expresses that the output of the enforcer for an extended input word σ' of an input word σ, extends the output produced by the enforcer for σ, i.e., E^φ is a growing function over relation $\preccurlyeq$. *Transparency* is expressed as a conjunction of constraints (Tr1) and (Tr2). (Tr1) expresses that for an input word σ, if there is no possible continuation of σ that can lead to the satisfaction of φ in the future (i.e., σ is not a prefix of a word that belongs to φ), the output produced by the enforcer is a subword of σ (i.e., obtained by discarding/suppressing some events from σ). (Tr2) expresses that for an input word σ, if there is any possible continuation of σ that can lead to the satisfaction of φ in the future (i.e., σ is a prefix of a word that belongs to φ), the output produced by the enforcer is a prefix of σ (i.e., no event from σ can be suppressed/discarded). *Optimal suppression* (Opt) expresses that for any word σ which is a prefix of a word that belongs to φ, when extended with an event $a \in \Sigma$ such that $\sigma \cdot a$ does not have any extension that satisfies φ, event a should be suppressed by the enforcer. Let us see the definition of an enforcement function that incrementally builds the output.

Definition 2 (Enforcement Function). *Given a property $\varphi \subseteq \Sigma^*$, the enforcement function is $E^\varphi : \Sigma^* \to \Sigma^*$, and is defined as $E^\varphi(\sigma) = \Pi_1(\mathrm{store}^\varphi(\sigma))$, where $\mathrm{store}^\varphi : \Sigma^* \to \Sigma^* \times \Sigma^*$ is defined as:*

$$\mathrm{store}^\varphi(\epsilon) = (\epsilon, \epsilon)$$

$$\mathrm{store}^\varphi(\sigma \cdot a) = \begin{cases} (\sigma_s \cdot \sigma_c \cdot a, \epsilon) & \text{if } \sigma_s \cdot \sigma_c \cdot a \in \varphi, \\ (\sigma_s, \sigma_c \cdot a) & \text{if } \sigma_s \cdot \sigma_c \cdot a \notin \varphi \wedge \sigma_s \cdot \sigma_c \cdot a \in \mathrm{pref}(\varphi), \\ (\sigma_s, \sigma_c) & \text{otherwise,} \end{cases}$$

with $(\sigma_s, \sigma_c) = \mathrm{store}^\varphi(\sigma)$.

Function store$^\varphi$ takes a word over Σ as input and returns a pair of words over Σ. The first element of the output of function store$^\varphi$ corresponds to the output of the enforcement function; it is a prefix of (a subword of) the input that satisfies φ; and the second element is a suffix of (a subword of) the input that the enforcer cannot output yet. It corresponds to the buffer of the enforcer. Function store$^\varphi$ is defined inductively: initially, for an empty input, both elements are empty; if σ is read, store$^\varphi(\sigma) = (\sigma_s, \sigma_c)$, and another new event $a \in \Sigma$ is observed, there are three possible cases depending on whether $\sigma_s \cdot \sigma_c \cdot a$ satisfies φ or not or is a prefix of a word that satisfies φ or not.

- If $\sigma_s \cdot \sigma_c \cdot a$ satisfies φ, then the concatenation of the buffer content (σ_c) and event a is released as output (i.e., appended to σ_s), and the buffer σ_c is emptied (i.e., σ_c is set to ϵ);
- If $\sigma_s \cdot \sigma_c \cdot a$ does not satisfy φ, but is a prefix of a word that satisfies φ (i.e., $\sigma_s \cdot \sigma_c \cdot a \in \mathrm{pref}(\varphi)$), then the output remains unchanged and the new event a is appended to the buffer σ_c;
- Otherwise ($\sigma_s \cdot \sigma_c \cdot a$ does not satisfy φ and also is not a prefix of a word that satisfies φ, i.e., $\sigma_s \cdot \sigma_c \cdot a \notin \mathrm{pref}(\varphi)$), then both the output and the buffer remain unchanged (i.e., the new event a is suppressed).

Proposition 1 (Soundness, Monotonicity, Transparency and Optimal suppression). *Given property* $\varphi \subseteq \Sigma^*$*, the enforcement function* E^φ *as per Definition 2 is an enforcer as per Definition 1.*

Example 1 (Enforcement Function). Let us consider property φ defined by automaton A_φ in Fig. 2. State q_0 is the initial and accepting state. Let the input word be *acbabbcacab*. Table 2 illustrates the behaviour of the enforcer when the considered input word is processed incrementally event-by-event.

When the enforcer receives the first event a (where σ_c and σ_s are initially both ϵ), φ is satisfied ($\sigma_s \cdot \sigma_c \cdot a \in \varphi$), i.e., the state reached (i.e., q_0), by the enforcer upon event a is an accepting state of A_φ, so the event a is emitted, as can be seen from the 1st row of Table 2. Upon receiving the second event c, the φ is not satisfied (i.e., $\sigma_s \cdot \sigma_c \cdot c \notin \varphi$), but $\sigma_s \cdot \sigma_c \cdot c$ is a prefix of a word that satisfies φ (i.e., $\sigma_s \cdot \sigma_c \cdot c \in \mathrm{pref}(\varphi)$), thus, the event c is added into the (empty) buffer σ_c. The events in rows 3–6 of Table 2 are also appended to the contents of σ_c, as $\sigma_s \cdot \sigma_c$ followed by the new input event does not satisfy φ, but is a prefix of a word that satisfies φ. When event c is received (row 7), neither φ is satisfied (i.e., $\sigma_s \cdot \sigma_c \cdot c \notin \varphi$) nor $\sigma_s \cdot \sigma_c \cdot c$ is a prefix of a word that satisfies φ (i.e., $\sigma_s \cdot \sigma_c \cdot c \notin \mathrm{pref}(\varphi)$) since, state reached (i.e., q_4) upon event c is a dead state of A_φ, thus, event c is suppressed. The events in rows 8–10 of Table 2 are also

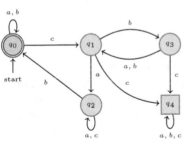

Fig. 2. Property φ of Example 1

Table 2. Incremental computation by the enforcement function of example 1

	Input(σ)	Buffer(σ_c)	Output(σ_s)
1	a	ϵ	a
2	ac	c	a
3	acb	cb	a
4	$acba$	cba	a
5	$acbab$	$cbab$	a
6	$acbabb$	$cbabb$	a
7	$acbabbc$	$cbabb$	a
8	$acbabbca$	$cbabba$	a
9	$acbabbcac$	$cbabbac$	a
10	$acbabbcaca$	$cbabbaca$	a
11	$acbabbcacab$	ϵ	$acbabbacab$

appended to the content of σ_c, as $\sigma_s \cdot \sigma_c$ followed by the new event consumed in each of those steps does not satisfy φ, but is a prefix of a word that satisfies φ. Then, φ is satisfied again (i.e., in row 11, $\sigma_s \cdot \sigma_c \cdot b \in \varphi$) meaning that the state reached (i.e., q_0) upon event b is an accepting state. Hence, the events in σ_c (i.e., $cbabbaca$) and the received event (i.e., b) are emitted by the enforcer (added to σ_s), and buffer σ_c is emptied.

4   Bounded-Memory Runtime Enforcement

In this section, we present the bounded-memory enforcement framework for some property $\varphi \subseteq \Sigma^*$ and buffer size $k \in \mathbb{N}$. Recall that, the enforcer defined in Sect. 3 is equipped with an unbounded buffer to store some events. We now lift the enforcement mechanism defined in Sect. 3 to the bounded-memory case; the buffer capacity is specified as an additional parameter to the enforcer.

4.1   Preliminaries for Bounded-Memory Enforcement

A bounded-memory enforcer is denoted by $E^{\varphi,k}$. Enforcer $E^{\varphi,k}$ for a given property φ is equipped with a buffer of size k and is able to transform an input word σ which is possibly incorrect w.r.t. φ into an output word that is correct w.r.t. φ. In addition, a bounded-memory enforcer also outputs status information indicating whether any event was discarded or not. Thus, enforcer $E^{\varphi,k} : \Sigma^* \rightarrow \Sigma^* \times \{\top, \bot\}$, outputs a tuple consisting of output word (element of Σ^*) and mode information (which is an element of $\{\top, \bot\}$) permitting to warn the user. For any input word $\sigma \in \Sigma^*$, we refer to the output word of the enforcer from the tuple using $E^{\varphi,k}_{\text{out}}(\sigma)$, and the information of the current mode of the enforcer using $E^{\varphi,k}_{\text{mode}}(\sigma)$. For any enforcer $E^{\varphi,k}$, $\text{buff}(E^{\varphi,k}(\sigma))$ is its buffer content after reading σ.

Mode of the Enforcer: The mode of the enforcer, $E^{\varphi,k}_{\text{mode}}$ can be $\{\top, \bot\}$, where $\top$ represents nominal mode (none of the elements from the buffer were suppressed; the output of the enforcer is a prefix of the input word), and $\bot$ represents degraded mode (some of the elements from the buffer were suppressed; the output of the enforcer is a subword of the input word) respectively.

Remark 1. When the buffer is full and cannot accommodate new events, it has to be cleaned (by discarding some events present in it) in order to store new events. When any event from the buffer is discarded, the mode of the enforcer changes from $\top$ to $\bot$, and the enforcer remains in $\bot$ mode from then onwards.

4.2 Bounded-Memory Runtime Enforcement: Problem Definition

We formalize the bounded-memory RE mechanism. Several constraints are required on how an enforcer transforms words. We consider that in order to correct an input sequence, the enforcer has abilities similar to the one defined in Sect. 3 such as buffering and suppressing an event when there is no possible continuation that will allow satisfying φ. Thus, constraints such as soundness and monotonicity are adapted from the unbounded setting.

In the bounded setting, since the internal buffer of the enforcer is finite, compared to the unbounded setting we need to handle the additional situation on how the enforcer can continue operating when its buffer is full. We introduce an additional optimality constraint that defines how to optimally (minimally) drop events present in the buffer to accommodate new events and to continue operating. The notion of transparency also slightly changes; it takes into account the mode of the enforcer indicating whether the buffer was full sometime and if any events were dropped or not.

Definition 3 (Bounded Enforcer). *A bounded enforcer for φ is a function,* $E^{\varphi,k} : \Sigma^* \to \Sigma^* \times \{\top, \bot\}$, *satisfying the following constraints:*

Soundness:

$$\forall \sigma \in \Sigma^* : E^{\varphi,k}_{\text{out}}(\sigma) \neq \epsilon \implies E^{\varphi,k}_{\text{out}}(\sigma) \in \varphi \qquad \text{(SndB)}$$

Monotonicity:

$$\forall \sigma, \sigma' \in \Sigma^* : \sigma \preccurlyeq \sigma' \implies E^{\varphi,k}_{\text{out}}(\sigma) \preccurlyeq E^{\varphi,k}_{\text{out}}(\sigma') \qquad \text{(MoB)}$$

Transparency:

$$\forall \sigma \in \Sigma^* : E^{\varphi,k}_{\text{mode}}(\sigma) = \bot \vee \sigma \notin \text{pref}(\varphi) \implies E^{\varphi,k}_{\text{out}}(\sigma) \triangleleft \sigma \qquad \text{(Tr1B)}$$

$$\forall \sigma \in \Sigma^* : E^{\varphi,k}_{\text{mode}}(\sigma) = \top \wedge \sigma \in \text{pref}(\varphi) \implies E^{\varphi,k}_{\text{out}}(\sigma) \preccurlyeq \sigma \qquad \text{(Tr2B)}$$

Optimal Suppression:

$$\forall \sigma \in \Sigma^*, \forall a \in \Sigma : E_{\text{mode}}^{\varphi,k}(\sigma) = \top \wedge \sigma \in \text{pref}(\varphi) \wedge \sigma \cdot a \notin \text{pref}(\varphi)$$
$$\implies \forall \sigma_{\text{con}} \in \Sigma^* : E_{\text{out}}^{\varphi,k}(\sigma \cdot a \cdot \sigma_{\text{con}}) = E_{\text{out}}^{\varphi,k}(\sigma \cdot \sigma_{\text{con}}) \tag{OptsB}$$

Optimal Mode Change:

$$E_{\text{mode}}^{\varphi,k}(\epsilon) = \top \wedge \forall \sigma \in \Sigma^*, \forall a \in \Sigma :$$
$$\{E_{\text{mode}}^{\varphi,k}(\sigma) = \top \wedge (|\sigma_{[|E_{\text{out}}^{\varphi,k}(\sigma)|+1\cdots]}| < k) \implies E_{\text{mode}}^{\varphi,k}(\sigma \cdot a) = \top\}$$
$$\wedge$$
$$\{E_{\text{mode}}^{\varphi,k}(\sigma) = \bot \vee ((|\sigma_{[|E_{\text{out}}^{\varphi,k}(\sigma)|+1\cdots]}| > k) \vee (\sigma \cdot a \notin \text{pref}(\varphi))) \implies$$
$$E_{\text{mode}}^{\varphi,k}(\sigma \cdot a) = \bot\}$$
$$\wedge$$
$$\{E_{\text{mode}}^{\varphi,k}(\sigma) = \top \wedge (|\sigma_{[|E_{\text{out}}^{\varphi,k}(\sigma)|+1\cdots]}| = k) \wedge (\sigma \cdot a \in \varphi) \implies E_{\text{mode}}^{\varphi,k}(\sigma \cdot a) = \top\}$$
$$\wedge$$
$$\{E_{\text{mode}}^{\varphi,k}(\sigma) = \top \wedge (|\sigma_{[|E_{\text{out}}^{\varphi,k}(\sigma)|+1\cdots]}| = k) \wedge (\sigma \cdot a \notin \varphi) \implies E_{\text{mode}}^{\varphi,k}(\sigma \cdot a) = \bot\}$$
$$\tag{OptmB}$$

Soundness **SndB** and *Monotonicity* **MoB** constraints are the same as in the unbounded case. *Transparency* is expressed as a conjunction of **Tr1B** and **Tr2B**. **Tr1B** expresses that for an input word σ, if the mode is degraded ($\bot$), or if there is no possible continuation of σ that can lead to the satisfaction of φ in the future (i.e., σ is not a prefix of a word that belongs to φ), the output produced is a subword of σ (i.e., obtained by suppressing some events from σ). **Tr2B** expresses that for an input word σ, if the mode is nominal ($\top$) and if there is at least one possible continuation of σ that can lead to the satisfaction of the φ in the future (i.e., σ is a prefix of a word that belongs to φ), the output produced is a prefix of σ (i.e., no event from σ can be suppressed). *Optimal suppression* **OptsB** expresses that for any word σ, if the mode is ($\top$), and σ is a prefix of a word that belongs to φ, when σ is extended with an event $a \in \Sigma$ such that $\sigma \cdot a$ does not have any extension that will satisfy φ, then event a should be suppressed. *Optimal mode change* **OptmB** is to ensure that the mode should change to $\bot$ only when necessary, and when the mode changes to $\bot$, it cannot revert back to $\top$. For any input σ if the mode is $\top$, it indicates that none of the input events from σ have been discarded (so the output is a prefix of the input and the remaining events from σ are stored in the buffer). If the mode is $\bot$, it indicates that some of the events from the input have been suppressed. It is defined inductively considering the mode reached when reading some given word σ and how the mode should change when a new event a is received, checking the conditions such as whether the input word belongs to φ (or the set of prefixes of words belonging to φ) or not, and if the number of elements in the suffix of the input word that is not released is less than (equal to/greater than) k.

4.3   Functional Definition

We define a bounded-memory enforcer as a function that incrementally builds the output. This definition provides an abstract view of the transformation of an input word performed by a bounded-memory enforcer for some property.

Definition 4 (Bounded Enforcement Function). *A bounded enforcement function is $E^{\varphi,k} : \Sigma^* \to \Sigma^* \times \{\top, \bot\}$, and is defined as:*
$E^{\varphi,k}(\sigma) = (\Pi_1(\text{store}^{\varphi,k}(\sigma)), \Pi_3(\text{store}^{\varphi,k}(\sigma)))$, *where:*

$\text{store}^{\varphi,k} : \Sigma^* \to \Sigma^* \times \Sigma^* \times \{\top, \bot\}$ *is defined as:*

- $\text{store}^{\varphi,k}(\epsilon) = (\epsilon, \epsilon, \top)$
- $\text{store}^{\varphi,k}(\sigma \cdot a) =$

$$
\begin{cases}
(\sigma_s \cdot \sigma_c \cdot a, \epsilon, mode) & \text{if } \sigma_s \cdot \sigma_c \cdot a \in \varphi, \\
(\sigma_s, \sigma_c \cdot a, mode) & \text{if } \sigma_s \cdot \sigma_c \cdot a \notin \varphi \wedge \sigma_s \cdot \sigma_c \cdot a \in \text{pref}(\varphi) \wedge |\sigma_c \cdot a| \leq k, \\
(\sigma_s, \text{clean}^{\varphi,k}(\sigma_s, \sigma_c \cdot a), \bot) & \text{if } \sigma_s \cdot \sigma_c \cdot a \notin \varphi \wedge \sigma_s \cdot \sigma_c \cdot a \in \text{pref}(\varphi) \wedge |\sigma_c \cdot a| > k, \\
(\sigma_s, \sigma_c, \bot) & \text{otherwise}
\end{cases}
$$

with:

- $(\sigma_s, \sigma_c, mode) = \text{store}^{\varphi,k}(\sigma)$
- $E_{\text{out}}^{\varphi,k}(\sigma) = \Pi_1(E^{\varphi,k}(\sigma))$, and $E_{\text{mode}}^{\varphi,k} = \Pi_3(E^{\varphi,k}(\sigma))$
- $\text{clean}^{\varphi,k} : \Sigma^* \times \Sigma^+ \to \Sigma^+$

$$
\begin{aligned}
\text{clean}^{\varphi,k}(\sigma_s, \sigma_{ca}) = \sigma_c' \in {}& \text{maxC}(\text{candidates}^{\varphi,k}(\sigma_s, \sigma_{ca})) \ \ s.t. \\
& \forall \sigma_c'' \in \text{maxC}(\text{candidates}^{\varphi,k}(\sigma_s, \sigma_{ca})), \\
& \exists i \in [1, |\sigma_{ca}|] : \sigma_{ca[i]} \neq \sigma_{c[i]}'' \\
& \implies \exists j \in [1, |\sigma_{ca}|] : \sigma_{ca[j]} \neq \sigma_{c[j]}' \wedge j < i.
\end{aligned}
$$

- $\text{maxC} : 2^{\Sigma^+} \to 2^{\Sigma^+}$

$$
\text{maxC}(W) = \{y \in W \mid \forall z \in W : |z| \leq |y|\}
$$

- $\text{candidates}^{\varphi,k} : \Sigma^* \times \Sigma^+ \to 2^{\Sigma^+}$

$$
\begin{aligned}
\text{candidates}^{\varphi,k}(\sigma_1, \sigma_2) = \{\sigma_{2[1\ldots i-1]} \cdot \sigma_{2[j+1\ldots k]} \mid {}& 1 \leq i \leq j < k \\
& \wedge \sigma_1 \cdot \sigma_2 \sim_\varphi \sigma_1 \cdot \sigma_{2[1\ldots i-1]} \cdot \sigma_{2[j+1\ldots k]}\}
\end{aligned}
$$

The bounded enforcement function $E^{\varphi,k}$ takes a word over Σ as input, and produces a word over Σ and mode (an element from the set $\{\top, \bot\}$) as output. Function $\text{store}^{\varphi,k}$ takes a word over Σ as input and computes a pair of words over Σ and mode as output. The first element of the output of function $\text{store}^{\varphi,k}$ corresponds to the output of the enforcement function; it is a prefix of (a subword of) the input that satisfies φ; and the second element is a suffix of (a subword of) the input that the enforcer cannot output yet. It corresponds to the buffer of the enforcer. The third element indicates the mode of the enforcer.

Function store$^{\varphi,k}$ is defined inductively: initially for ϵ, the output and buffer content are both ϵ and mode is initially $\top$; if σ is read, store$^{\varphi,k}(\sigma) = (\sigma_s, \sigma_c, mode)$, and another new event $a \in \Sigma$ is observed, then there are four possible cases based on whether $\sigma_s \cdot \sigma_c \cdot a$ satisfies φ or not, etc.

- If $\sigma_s \cdot \sigma_c \cdot a$ satisfies φ then the concatenation of the buffer (σ_c) and the event a is released as output (i.e., appended to σ_s), and the buffer σ_c is emptied (i.e., σ_c is set to ϵ);
- If $\sigma_s \cdot \sigma_c \cdot a$ does not satisfy φ, but is a prefix of a word that satisfies φ (i.e., $\sigma_s \cdot \sigma_c \cdot a \in \text{pref}(\varphi)$), and the buffer has capacity to accommodate the received event a (i.e., $|\sigma_c \cdot a| \leq k$) then the output remains unchanged and the new event a is appended to buffer σ_c;
- If $\sigma_s \cdot \sigma_c \cdot a$ does not satisfy φ, but is a prefix of a word that satisfies φ (i.e., $\sigma_s \cdot \sigma_c \cdot a \in \text{pref}(\varphi)$), and the buffer is full (i.e., $|\sigma_c \cdot a| > k$) then the output remains unchanged and function clean$^{\varphi,k}$ is called to clean the buffer (received event is also considered for cleaning) in order to accommodate the event. The mode changes to $\bot$;
- If $\sigma_s \cdot \sigma_c \cdot a$ does not satisfy φ nor is a prefix of a word that satisfies φ (i.e., $\sigma_s \cdot \sigma_c \cdot a \notin \text{pref}(\varphi)$), then both the output and the buffer remain unchanged (i.e., the new event a is suppressed). The mode changes to $\bot$.

Function clean$^{\varphi,k}$ takes two words over Σ as input; one that corresponds to word released as output (σ_s) and another σ_{ca} which is the current buffer content (σ_c) followed by the received event (a). It produces a word σ_c' as output which should be a subword of $\sigma_c \cdot a$ (obtained by minimally removing events from σ_{ca} such that equivalence of $\sigma_s \cdot \sigma_c'$ is preserved w.r.t $\sigma_s \cdot \sigma_{ca}$). The output word σ_c' should be of maximal length among all the subwords of $\sigma_c \cdot a$ that preserve equivalence and the events discarded from $\sigma_c \cdot a$ are the most obsolete (earliest received events are considered for deletion in this approach; this is an implementation choice but one could choose another strategy) ones.

For this purpose, first function candidates$^{\varphi,k}$ provides the (non-empty) set of all possible candidate subwords of $\sigma_c \cdot a$ preserving equivalence, then function maxC selects all the longest subwords (so that least number of events are discarded from $\sigma_c \cdot a$ and the output is as close as possible to the input). Then, one subword is selected uniquely (the subword discarding the most *obsolete* event from $\sigma_c \cdot a$). This is done by comparing the indexes of $\sigma_c \cdot a$ with the indexes of received subwords from function maxC. The contents of the buffer is then substituted by the output of function clean$^{\varphi,k}$.

Example 2. To illustrate the enforcement function in Definition 4, let us consider the same property φ and the input sequence *acbabbcacab* considered in Example 1. Suppose the max size of the buffer is 7.

The behaviour of the enforcement function in Definition 4 is the same as the enforcement function in Definition 2 in rows 1–9 of Table 3 as the buffer is not full. But, in the 10th row, when event a is received, φ is not satisfied (i.e., $\sigma_s \cdot \sigma_c \cdot a \not\models \varphi$), but $\sigma_s \cdot \sigma_c \cdot a$ is a prefix of a word that satisfies φ (i.e., $\sigma_s \cdot \sigma_c \cdot a \in \mathrm{pref}(\varphi)$); however, the buffer is already full (i.e., $|\sigma_c \cdot a| > k$). So, function $\mathrm{clean}^{\varphi,k}$ is invoked to accommodate the received event. The possible candidate subwords provided by function $\mathrm{candidates}^{\varphi,k}$ and the set of longest subwords picked by function maxC are:

Table 3. Incremental computation by the bounded enforcement function (for φ in Fig. 2).

	Input(σ)	Buffer(σ_c)	Output(σ_s)
1	a	ϵ	a
2	ac	c	a
3	acb	cb	a
4	$acba$	cba	a
5	$acbab$	$cbab$	a
6	$acbabb$	$cbabb$	a
7	$acbabbc$	$cbabb$	a
8	$acbabbca$	$cbabba$	a
9	$acbabbcac$	$cbabbac$	a
10	$acbabbcaca$	$cbabba\!\!\not{c}a$	a
11	$acbabbcacab$	ϵ	$acbabbaab$

$$\mathrm{candidates}^{\varphi,7}\,(a, cbabbac \cdot a) = \{cbbaca, cbaaca, cbabbac, cbabbaa, caca, cbabba\}$$
$$\mathrm{maxC}\{cbbaca, cbaaca, cbabbac, cbabbaa, caca, cbabba\} = \{cbabbac, cbabbaa\}$$

Function $\mathrm{clean}^{\varphi,k}$ chooses $cbabbaa$ which is formed after removing event c from $\sigma_c \cdot a$, since event c is the event engaged in minimal cycle (the longest subword of $\sigma_c \cdot a$) and is the most obsolete (cycle) event of $\sigma_c \cdot a$. Thus, the content of σ_c is replaced by $cbabbaa$ in the 10th row.

Remark 2. If $n \in \mathbb{N}$ is the number of states in A_φ, and the buffer size $k \geq n$, then it is ensured that the set computed by the function $\mathrm{candidates}^{\varphi,k}$ in Definition 4 will be non-empty. This is because the length of a path without cycles between 2 states cannot be greater than the number of states.

Proposition 2 (SndB, MoB, Tr1B, Tr2B, OptsB and OptmB). *Let* $n \in \mathbb{N}$ *be the number of states in* A_φ. *If* $k \geq n$, $E^{\varphi,k}$ *as per Definition 4 is a bounded enforcer for* φ *as per Definition 3.*

The following proposition states that when k is considered to be ∞, for any word σ, the output produced by the bounded enforcer for σ is equal to the output produced by the ideal enforcer (as per Definition 2).

Proposition 3 (Case of an infinite/unbounded buffer).
$\forall \sigma \in \Sigma^* : E^{\varphi,\infty}(\sigma) = E^\varphi(\sigma).$

Definition 5 (∞-compatible). *Enforcer* $E^{\varphi,k}$ *is compatible with* $E^{\varphi,\infty}$, *noted* ∞-*compatible*($E^{\varphi,k}$), *if* $\forall \sigma \in \Sigma^* : E^{\varphi,\infty}(\sigma) \cdot \mathrm{buff}(E^{\varphi,\infty}(\sigma)) \sim_\varphi E^{\varphi,k}_{\mathrm{out}}(\sigma) \cdot \mathrm{buff}(E^{\varphi,k}(\sigma)).$

A bounded enforcer $E^{\varphi,k}$ is compatible with an ideal unbounded enforcer $E^{\varphi,\infty}$ for φ, if for any input word σ, the concatenation of the output and the buffer content of the unbounded enforcer $E^{\varphi,\infty}$ is φ-equivalent to the concatenation of the output and the buffer content of the bounded enforcer $E^{\varphi,k}$.

Proposition 4 (Optimality of enforcement functions). *Consider any bounded enforcer* $F^{\varphi,k}$ *(Definition 3). We have:* $\forall \sigma \in \Sigma^*, \forall a \in \Sigma$:

$$(E_{\text{out}}^{\varphi,k}(\sigma) \cdot \text{buff}(E^{\varphi,k}(\sigma)) = F_{\text{out}}^{\varphi,k}(\sigma) \cdot \text{buff}(F^{\varphi,k}(\sigma)))\wedge$$
$$(|E_{\text{out}}^{\varphi,k}(\sigma \cdot a) \cdot \text{buff}(E^{\varphi,k}(\sigma \cdot a))| < |F_{\text{out}}^{\varphi,k}(\sigma \cdot a) \cdot \text{buff}(F^{\varphi,k}(\sigma \cdot a))|)$$
$$\implies \neg(\infty\text{-}compatible(F^{\varphi,k}))$$

Proposition 4 expresses that an enforcer $E^{\varphi,k}$ as per Definition 4 is optimal; if for any other enforcer $F^{\varphi,k}$, the length of the concatenation of its output and the buffer content is greater than the length of the concatenation of output and the buffer content of $E^{\varphi,k}$ for some input, then the output produced by $F^{\varphi,k}$ is not ∞-compatible. Proposition 4 means that there does not exist an enforcer that can clean the buffer in a better way (by discarding less events and being ∞-compatible with the ideal enforcer).

4.4   Enforcement Algorithm

In Sect. 4.3, we provided an abstract view of our bounded-memory enforcement monitoring mechanism, defining it as a function that transforms words. In this section, we provide the overall enforcement algorithm.

Let automaton $A_\varphi = (Q_\varphi, q_0, \Sigma, \delta_\varphi, F_\varphi)$ define φ. We recall that φ models the property that we want to enforce. We devise an online algorithm, which takes A_φ, and the buffer size $k \in \mathbb{N}$ as input parameters.

Enforcement algorithm: In the Algorithm 1, sequence σ_c is the same as in Definition 4. State q holds the state of A_φ reached by taking events that have been emitted by the enforcer, which correspond to events in σ_s in Definition 4. Function $\texttt{await\_event}$ is used to wait for a new input event. Function $\texttt{release}$ takes a sequence of events and releases it as output of the enforcer. Function $\texttt{suppress}$ removes an event. Function $\texttt{clean}$ deletes events from the buffer in case the buffer is full for an incoming event.

1 Algorithm Enforcer(A_φ, k)

```
1: σc ← ε
2: q ← q0
3: while true do
4:     a ← await_event()
5:     if δφ(q, σc · a) ∈ Fφ then
6:         q ← δφ(q, σc · a)
7:         release(σc · a)
8:         σc ← ε
9:     else
10:         if L(Aφ, δφ(q, σc · a))=∅
11:         then
12:             suppress(a)
13:         else
14:             if |σc · a| ≤ k then
15:                 σc ← σc · a
16:             else
17:                 σc ← clean(σc · a, Aφ, k, q)
```

Function clean$(\sigma_{ca}, A_\varphi, k, q)$

```
1: function CLEAN(σca, Aφ, k, q)
2:     for i in 1... k+1   do
3:         j=1
4:         while (i + j ≤ k + 2) do
5:             if j = 1 then
6:                 if δφ(q, σca[j...j+i−1]) = q then
7:                     return σca[j+i...k+1]
8:             else
9:                 if δφ(q, σca[1...j−1] · σca[j...j+i−1]) =
10:                    δφ(q, σca[1...j−1]) then
11:                     return σca[1...j−1] · σca[j+i...k+1]
12:             j++
```

The algorithm proceeds as follows. Buffer σ_c is initialized to ϵ, and q is initialized with the initial state of A_φ (i.e., q_0). It then enters into an infinite loop waiting for an input event. Upon receiving an event a, if the state reached from q upon $\sigma_c \cdot a$ is an accepting state (i.e., state in F_φ), then state q is updated $(q \leftarrow \delta_\varphi(q, \sigma_c \cdot a))$, all the events of $\sigma_c \cdot a$ are released as output, and σ_c is emptied (set to ϵ). However, if $\delta_\varphi(q, \sigma_c \cdot a)$ is a dead state $(L(A_\varphi, \delta_\varphi(q, \sigma_c \cdot a)) = \emptyset)$, then the received event is suppressed and the enforcer continues with the next event, otherwise it is buffered into σ_c (i.e., $\sigma_c \leftarrow \sigma_c \cdot a$), provided the buffer is not full. If the buffer is full, then function clean is invoked with $\sigma_c \cdot a$.

Function clean enters a loop where in every iteration i ($1 \leq i \leq k + 1$), it checks if A_φ makes a cycle upon substrings of length i at every index j ($j = 1, ..$) of σ_{ca} (representing $\sigma_c \cdot a$). If a substring of length i from index j of σ_{ca} can be read on a cycle, then the subword formed by removing that substring from σ_{ca} is returned by function clean . For instance, in 10th row of Table 3, in Example 2, since the state reached (i.e., s_2) upon event a is not in F_φ, $L(A_\varphi, \delta_\varphi(s_1, cbabbaca)) \neq \emptyset$, and the buffer is full, thus, function clean is invoked with $cbabbaca$. In iteration $i = 1$, for every index j ($j = 1, ..$) of σ_{ca}, the substrings of length 1 are computed, which are: {[c], [b], [a], [b], [b], [a], [c], [a]}. Function clean checks if A_φ makes a cycle upon these substrings. Since by taking event c at index $j = 7$ of σ_{ca}, A_φ makes a cycle, thus the substring c is removed from σ_{ca} and $cbabbaa$ (subword of $\sigma_c \cdot a$) is returned to the enforcer by function clean. Following it, the enforcer continues with the next event.

Remark 3. Note that function clean in Algorithm 1 produces the same output as function clean$^{\varphi,k}$ in Definition 4. Instead of providing σ_s (which corresponds to the output of the enforcement function in Definition 4) as input, we here provide the state q reached in A_φ upon the sequence released as output. Also the time complexity of function clean$^{\varphi,k}$ in Definition 4 is $\mathcal{O}(k^2)$, however, in the implementation, for efficiency reasons, function clean in Algorithm 1 directly computes the maximal subword of σ_{ca} by discarding the most obsolete elements that correspond to a (minimal) cycle in A_φ, which is chosen by function clean$^{\varphi,k}$ in Definition 4 from all the maximal candidate subwords.

5   Implementation and Evaluation

We implemented algorithms of Sect. 4.4 and work out some examples mainly *i)* to measure the performance[2] of the bounded-memory enforcer; how its performance varies compared to the ideal enforcer (mainly the additional overhead that will be induced by clean), by varying the complexity of the properties, input and buffer size and *ii)* to see the practicability and usefulness of the bounded-memory enforcer using example application scenarios. The bounded-memory enforcer and the ideal enforcer are implemented in 140 and 88 LoC respectively

---

[2] Experiments were conducted on an Intel Core i7-9700K CPU at 3.60GHz × 8, with 32 GB RAM, and running on Ubuntu 18.04.5 LTS.

in Python. The implementation along with a brief description about the application scenarios, properties and the performance analysis using them is provided at https://github.com/saumyashankarsinha/BMRE.git.

5.1   Performance Analysis

We take an example property P_1 which expresses, *"The word should start with one or more elements from set $C=\{a, b, c\}$ and should end with one or more elements from set $D=\{1, 2\}$"*. P_1 is defined by the automaton A_{P_1} in Fig. 3, where state q_0 is the initial state and q_2 is the accepting state. This example has been chosen because it allows the automaton's size to be readily scaled up while maintaining its structure.

For measuring the performance, the size of buffer $(k = 4)$ and number of states in A_{P_1} (=4) were fixed and the length of input sequence was varied from 10 to 10,000 with an increment of 1000 each time. The input sequences were chosen in such a way that the P_1 is satisfied by the latter events, so that the events are buffered and function `clean` is invoked everytime. It permits to calculate the worst time taken by the bounded-memory enforcer. The time taken by both the ideal enforcer (E^{P_1}) and the bounded-memory enforcer $(E^{P_1,4})$ was measured (all in seconds) and was averaged over 100 iterations. Table 4 summarises the result where, `Input` indicates the length of the input word, `Time(s)` indicates the time taken by E^{P_1} to output the word, `No.` and `T1(s)` under `clean` indicate number of times function `clean` is called and the total time taken by it respectively (i.e., time taken to check if the buffer if full or not, time taken by function `clean` to delete events from the buffer and time taken to update the buffer with the word returned by function `clean`), and `T2(s)` indicates the time taken by $E^{P_1,4}$.
Considering $k = 4$, for A_{P_1}, we have the following observations from Table 4:

- The time taken by both unbounded and bounded enforcers increases linearly with the trace length (by considering traces such that the number of times function `clean` is invoked increases linearly).
- When comparing the time taken by the bounded and unbounded enforcer, if we subtract the additional time (T1) taken by the bounded enforcer to clean the buffer from the total time (T2) taken by it, then the resultant time (T2-T1) is similar to the time taken by the unbounded enforcer. Thus, when cleaning the buffer is not necessary (e.g., for some input traces/when the buffer size is large), the performance of the bounded enforcer is similar to the unbounded enforcer.
- The average time taken for cleaning (per call) is 0.0048 ms is low/reasonable.

Varying the Complexity of the Property. We also considered properties with similar structures as P_1 but with an increasing number of states, and evaluated them with input sequences of varying sizes. It was observed that the time taken by both the enforcers increases linearly with the number of states (as the number of transitions increase).

Table 4. Effect on time taken by enforcers by varying the length of input sequences.

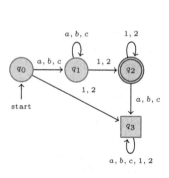

a, b, c

Fig. 3. A_{P_1}

Input	E^{P_1}	$E^{P_1,4}$			
	Time(s)	clean			
		No.	T1(s)	T2(s)	T2-T1(s)
10	0.00001	4	0.00002	0.00003	0.00001
1000	0.00094	994	0.00492	0.00586	0.00094
2000	0.00185	1994	0.00952	0.01136	0.00184
3000	0.00276	2994	0.01426	0.01701	0.00275
4000	0.00364	3994	0.01877	0.02239	0.00362
5000	0.00457	4994	0.02350	0.02806	0.00456
6000	0.00548	5994	0.02814	0.03360	0.00546
7000	0.00642	6994	0.03314	0.03956	0.00642
8000	0.00736	7994	0.03784	0.04518	0.00734
9000	0.00827	8994	0.04247	0.05068	0.00821
10000	0.00922	9994	0.04754	0.05679	0.00924

Varying the buffer size. On increasing the buffer size, the average time taken by function clean increases linearly, however the time taken by $E^{\varphi,k}$ decreases linearly, since the number of times function clean is called decreases.

These are further discussed at varying_complexity_of_property_and_buffer_sizes.

Remark 4. We choose to clean the buffer when it is full. Indeed we consider that the computing time of the cleaning function is lower than the time between two received events. One may clean the buffer when it is partially full. This can be done with a simple modification in the framework by considering another additional parameter as input indicating when function clean should be triggered (when the buffer is 80% full, 90% full etc.).

Remark 5 (Enforcing multiple properties). Our framework is able to consider multiple properties. It consists of computing their intersection and then synthesize the corresponding enforcer.

6   Potential Application Scenarios

We discuss the usefulness and applicability of the bounded-memory enforcer in real-world context. We formulate some example properties in different scenarios to express the desired behaviour in domains like autonomous vehicle, operating system, databases, etc. The formulated properties are such that it deals with the suppression of the *idempotent* events when required, making them suitable to be enforced by a bounded-memory runtime enforcer. We also analyse the performance of the bounded-memory enforcer against these real-world properties.

Scenario 1. Autonomous Vehicle (AV): An AV or a self-driving car is a vehicle that is capable of sensing its environment and moving safely with little or no human intervention. They rely on sensors, actuators, complex algorithms, machine learning systems, and powerful processors to execute software. Let us consider two example properties in AVs to express some desired behaviour.

(a) Logging in AV: *"When the path planning steering commands, like {Move Left, Move Right, Move Forward, Stop} are logged for better testing and validation solutions, each time it is issued, to a remote location (due to memory constraints in AV), then logging of these commands should be done, when the vehicle reaches a Stop state, on the remote logging application."*

(b) Switching to manual driving mode in autonomous vehicle: *"Upon pressing of the manual mode button, the switching of manual driving mode from autonomous driving mode will be done if the following three conditions are satisfied: checking whether a driver's hand is holding a steering wheel; checking whether the driver's foot is placed on a brake pedal; checking whether the driver's gaze is facing forward."* It is here assumed that once an event is received, meaning that the condition respective to that event is satisfied, it remains satisfied.

Scenario 2. Concurrency: In the context of concurrent systems, each hardware/software component is designed to obey or to meet certain consistency rules. Concurrent use of shared resources can be a source of indeterminacy leading to issues such as deadlocks, and resource starvation. Let us consider two example properties related to concurrency.

(a) Lock: *"For database items {A, B}, any transaction accessing both A and B must access A before accessing B."*

(b) Critical Section Problem: *"If a process wishes to enter the critical section, it must first execute the try section and wait until it acquires access to the critical section. After the process has executed its critical section and is finished with the shared resources, it can release them for other processes' use."*

Remark 6. We modeled all the policies for each of the scenarios as DFA, obtained the respective bounded-memory enforcers and have measured their performance. More details, including description about the scenarios, policies and their formulation as DFA, and the performance analysis using them is provided along with the implementation in our repository at: Potential_Application_Scenarios.

7   Related Work

RE has been pioneered by Schneider et al. in [21]. In this framework the enforcement mechanism enforces properties described as Büchi automata and synthesizes a *security automaton (SA)* which is executed in parallel with the system under scrutiny and terminates whenever the property is going to be violated. Later, Bloem et al. propose in [3] an approach to synthesize an enforcement mechanism (named *shield*) using a 2-player game approach. A shield is *k-stabilizing* i.e., whenever a property violation is unavoidable, it allows deviating from the property for k consecutive steps. A similar approach is proposed by Wu et al. in [23] adding the ability to handle burst errors and Bielova et al. in [2] who specified how bad traces are fixed so that the system exhibits a reasonable behaviour. All these approaches deal only with safety properties and cannot memorize actions.

In [12], Ligatti et al. extend the work of Schneider et al. by noticing that SA (only) act as a sequence recognizer, thus they propose the model of *edit-automata (EA)*: this models allows inserting or suppressing events during the RE and to use a memory in order to store the suffix of an invalid execution until it becomes valid. EA permits enforcing a larger set of properties, namely the *renewal* properties. Later, Falcone et al. generalise in [9] EA with the *generalised enforcement monitors*. Their model enforces *response* properties (from the *Safety-Progress* classification [5]), which are similar to *infinite renewal* properties, but separates explicitly the specification of the property to enforce from the enforcer. Many extensions of these approaches exist, e.g. in a timed context [7,13,14,16] or considering uncontrollable events [17–19].

The above models do not consider memory constraints. Few attempts with memory limitations of the enforcer have been proposed. Fong proposes in [10] the model of *Shallow History Automata (SHA)* as SA that do not keep track of the order of event occurring, and generalizes it as α-SA, a variant of SA endowed with a morphism abstracting the current input sequence. Then he defines a complete lattice of security policy classes. Talhi et al. [22] extend SA and EA to define their bounded-history versions, that is the versions of the mechanism that can remember up to a certain number of events in the trace. Beauquier et al. [1] consider finite set of states as a memory limitation on EAs and show that finite EAs are strictly less expressive than EAs and characterize the conditions of the enforceability of a property. These approaches, considering a limited memory, mainly focus on characterizing the set of enforceable properties. To the best of our knowledge, our framework is the first to define how to synthesize an enforecr that provides a solution when the memory of the enforcer is full at runtime.

8   Conclusion and Future Work

This paper presents a complete RE framework for regular properties with a bounded memory. In this approach, the enforecr has the ability to delay (buffer) or suppress events, and the maximal size of the memory is known. We introduce the notion of nominal and degraded modes, the last one corresponding to the situation where the maximal size of the memory has been reached. We redefine the notion of transparency and propose a way to reduce optimally the content of the memory in order to maintain a behaviour satisfying the property. We provide a functional definition of the enforcer and an algorithmic version. We have implemented the framework in a prototype and evaluated its performance using multiple example properties.

Future works include enriching the framework in order to consider the possibility to recover a nominal behaviour when the degraded one has been reached, and to extend the proposed approach in a timed context.

References

1. Beauquier, D., Cohen, J., Lanotte, R.: Security policies enforcement using finite and pushdown edit automata. Int. J. Inf. Sec. **12**(4), 319–336 (2013). https://doi.org/10.1007/s10207-013-0195-8, http://dx.doi.org/10.1007/s10207-013-0195-8
2. Bielova, N., Massacci, F.: Predictability of enforcement. In: Erlingsson, Ú., Wieringa, R., Zannone, N. (eds.) ESSoS 2011. LNCS, vol. 6542, pp. 73–86. Springer, Heidelberg (2011). https://doi.org/10.1007/978-3-642-19125-1_6
3. Bloem, R., Könighofer, B., Könighofer, R., Wang, C.: Shield synthesis. In: Baier, C., Tinelli, C. (eds.) TACAS 2015. LNCS, vol. 9035, pp. 533–548. Springer, Heidelberg (2015). https://doi.org/10.1007/978-3-662-46681-0_51
4. Dolzhenko, E., Ligatti, J., Reddy, S.: Modeling runtime enforcement with mandatory results automata. Int. J. Inf. Secur. **14**(1), 47–60 (2015). https://doi.org/10.1007/s10207-014-0239-8
5. Falcone, Y., Fernandez, J.-C., Mounier, L.: Runtime verification of safety-progress properties. In: Bensalem, S., Peled, D.A. (eds.) RV 2009. LNCS, vol. 5779, pp. 40–59. Springer, Heidelberg (2009). https://doi.org/10.1007/978-3-642-04694-0_4
6. Falcone, Y., Fernandez, J., Mounier, L.: What can you verify and enforce at runtime? Int. J. Softw. Tools Technol. Transf. **14**(3), 349–382 (2012). https://doi.org/10.1007/s10009-011-0196-8
7. Falcone, Y., Jéron, T., Marchand, H., Pinisetty, S.: Runtime enforcement of regular timed properties by suppressing and delaying events. Syst. Control Lett. **123**, 2–41 (2016). https://doi.org/10.1016/j.scico.2016.02.008
8. Falcone, Y., Mariani, L., Rollet, A., Saha, S.: Runtime failure prevention and reaction. In: Bartocci, E., Falcone, Y. (eds.) Lectures on Runtime Verification. LNCS, vol. 10457, pp. 103–134. Springer, Cham (2018). https://doi.org/10.1007/978-3-319-75632-5_4
9. Falcone, Y., Mounier, L., Fernandez, J., Richier, J.: Runtime enforcement monitors: composition, synthesis, and enforcement abilities. Formal Methods Syst. Des. **38**(3), 223–262 (2011). https://doi.org/10.1007/s10703-011-0114-4
10. Fong, P.W.L.: Access control by tracking shallow execution history. In: IEEE Symposium on Security and Privacy, 2004. Proceedings. 2004, pp. 43–55 (2004). https://doi.org/10.1109/SECPRI.2004.1301314
11. Ligatti, J., Bauer, L., Walker, D.: Edit automata: enforcement mechanisms for run-time security policies. Int. J. Inf. Sec. **4**(1-2), 2–16 (2005). https://doi.org/10.1007/s10207-004-0046-8
12. Ligatti, J., Bauer, L., Walker, D.: Run-time enforcement of nonsafety policies. ACM Trans. Inf. Syst. Secur. **12**(3) (2009). https://doi.org/10.1145/1455526.1455532, https://doi.org/10.1007/s10207-004-0046-8

13. Pinisetty, S., Falcone, Y., Jéron, T., Marchand, H., Rollet, A., Nguena Timo, O.: Runtime enforcement of timed properties revisited. Formal Methods Syst. Des. **45**(3), 381–422 (2014). https://doi.org/10.1007/s10703-014-0215-y
14. Pinisetty, S., Falcone, Y., Jéron, T., Marchand, H., Rollet, A., Nguena Timo, O.L.: Runtime enforcement of timed properties. In: Qadeer, S., Tasiran, S. (eds.) RV 2012. LNCS, vol. 7687, pp. 229–244. Springer, Heidelberg (2013). https://doi.org/10.1007/978-3-642-35632-2_23
15. Pinisetty, S., Preoteasa, V., Tripakis, S., Jéron, T., Falcone, Y., Marchand, H.: Predictive runtime enforcement. Formal Methods Syst. Des. **51**(1), 154–199 (2017). https://doi.org/10.1007/s10703-017-0271-1
16. Pinisetty, S., Roop, P.S., Smyth, S., Tripakis, S., Hanxleden, R.V.: Runtime enforcement of reactive systems using synchronous enforcers. In: Proceedings of the 24th ACM SIGSOFT International SPIN Symposium on Model Checking of Software, pp. 80–89 (2017)
17. Renard, M., Falcone, Y., Rollet, A., Jéron, T., Marchand, H.: Optimal enforcement of (timed) properties with uncontrollable events. Math. Struct. Comput. Sci. 1–46 (2017). https://doi.org/10.1017/S0960129517000123
18. Renard, M., Falcone, Y., Rollet, A., Pinisetty, S., Jéron, T., Marchand, H.: Enforcement of (timed) properties with uncontrollable events. In: Theoretical Aspects of Computing - ICTAC 2015–12th International Colloquium Cali, Colombia, October 29–31, 2015, Proceedings, pp. 542–560 (2015). https://doi.org/10.1007/978-3-319-25150-9_31
19. Renard, M., Rollet, A., Falcone, Y.: Runtime enforcement of timed properties using games. Formal Aspects Comput. **32**(2), 315–360 (2020)
20. Roc SU, G.: On safety properties and their monitoring. Sci. Ann. Comput. Sci. **22**(2), 327–365 (2012). https://doi.org/10.7561/SACS.2012.2.327
21. Schneider, F.B.: Enforceable security policies. ACM Trans. Inf. Syst. Secur. **3**(1), 30–50 (2000). https://doi.org/10.1145/353323.353382
22. Talhi, C., Tawbi, N., Debbabi, M.: Execution monitoring enforcement under memory-limitation constraints. Inf. Comput. **206**(2), 158–184 (2008). https://doi.org/10.1016/j.ic.2007.07.009, https://www.sciencedirect.com/science/article/pii/S0890540107001320, joint Workshop on Foundations of Computer Security and Automated Reasoning for Security Protocol Analysis (FCS-ARSPA 2006)
23. Wu, M., Zeng, H., Wang, C.: Synthesizing runtime enforcer of safety properties under burst error. In: NASA Formal Methods - 8th International Symposium, NFM 2016, Minneapolis, MN, USA, 7–9 June 2016, Proceedings, pp. 65–81 (2016). https://doi.org/10.1007/978-3-319-40648-0_6

Solving String Theories Involving Regular Membership Predicates Using SAT

Mitja Kulczynski[1] , Kevin Lotz[1][(✉)] , Dirk Nowotka[1],
and Danny Bøgsted Poulsen[2]

[1] Department of Computer Science, Kiel University, Kiel, Germany
{mku,kel,dn}@informatik.uni-kiel.de
[2] Department of Computer Science, Aalborg University, Aalborg, Denmark
dannybpoulsen@cs.aau.dk

Abstract. String solvers gained a more prominent role in the formal analysis of string-heavy programs, causing an ever-growing need for efficient and reliable solving algorithms. Regular constraints play a central role in several real-world queries. To emerge this field, we present two approaches to encode regular constraints as a Boolean satisfiability problem, one making use of the inductive structure of regular expressions and one working on nondeterministic finite automata. We implement both approaches using WOORPJE, a recently developed purely SAT-based string solver, as a framework. An evaluation of our approaches shows that they are competitive to state-of-the-art string solvers and even outperform them in many cases.

1 Introduction

Guaranteeing that software behaves correctly has garnered widespread attention since the late 80s/early 90s. It was pioneered by tools like SPIN [18] that model a computer system as a finite state machine and verify properties of that model. Obviously, this relies on the model capturing the behavior of the real code.

Gradually, works started appearing where formal methods were applied directly to source code. In particular, the techniques *Counter Example Guided Abstraction Refinement*—used by tools as BLAST [8], SLAM [3] and CPA-CHECKER [9]—*Bounded Model Checking*—used by CBMC [20]—and *Symbolic Execution*—used by KLEE [13]—have been successful in analyzing C-code. Although these techniques are conceptually different, they are all based on encoding properties of the program into logical formulae that are later on dispatched to a SAT/SMT-solver. The kind of programs that can be analyzed by these tools, thus, inherently depends on the theories supported by SMT-solvers. Since SMT-solvers, to a large extent, evolved side-by-side with the software verification tools, they primarily support theories for reasoning on natural numbers, bit vectors, and arrays.

A fairly new addition required by software verifiers is that of theories involving relations over string variables. The need for this is two-fold. Firstly, strings appear in most higher-level languages, so applying verification to programs in these languages demands to reason on strings. Secondly, the root cause of many vulnerabilities in web applications is often related to improper string usage. An example could be using the regular expression /[A-Za-z0-9 .-@:/]/ to validate a string only contains alphanumeric characters and the special symbols ., -, @, :, /. The intention is to avoid Javascript injections in a web application. However, this regular expression is flawed due to the semantics of the unescaped - symbol. It instead expresses that characters between . and @ in the ASCII alphabet are allowed—this includes < and >, possibly enabling an attacker to inject code into an HTML-output.

The theory of strings in SMT-LIB 2.6 [28] includes many constraints needed to support the analysis of string operations in programs. In particular, it includes regular language membership constraints. The theory defined in the SMT-LIB standard is unfortunately undecidable [16], so many string solvers implement smaller, decidable fragments. Targeting even the simplest sub-theory—word equations—is troublesome: solving word equations is NP-hard [25]. The complexity of solving theories with regular membership constraints is even worse. Even when restricted to simple regular languages, i.e., without complements, the problem is known to be PSPACE-complete (see, e.g., [5]).

The above complexity results are discouraging. However, previous work [15] has shown that a SAT-based encoding of word-equations is competitive with state of the art solvers like CVC4 [4], Z3SEQ [27] and Z3STR3 [6]. Encouraged by this result, we theorize that SAT-solvers are generally good at coping with the complexities of string solving and that a proper encoding of regular membership constraints into SAT will also prove competitive. Therefore we experiment with two different encodings of regular membership constraints using WOORPJE [15] as the underlying framework. In particular we present: 1. two approaches for encoding bounded regular constraints in propositional logic such that a satisfying assignment for the formula directly gives a solution for the constraint, 2. methods for pruning the search space which we use to speed up the encoding process and to reduce the size of the resulting formula, and 3. an evaluation, where we compare both approaches with each other as well as with state-of-the-art SMT string solvers.

1.1 Related Work

To the best of our knowledge, other than WOORPJE, no attempts have been made to solve string constraints as the Boolean satisfiability problem. However, the field of string constraint solving, especially solving regular constraints, is widely discussed in the literature. The majority of modern string constraint solvers are based on the SMT paradigm. Arguably, Z3 and CVC4 are the most prominent general purpose SMT solvers. These solvers are designed to support a rich theory of string constraints. However, there is also research specifically focussed on the topic of solving regular constraints. Berzish et al. investigated a wide variety of real-world string constraint problems containing regular membership predicates towards their decidability [5]. They conclude that most of these problems belong to decidable fractions of first-order logic theories but are PSPACE-complete. The

$$
\begin{array}{lll}
F & ::= Atom \;\|\; F \wedge F \\
Atom & ::= t_{str} \in R \\
R & ::= w \;\|\; R \cdot R \;\|\; R \mid R \;\|\; R^* \;\|\; \emptyset, \text{ with } w \in \Sigma^* \\
t_{str} & ::= \alpha, \text{ with } \alpha \in \Xi^*
\end{array}
$$

Fig. 1. Syntax of the input language.

latter also applies to the theory our approach copes with. However, the theoretical landscape is not yet fully mapped. There are still theories involving regular constraints whose decidability remains unknown. As a secondary result of their research, they implemented a novel solver aimed at solving the most frequently occurring problems involving regular constraints, Z3STR3RE [7]. It is based on Z3STR3 but solves regular expressions by conversion to an automaton. Another approach for solving regular constraints was given by Stanford et al. They tackled the problem of solving Boolean combinations of regular constraints over arbitrary character theories, which may or may not be finite alphabets. To this end, they introduce a generalization of derivatives for regular expressions, named *symbolic Boolean derivates*, that may additionally contain Boolean predicates. The implementation thereof is built upon Z3 and referred to as Z3SEQ [27].

2   Preliminaries

For a finite set Δ of symbols, we let Δ^* be the set of all words over Δ and ε be the empty word. For an alphabet Δ and $a \notin \Delta$, we let Δ_a denote the set $\Delta \cup \{\,a\,\}$. A word $v \in \Delta^*$ is a *factor* of a word $w \in \Delta^*$ if $w = xvy$ for some $x, y \in \Delta^*$. If $x = \varepsilon$ ($y = \varepsilon$), we call v a *prefix* (*suffix*) of w. For a word $w = a_1 a_2 \ldots a_n$ with $a_i \in \Delta$ for all $1 \leq i \leq n$ we refer with $|w| = n$ to its length and with $|w|_a$ for an $a \in \Delta$ to the count of a's occurring in w. Moreover, for $1 \leq i \leq j \leq n$, $w[i]$ denotes i^{th} symbol in w and $w[i : j]$ denotes the factor $w_i \ldots w_j$. We define $w[i : j] = \varepsilon$ if $i > j$ and $w[k] = \varepsilon$ for all $k > |w|$. A *non-deterministic finite automaton* (NFA) is a structure $A = (Q, \Delta, \delta, q_0, F)$ where Q is the set of states, Δ an alphabet, $\delta : Q \times \Delta \to 2^Q$ a transition function, $q_0 \in Q$ the initial state, and $F \subseteq Q$ a set of accepting states. We say A *accepts* a word $w \in \Delta^*$ if there is a path via δ leading from q_0 to some $f \in F$ (shortly $w \in \mathcal{L}(A)$). In the remainder of the paper, we let $\Xi = \Sigma \cup \Gamma$ where Σ (Γ) is a set of symbols called letters (variables) and $\Sigma \cap \Gamma = \emptyset$. We call a word $\alpha \in \Xi^*$ a *pattern* over Ξ. For a pattern $\alpha \in \Xi^*$ we let $\text{var}(\alpha) \subseteq \Gamma$ denote the set of variables from Γ occurring in α. A *substitution* for Ξ is a morphism $h : \Xi^* \to \Sigma^*$ with $h(a) = a$ for every $a \in \Sigma$ and $h(\varepsilon) = \varepsilon$. Note that to define a substitution h, it suffices to define $h(x)$ for all $x \in \Gamma$.

Our procedure accepts quantifier-free many-sorted first-order logic formulae of the syntax given in Fig. 1. The only atoms we are concerned with are *regular constraints*. We state Boolean combinations of atoms asking whether a pattern $\alpha \in \Xi^*$ is a member of a regular language given as a regular expression. Expressions are stated recursively over concatenation, union, Kleene star, and string constants $w \in \Sigma^*$. Note that all regular expression terms must be grounded, i.e., they must not contain variables. We denote the set of all regular expressions by Reg_Σ. The semantics of regular constraints are defined in terms of a substitution h as follows. Let $\alpha \in \Xi^*$, $R_1, R_2 \in \mathsf{Reg}_\Sigma$, and $w \in \Sigma^*$. We have $h \models \alpha \mathbin{\dot\in} w$ iff $h(\alpha) = w$, $h \models \alpha \mathbin{\dot\in} R_1 \mid R_2$ iff $h(\alpha) \in \mathcal{L}(R_1)$ or $h(\alpha) \in \mathcal{L}(R_2)$, $h \models \alpha \mathbin{\dot\in} R_1 \cdot R_2$ iff there exists an $0 \leq i \leq |h(\alpha)|$ such that $h(\alpha)[1:i] \in \mathcal{L}(R_1)$ and $h(\alpha)[i+1:|h(\alpha)|] \in \mathcal{L}(R_2)$, and $h \models R_1^*$ iff $h(\alpha) = \varepsilon$ or there exists $n \in \mathbb{N}$ such that $h(\alpha) = w_1 w_2 \ldots w_n$ and $w_i \in \mathcal{L}(R_1)$ for $1 \leq i \leq n$, whereas $\mathcal{L}(R)$ denotes the common semantics of a regular expression. There does not exist a substitution h that satisfies $\alpha \mathbin{\dot\in} \emptyset$. If there exists a substitution h satisfying a regular constraint $\alpha \mathbin{\dot\in} R$, respectively there does not exist such a substitution, we simply write $\models \alpha \mathbin{\dot\in} R$, respectively $\not\models \alpha \mathbin{\dot\in} R$.

A natural sub-problem of solving regular constraints is that of *bounded regular constraints*. Here we are both given a formula containing regular constraints and a set of upper bounds $\{ |x| \leq b_x \mid x \in \Gamma \wedge b_x \in \mathbb{N} \}$ for each variable occurring in our formula. A bounded regular constraints $\alpha \mathbin{\dot\in} R$ is satisfiable if there exists a substitution h such $h \models \alpha \mathbin{\dot\in} R$ and $|h(x)| \leq b_x$ for each $x \in \Gamma$. Whenever reasoning with bounds, we replace each variable x with a sequence of new *'filled variables'* $x^{(1)} \cdots x^{(b_x)}$, which we restrict to be only substituted by either a single letter or the empty word denoted by the special symbol λ in this context. A pattern containing only filled variables, as well as letters, is called a *filled pattern*. For a pattern $\alpha \in \Xi^*$, we denote its corresponding filled pattern by $\check\alpha$. In the following, we refer to the alphabet of filled variables by $\check\Gamma$ and by $\check\Xi = \Sigma \cup \check\Gamma$ to the alphabet of the filled patterns. Let $h : \Xi^* \to \Sigma^*$ be a substitution for $\alpha \in \Xi^*$. We can canonically define the induced substitution for filled patterns as $\check h : (\Sigma \cup \check\Gamma) \to \Sigma_\lambda$ with $\check h(a) = h(a)$ for all $a \in \Sigma$, $\check h(x^{(i)}) = h(x)[i]$ for all $x^{(i)} \in \check\Gamma$ and $i \leq |h(x)|$, and $\check h(x^{(j)}) = \lambda$ for all $x^{(j)} \in \check\Gamma$ and $|h(x)| < j \leq b_x$, where $\lambda \notin \check\Xi$. In the other direction, if we have found a satisfying filled substitution, we can transform it to a substitution for our original constraint by defining $h(x)$ as the concatenation $\check h\left(x^{(1)}\right) \cdots \check h\left(x^{(b_x)}\right)$ in which each occurrence of λ is replaced by ε.

For convenience, we call the set $\{ n \in \mathbb{N} \mid \exists w \in L : |w| = n \}$ the *length abstraction* of a regular language L and denoted it with $\mathrm{rAbs}(L)$. Likewise, for a pattern $\alpha \in \Xi^*$ with upper bounds $\{ |x| \leq b_x \mid x \in \Gamma \wedge b_x \in \mathbb{N} \}$, we define its *length abstraction* $\mathrm{rAbs}(\alpha) = \{ n \in \mathbb{N} \mid n = c + j \wedge 0 \leq j \leq v \}$, where $c = \sum_{a \in \Sigma} |\alpha|_a$ is the number of constants in α and $v = \sum_{x \in \Gamma} (|\alpha|_x \cdot b_x)$ is the sum of upper bounds of each variable occurrence.

We define propositional formulae in the classical way stated in 1847 by Boole [11] and refer to the set of all propositional formulae with $\mathscr{F}_{PL}$. If a propositional formula φ is satisfiable, we write $\models \varphi$. Conversely, if it is not satisfiable, we write $\not\models \varphi$. We recall that any propositional formula can be converted to an equisatisfiable formula in Conjunctive Normal Form (CNF) by the *Tseitin transformation* [30]. This is important as the SAT-solver we use requires formula to be in CNF.

The underlying solver. Since our approach is based on WOORPJE, we quickly overview the inner workings of this framework. WOORPJE is a SAT-based approach for solving word equations with linear length constraints. The pair of two

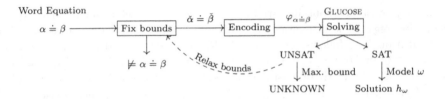

Fig. 2. Architecture of WOORPJE.

patterns $\alpha, \beta \in \Xi^*$ written $\alpha \doteq \beta$ is called a word equation. WOORPJE was primarily build to solve word equations – that is trying to find a substitution h unifying both sides of equation such that $h(\alpha) = h(\beta)$. For a word equation $\alpha \doteq \beta$ and upper bounds, the solver constructs a propositional logic formula $\varphi_{\alpha \doteq \beta}$ which is satisfiable if and only if the equation has a solution w.r.t. the given bounds. The formula is forwarded to the SAT solver GLUCOSE [2] that either determines $\not\models \varphi_{\alpha \doteq \beta}$ or generates an assignment ω with $\omega \models \varphi_{\alpha \doteq \beta}$. In the latter case, WOORPJE uses ω to construct a substitution h_ω such that $h_\omega \models \alpha \doteq \beta$.

If there is no upper bound given for a variable $x \in \Gamma$, WOORPJE tries solving the problem with increasing bounds iteratively until a maximum bound is reached. The encoding makes use of the *filling the position* [19,26] approach. Thus, the word equation is converted into its filled counterpart $\check{\alpha} \doteq \check{\beta}$ over the filled alphabet $\check{\Xi}$.

The encoding consists of a set of propositional formulae that constraint both sides of the equation to be identical position by position. For this purpose, WOORPJE introduces multiple Boolean variables which model the mappings between two constants or a filled variable and a constant, i.e., the substitution. More detailed, to match constants the variables $C_{a,b}$ for all $a, b \in \Sigma_\lambda$ are introduced, along with the formulae $C_{a,a} \leftrightarrow \top$ and $C_{a,b} \leftrightarrow \bot$ with $a \neq b$. To model the mappings between filled variables and constants, WOORPJE uses the Boolean variables $K^a_{x^{(i)}}$ for all $x^{(i)} \in \check{\Gamma}$ and $0 \leq i \leq b_x$. WOORPJE constraints that if $K^a_{x^{(i)}}$ is set to 1, then the variable $x^{(i)}$ is substituted with a. Thus, the C variables represent the substitution for constants, and the K variables model the substitution for each variable. Both are summarized under the Boolean variables $\text{word}^a_{w[i]}$ with

$$\text{word}^a_{w[i]} \leftrightarrow \begin{cases} C^a_{w[i]} & \text{if } w[i] \in \Sigma_\lambda \\ K^a_{w[i]} & \text{if } w[i] \in \check{\Gamma} \end{cases}$$

for all $w \in \{\check{\alpha}, \check{\beta}\}$, $1 \leq i \leq |w|$, and $a \in \Sigma_\lambda$. Hence, a substitution h_ω can be derived from the assignment of the word variables under a model ω. WOORPJE constructs a formula that constraints the variables to express this relation. Consider, i.e., a word equation $ax_1 b \doteq x_2$ and upper bounds $b_{x_1} = 1$ and $b_{x_2} = 3$. WOORPJE constructs the following formula: $\bigwedge_{i \in \{1,...,|\check{\alpha}|\}} \bigvee_{c \in \{a,b\}} \text{word}^c_{\check{\alpha}[i]} \leftrightarrow \text{word}^c_{\check{\beta}[i]}$ and potentially returns a solution ω mapping $\text{word}^a_{w[1]}, \text{word}^a_{w[2]}$, and $\text{word}^b_{w[i]}$ for $w \in \{\check{\alpha}, \check{\beta}\}$ to true. This allows the construction of $h_\omega = \{x_1 \mapsto a, x_2 \mapsto aab\}$ which is an actual solution to the given equation. The general way of WOORPJE's inner working is depicted in Fig. 2.

3   Encoding Regular Constraints

In the following, we present two approaches on how to express a bounded regular constraint $\alpha \doteq L$ as a propositional formula $\varphi_{\alpha \doteq L} \in \mathscr{F}_{PL}$ that is satisfiable if the predicate itself is. The first, which we call the *word-based* approach, essentially reduces the constraint to a pattern matching problem by translating regular operators into Boolean counterparts. The other approach takes a detour to the NFA equivalent to the regular expression first. We hence call it the *automaton-based* approach. Both approaches make use of the filled version of the predicate, $\breve{\alpha} \doteq L$, and we use both representations interchangeably without further notice. As both approaches naturally extend to solving multiple constraints by Boolean conjunction/disjunction, we only consider single regular constraints.

3.1   Word-Based Encoding

Regular expressions are built by inductively applying regular operations to existing expressions. We use this inductive structure to express the semantics of the regular operations in propositional logic. To avoid treating edge cases separately, we assume $\text{word}_\varepsilon^\lambda \leftrightarrow \top$ and $\text{word}_a^\varepsilon \leftrightarrow \bot$ for all $a \in \Sigma$.

Definition 3.1 (Word-based Encoding). *Let $\alpha \doteq \mathcal{L}(E)$ be a bounded regular membership predicate with $\alpha \in \Xi^*$ and $E \in \text{Reg}_\Sigma$. We define the* word-based *encoding $\varphi : \Xi^* \times \text{Reg}_\Sigma \to \mathscr{F}_{PL}$ inductively over the structure of regular expressions as follows. For $E = \emptyset$ we define $\varphi(\breve{\alpha}, E) = \bot$. Let $E = w$ for some $w \in \Sigma^*$. If $|\breve{\alpha}| < |w|$ then $\varphi(\breve{\alpha}, w) = \bot$. Furthermore, if $|\breve{\alpha}| = 0$, we set $\varphi(\breve{\alpha}, \varepsilon) = \top$ and elsewise $\varphi(\breve{\alpha}, \varepsilon) = \bigwedge_{i=1}^{|\breve{\alpha}|} \text{word}_{\breve{\alpha}[i]}^\lambda$. If $0 < |w| \le |\breve{\alpha}|$ then we set*

$$\varphi(\breve{\alpha}, w) = \bigvee_{j=0}^{|w|} \bigwedge_{i=1}^{j} (\text{word}_{\breve{\alpha}[i]}^{w[i]}) \wedge \text{word}_{\breve{\alpha}[j+1]}^\lambda \wedge \varphi(\breve{\alpha}[j+2:|\breve{\alpha}|], w[j+1:|\breve{\alpha}|]).$$

Let $R_1, R_2 \in \text{Reg}_\Sigma$ then, for a fixed bound $b_* \in \mathbb{N}$, we define

$$\varphi(\breve{\alpha}, E) = \begin{cases} \varphi(\breve{\alpha}, R_1) \vee \varphi(\breve{\alpha}, R_2) & \text{if } E = R_1 | R_2 \\ \bigvee_{i=0}^{|\breve{\alpha}|} \varphi(\breve{\alpha}[1:i], R_1) \wedge \varphi(\breve{\alpha}[i+1:|w|], R_2) & \text{if } E = R_1 \cdot R_2 \\ \bigvee_{i=0}^{b_*} \varphi(\breve{\alpha}, R_1^i) & \text{if } E = R_1^* \end{cases}$$

Intuitively, the above encoding descents down the subexpressions a regular expression is composed of and expresses their semantics in propositional logic. Whenever an atomic expression, i.e., a constant word or the empty word, is encountered, a matching between the expression and the currently considered pattern is encoded, utilizing the word variables provided by WOORPJE. This is realized by encoding that each position in the pattern is either substituted by the symbol in the expression at the same position or by a λ. In the latter case, it is necessary to encode that the suffix of the pattern (after the λ substitution) matches the remaining part of the expression. The cases are illustrated in Fig. 3.

$E = \varepsilon$

(a) The expression is empty and $\breve{\alpha}$ contains only variables (SAT).

$E = \varepsilon$

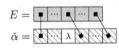

(b) The expression is empty but $\breve{\alpha}$ contains constants (UNSAT).

$E =$

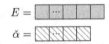

(c) The expression is longer than the filled pattern (UNSAT).

$E =$

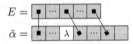

(d) The expression and the pattern have the same size and must match position by position.

(e) The expression is longer than the pattern. A sufficient amount of variables must be substituted with λ.

(f) The expression is longer than the pattern but the pattern does not contain sufficiently many positions to map to λ (UNSAT).

Fig. 3. The cases to consider for encoding the matching between a constant word and a pattern. Constants are grey, variables are white, and hatched fields may either be a variable or a constant. The cases (d) to (f) are included in the formula for encoding a nonempty word not longer than the filled pattern.

In our implementation, trivially unsatisfiable matchings (e.g., containing word_a^b with $a \neq b$) are omitted from encoding directly. As an example, consider the constraint $axd \doteq \mathcal{L}((ab|ac)(ad|bd))$ with bound $b_x = 2$. At the topmost level, i.e., the concatenation, $\varphi(a x^{(1)} x^{(2)} d, (ab|ac)(ad|bd))$ equals

$$
\begin{array}{lll}
\varphi(\varepsilon, (ab|ac)) & \wedge & \varphi(a x^{(1)} x^{(2)} d, (ad|bd)) \\
\vee \varphi(a, (ab|ac)) & \wedge & \varphi(x^{(1)} x^{(2)} d, (ad|bd)) \\
\vee \varphi(a x^{(1)}, (ab|ac)) & \wedge & \varphi(x^{(2)} d, (ad|bd)) \qquad (*) \\
\vee \varphi(a x^{(1)} x^{(2)}, (ab|ac)) & \wedge & \varphi(d, (ad|bd)) \\
\vee \varphi(a x^{(1)} x^{(2)} d, (ab|ac)) & \wedge & \varphi(\varepsilon, (ad|bd)).
\end{array}
$$

By observing the lengths of the filled patterns and the regular expression, no formula but the one marked with (*) can be satisfied. All others can be pruned, as explained later on. Encoding $\varphi(a x^{(1)}, (ab|ac)) \wedge \varphi(x^{(2)} d, (ad|bd))$ further gives

$$(\varphi(a x^{(1)}, ab) \vee \varphi(a x^{(1)}, ac)) \wedge (\varphi(x^{(2)} d, ad) \vee \varphi(x^{(2)} d, bd)).$$

The last step is to encoding the pattern matchings. The first term of the example, $\varphi(a x^{(1)}, ab)$, results in

$$\underbrace{\mathrm{word}_a^\lambda \wedge \varphi(x^{(1)}, ab)}_{\text{Unsatisfiable}} \vee \underbrace{\mathrm{word}_a^a \wedge \mathrm{word}_{x^{(1)}}^\lambda \wedge \varphi(\varepsilon, b)}_{\text{Unsatisfiable}} \vee \underbrace{\mathrm{word}_a^a \wedge \mathrm{word}_{x^{(1)}}^b \wedge \varphi(\varepsilon, \varepsilon)}_{\text{Satisfiable}}.$$

Repeating this for the other matchings yields the final formula, which is satisfiable with the four different assignments that correspond to the solution words $abad$, $abbd$, $acad$, and $acbd$. It is easy to see that for any filled pattern $\breve{\alpha}$ and regular expression $E \in \mathsf{Reg}_\Sigma$, $\varphi(\breve{\alpha}, E)$ is finite.

Theorem 3.1 (Word-based Encoding Soundness). *Let* $\alpha \overset{.}{\in} \mathcal{L}(E)$ *be a bounded regular membership predicate. If* $\models \varphi(\breve{\alpha}, E)$, *then* $\models \alpha \overset{.}{\in} \mathcal{L}(E)$.

The other direction of Theorem 3.1 does not hold if a Kleene star occurs in E. The encoding replaces the infinite nature of the Kleene star by only finitely many disjunctions, according to some bound $b_* \in \mathbb{N}$. The result is equivalent to encoding a regular constraint in which each Kleene star R^* is replaced with $(\varepsilon|R|RR|...|R^{b_*})$. This procedure is called *unrolling*, and b_* is called the *unroll bound*. If we have $\not\models \alpha \in (\breve{\alpha}, E)$, the result is only valid for that particular chosen unroll bound b_*. It could as well be the case that the predicate is, in fact, satisfiable, but b_* was set too small.

By comparing the length abstraction of regular languages and patterns, we can identify and prune unsatisfiable instances during the encoding. Intuitively, a satisfying solution can only substitute variables such that the total length of the solution word is contained in the length abstraction of the regular language. If there is no such solution, then the predicate is unsatisfiable, as stated in the following theorem[1].

Theorem 3.2. *Let* $\alpha \overset{.}{\in} L$ *be a bounded regular membership predicate with bounds* $b_x \in \mathbb{N}$ *for each* $x \in \Gamma$. *If* $\mathrm{rAbs}(\alpha) \cap \mathrm{rAbs}(L) = \emptyset$ *then* $\not\models \alpha \overset{.}{\in} L$.

This result can be integrated into the recursive encoding procedure. In particular, for a regular expression E and pattern α we have $\varphi(\breve{\alpha}, E) \Leftrightarrow \bot$ if $\mathrm{rAbs}(\alpha) \cap \mathrm{rAbs}(E) = \emptyset$. If E is compound, i.e., not a constant word, we apply the criterion to each subexpression E consists of. If any of the subexpressions does not meet the condition, the encoding of it can be omitted altogether, since it is used in disjunction with the encoding of the other subexpressions[2]. For example, let $E = R_1 | R_2$ for some regular expression R_1 and R_2 with $\mathrm{rAbs}(\alpha) \cap \mathrm{rAbs}(R_1) = \emptyset$, then $\varphi(\breve{\alpha}, E) = \varphi(\breve{\alpha}, R_1) \vee \varphi(\breve{\alpha}, R_2) \Leftrightarrow \varphi(\breve{\alpha}, R_1) \vee \bot \Leftrightarrow \varphi(\breve{\alpha}, R_2)$. Hence, we can omit the encoding of $\varphi(\alpha, R_2)$ from the final formula. The same principle is applicable in the other induction steps. The length abstraction for a regular expression can be computed efficiently (see, e.g., [23]).

The word-based encoding suffers from two problems. First, as noted above, it is not refutation complete. That is, for a satisfiable bounded regular membership predicate $\alpha \overset{.}{\in} L$ where L is a regular language that contains a Kleene star, the resulting encoding might be unsatisfiable due to a poor choice of b_*. To evade this, we currently set $b_* = |\breve{\alpha}|$. This way, it is guaranteed that the resulting union contains an operand at least as long as the filled pattern itself (given the expression does not only consist of ε or $\emptyset$). However, this usually introduces more complexity than necessary. Furthermore, as we'll present in the evaluation, the encoding falls behind the automaton-based encoding performance-wise. We recon the reason to be the combinatorial explosion caused by the recursive pattern matching along with the encoding of the concatenation, which considers all

---

[1] All proofs are omitted due to space constraints but made available in the appendix for reviewing purpose.

[2] This is due to the fact that for all $\psi \in \mathscr{F}_{PL}$ we have $\psi \vee \bot \Leftrightarrow \psi$.

quotients of a pattern. That further amplifies with occurrences of Kleene stars which, as noted above, are expressed as concatenation.

3.2   Automaton-Based Encoding

Let $\alpha \doteq \mathcal{L}(E)$ be a bounded regular membership predicate with $E \in \mathsf{Reg}_\Sigma$. Instead of processing the regular expression directly, the first step of the automaton-based encoding is to construct an NFA $\mathcal{M} = (Q, \Sigma, \delta, q_0, F)$ with $\mathcal{L}(M) = \mathcal{L}(E)$. After that, the general idea is to introduce Boolean variables S_q^i that encode whether there exist a substitution h such that q is reachable after i transitions when reading $h(\alpha)$, i.e., $q \in \hat{\delta}(\{q_0\}, h(\alpha)[1:i])$. Since we are working on filled patterns, we need to prepare for reading λ symbols, which leads us to the following natural extension definition of a *filled automaton*. For an NFA $\mathcal{M} = (Q, \Sigma, \delta, q_0, F)$ we define the corresponding filled automaton $\check{\mathcal{M}} = (Q, \Sigma_\lambda, \check{\delta}, q_0, F)$ where for all $q \in Q$ and $a \in \Sigma_\lambda$ if $a = \lambda$ we have $\check{\delta}(q,a) = \{q\}$ and $\check{\delta}(q,a) = \delta(q,a)$ otherwise. Essentially, the filled automaton is a version of the original automaton that allows self-transition on all states by reading λ.

It is immediate that for any automaton $\mathcal{M}$ and bounded pattern α we have $\models \alpha \doteq \mathcal{L}(\mathcal{M})$ if and only if $\models \check{\alpha} \doteq \mathcal{L}(\check{\mathcal{M}})$. Due to this relationship, we can specify an encoding for the filled automaton without further considerations. The encoding makes use of the *predecessor* function for the filled NFA, pred $: Q \to \mathcal{P}(Q \times \Sigma_\lambda)$, which we define for $q' \in Q$ by $\mathrm{pred}(q') = \{(q,a) \in Q \times \Sigma_\lambda \mid q' \in \check{\delta}(q,a)\}$. That is, $\mathrm{pred}(q')$ contains all pairs (q,a) such that q' can be reached from q by reading a.

Definition 3.2 (Automaton-based Encoding). *Let $\alpha \doteq \mathcal{L}(\mathcal{M})$ be a bounded regular membership predicate where $\alpha \in \Xi^*$ is a pattern and $\mathcal{M} = (Q, \Sigma, \delta, q_0, F)$ is an NFA. Let S_q^i be Boolean variables for all $q \in Q$ and $0 \leq i \leq |\alpha|$. The automaton-based encoding is the conjunction of the following formulae:*

1. $\bigwedge_{i=0}^{|\check{\alpha}|-1} \bigwedge_{(q,a)\in\mathrm{dom}(\check{\delta})} \bigwedge_{q'\in\check{\delta}(q,a)} (S_q^i \wedge \mathrm{word}_{\check{\alpha}[i+1]}^a \to S_{q'}^{i+1})$ *(Transition)*

2. $\bigwedge_{i=1}^{|\check{\alpha}|} \bigwedge_{q'\in Q} (S_{q'}^i \to \bigvee_{(q,a)\in\mathrm{pred}(q')} (S_q^{i-1} \wedge \mathrm{word}_{\check{\alpha}[i]}^a))$ *(Predecessor)*

3. $S_{q_0}^0 \wedge \bigwedge_{q\in Q\setminus\{q_0\}} \neg S_q^0$ *(Initial State)*

4. $\bigvee_{q\in F} S_q^{|\check{\alpha}|}$ *(Accepting States)*

We want the variable S_q^i to encode whether there is a substitution h such that state $q \in Q$ is reachable from q_0 when reading $h(\check{\alpha})[1:i]$, i.e., after i transitions. The first three formulae specified in Definition 3.2 constraint S_q^i to expresses exactly this property. Recall that in our SAT encoding, a substitution h is given by means of the word variables. The *Transition* constraint models that the automaton follows the existing transitions. That is, if after i transitions h maps the i+1th symbol of $\check{\alpha}$ to an $a \in \Sigma$, and there is a transition from q to $q' \in Q$ labeled with a, then the state q' is reachable after $i + 1$ transitions. The *Predecessor* constraint restricts that any state reachable after $i \geq 1$ transitions must have a predecessor reachable in $i - 1$ transitions. In particular, if state q' is reachable after $i \geq 1$ transitions, then there must be a state q that is reachable

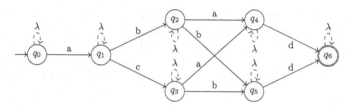

Fig. 4. The filled automaton $\mathcal{M}_\xi$ for the automaton $\mathcal{M}$ with $\mathcal{L}(M) = \mathcal{L}((ab|ac)(ad|bd))$.

with $i - 1$ transitions and a transition from q to q' labeled with the symbol the i-th position of the pattern is mapped to. Generally, it is necessary to iterate over all $q' \in Q$ and not only over the reachable states to assure that unreachable states remain unused. Meaning, if $\text{pred}(q') = \emptyset$ we get $S_{q'}^i \to \bot$ for all $i \in \{1, ..., |\alpha|\}$, which falsifies the whole formula if we assign 1 to $S_{q'}^i$. The *Initial State* constraint states that after 0 transitions, the initial state q_0, and only this state, is reachable. The *Accepting States* constraint models the acceptance of the automaton. The encoded substitution is a solution if and only if after reading the word, i.e., after $|\breve{\alpha}|$ transitions, the automaton is in any state $q_f \in F$.

Consider the example from the word-based encoding again. The filled automaton equivalent to the expression $(ab|ac)(ad|bd)$ is shown in Fig. 4. By the *Initial State* constraint we have $S_{q_0}^0 \wedge \neg S_{q_1}^0 \wedge \neg S_{q_2}^0 \cdots \wedge \neg S_{q_6}^0$. The encoding of the transition for the path $(q_0, q_1, q_2, q_4, q_6)$ is given by

$$\underbrace{(S_{q_0}^0 \wedge \text{word}_a^a \to S_{q_1}^1)}_{q_1 \text{ reachable after 1 transition}} \qquad \wedge \qquad \underbrace{(S_{q_1}^1 \wedge \text{word}_{x(1)}^b \to S_{q_2}^2)}_{\substack{q_2 \text{ reachable after 2 transitions if } q_1 \text{ is} \\ \text{reachable after 1 transition and } h(x^{(1)})=b}}$$

$$\wedge \qquad \underbrace{(S_{q_2}^2 \wedge \text{word}_{x(2)}^a \to S_{q_4}^3)}_{\substack{q_4 \text{ reachable after 3 transitions if } q_2 \text{ is} \\ \text{reachable after 2 transition and } h(x^{(2)})=a}} \qquad \wedge \qquad \underbrace{(S_{q_4}^3 \wedge \text{word}_d^d \to S_{q_6}^4)}_{\substack{q_6 \text{ reachable after 4 transitions if } q_4 \text{ is} \\ \text{reachable after 3 transition}}}$$

Further, the *Accepting States* constraint requires $S_{q_6}^4$ to be set to true. Thus, *abad* is a solution word given only this fraction of the encoding. All other paths are encoded in the same manner. We omitted the encoding of the predecessor constraints for brevity.

Theorem 3.3. *Let* $\mathcal{M} = (Q, \Sigma, \delta, q_0, F)$ *an NFA and,* $\alpha \,\dot{\in}\, \mathcal{L}(\mathcal{M})$ *be a bounded regular membership predicate. We have* $\models \varphi(\breve{\alpha}, \breve{\mathcal{M}})$ *if and only if* $\models \alpha \,\dot{\in}\, \mathcal{L}(\mathcal{M})$.

Likewise to the word-based encoding, we can make use of the length abstraction to reduce the number of cases to encode and thus the size of the resulting propositional formula. Both, the *Transition* and the *Predecessor* constraint encode substitutions that cannot be solutions based on the length of the pattern alone. This is due to the fact that, given some $i \in \{1, \ldots, |\breve{\alpha}|\}$, the constraints do not take into account whether the currently considered state leads to an accepting state or is reachable from the initial state. That results in a disjunction of many unsatisfiable sub-formulae that do not carry any valuable information. Analyzing the length of paths between states, we can omit a large fraction of such cases. Using the *reachability* relation defined for an NFA $\mathcal{M} = (Q, \Sigma, \delta, q_0, F)$ for each pair of states $q, q\prime \in Q$ by $\text{reach}_{\mathcal{M}}(q, q\prime) = \{\, n \in \mathbb{N} \mid \exists u \in \Sigma^* : q\prime \in \hat{\delta}(\{q\}, u) \wedge |u| = n \,\}$ allows identifying paths that cannot be part of a solution. For $q \in Q$, $\alpha \in \Xi^*$, and $i \in \{0, \dots, |\breve{\alpha}|\,\}$, we immediately get that if $\text{rAbs}(\breve{\alpha}[1 : i]) \cap \text{reach}_{\mathcal{M}}(q_0, q) = \emptyset$, then there is no substitution h with $q \in \hat{\delta}(\{q_0\}, h(\alpha)[1 : i])$. Put simply, if for a substitution h we have that state q is reachable after reading $h(\alpha)[1 : i]$, then necessrily there must be a path from q_0 to q of length $|h(\alpha)[1 : i]|$. If there is no path from q_0 to q with length in $\text{rAbs}(\breve{\alpha}[1 : i])$, then such an h cannot exist. In this case, we simply set $S_q^i \Leftrightarrow \bot$ and omit encoding the *Predecessor* constraint for q. We get a similar result for the reachability of final states from a given state q. If $\text{rAbs}(\breve{\alpha}[i : |\breve{\alpha}|]) \cap \bigcup_{q_f \in F} \text{reach}_{\mathcal{M}}(q, q_f) = \emptyset$, then there is no substitution h with $\hat{\delta}(\{q\}, h(\alpha)[i : |\breve{\alpha}|]) \cap F \neq \emptyset$. In other words, if the automaton is in state q after i transition, all remaining $i + 1$ to $|\breve{\alpha}|$ positions of the pattern must be filled in order for the substitution to be a solution. If the existing path lengths and the length abstraction of the pattern make this impossible, we skip encoding all transitions from q to any state for position $i + 1$. Especially, we can directly proof the predicate invalid, if $\text{rAbs}(\breve{\alpha}) \cap \bigcup_{q_f \in F} \text{reach}_{\mathcal{M}}(q_0, q_f) = \emptyset$.

Approximating Reachability. Essentially, for an NFA $\mathcal{M} = (Q, \Sigma, \delta, q_0, F)$, we are interested in the sets $\text{reach}_{\mathcal{M}}(q_0, q)$ and $\bigcup_{q_f \in F} \text{reach}_{\mathcal{M}}(q, q_f)$ for each $q \in Q$. While these sets, in general, can be infinite, they can be described in a succinct way as sets of arithmetic progressions. This representation can be found by transforming the NFA into *Chrobak normalform* [14], which, however, only yields $\bigcup_{q_f \in F} \text{reach}_{\mathcal{M}}(q_0, q_f)$. Hence, calculating $\text{reach}_{\mathcal{M}}(q_0, q)$ and $\bigcup_{q_f \in F} \text{reach}_{\mathcal{M}}(q, q_f)$ necessitates repeated calculations of the normal form using each state q as each, the initial and final state. Unfortunately, preliminary tests have shown that this computation exceeds the potential speed-up by large. Thus, instead of an exact calculation, we use an approximation based on the following observation.

Lemma 3.1. *Let* $\mathcal{M} = (Q, \Sigma, \delta, q_0, F)$ *be an NFA and* $\alpha \in \Xi^*$. *The following conditions hold for all* $i \in \{1, \dots, |\breve{\alpha}|\,\}$ *and* $q \in Q$.

1. *If* $\max(\text{rAbs}(\breve{\alpha}[i : |\breve{\alpha}|])) < \min(\bigcup_{q_f \in F} \text{reach}_{\mathcal{M}}(q, q_f))$ *or* $\min(\text{rAbs}(\breve{\alpha}[i : |\breve{\alpha}|])) > \max(\bigcup_{q_f \in F} \text{reach}_{\mathcal{M}}(q, q_f))$, *then* $\text{rAbs}(\breve{\alpha}[i : |\breve{\alpha}|]) \cap \bigcup_{q_f \in F} \text{reach}_{\mathcal{M}}(q, q_f) = \emptyset$.
2. *If* $\max(\text{rAbs}(\breve{\alpha}[1 : i])) < \min(\text{reach}_{\mathcal{M}}(q_0, q))$ *or* $\min(\text{rAbs}(\breve{\alpha}[1 : i])) > \max(\text{reach}_{\mathcal{M}}(q_0, q))$, *then* $\text{rAbs}(\breve{\alpha}[1 : i]) \cap \text{reach}_{\mathcal{M}}(q_0, q) = \emptyset$

Hence, as an approximation, it is sufficient to know the longest and shortest path from each state to an accepting state and from the initial state to each state. Fortunately, this information can be computed during the construction of the NFA using the *Thompson construction* with negligible additional effort.

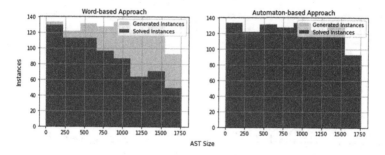

Fig. 5. Distribution of generated and solved instance per approach, based on expression size.

4   Empirical Evalutation

We have implemented both approaches in WOORPJE[3] and evaluated them in two ways. First, we conducted a performance analysis to gain insight into their inner workings. Second, we evaluated if our solutions are competitive with other string solvers.For both experiments, we only consider satisfiable instances due to a known limitation of WOORPJE: WOORPJE can only classify a regular membership predicate as UNSAT if, after preprocessing, the regular expression defines an empty language. Constraints that are unsatisfiable but consist of a non-empty regular expression cannot be determined as unsatisfiable. WOORPJE instead tries to solve the problem with increasing upper bounds and fails to find a solution for any of them. We recognize that a tool's ability to classify unsatisfiable instances is of interest but focus on satisfiable cases since they will provide the most insights into the working of our techniques.

All experiments were performed on a 1.5 TiB machine with two 6th generation Intel Xeon CPUs, providing 56 logical cores in total, usingUbuntu version 1.20 as the operating system.

4.1   Performance Analysis

We ran both approaches against a benchmark set of 1000 satisfiable regular membership predicates generated by STRINGFUZZ [10]. Each has the form $x \in \mathcal{L}(E)$ where x is a single variable and E is a regular expression. The expressions have between 1 and 1800 nodes in the AST (counting each character as a single node). The two approaches were each run with a timeout of two minutes per instance.

Results. The automaton-based approach solved all instances, while the word-based approach solved 725 instances. Figure 5 shows the distribution of solved compared to generated instances, based on the expressions AST size (number of nodes). The automaton-based approach surpasses the word-based approach w.r.t.

---

[3] https://git.zs.informatik.uni-kiel.de/dbp/wordsolve/-/tree/spin22

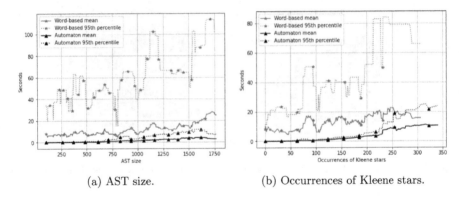

(a) AST size.   (b) Occurrences of Kleene stars.

Fig. 6. Encoding time based on AST size and Kleene star occurrences, smoothed with a rolling window.

this ratio at all input sizes. Furthermore, the number of samples solved by the word-based approach decreases, seemingly linearly, with increasing expression size. In the following, we analyze the impact that various parameters of regular expressions have on the performance. The results are independent of the number of iterations needed by WOORPJE to find the bound that renders the constraint satisfiable. That is, if WOORPJE tried multiple bounds for a single constraint, the presented results cumulate the time taken for all attempted bounds. That does not affect the comparability, as the number of iterations per instance is always identical in both approaches.

Expression Size. Figure 6a compares the time to encode based on the size of the expression's AST. The effect of growing expressions on the automaton-based approach seems limited. The durations range from a few milliseconds to three seconds for the largest expressions, on average. The word-based approach performs worse across the whole range of considered instances. Furthermore, the time taken to encode the constraints increases steadily with the size of expressions. Additionally, the mean and 95th percentile show a volatile behavior, indicating that other factors influence the encoding time of the word-based approach.

Star Operations. A similar picture shows when investigating the encoding time based on the occurrences of star operations. The results are shown in Fig. 6b. Generally, both approaches took more time to encode the predicate the more stars occurred in the expression. Again, the automaton-based approach shows better results than the word-based. The latter approach did not solve constraints with expressions containing more than 310 Kleene stars. Moreover, it shows an even more volatile behavior. We reckon this to be due to the unrolling procedures, for two reasons. First, it additionally depends on the size of the pattern, i.e., the upper bound of the variable. Second, the measurement does not capture where the stars occur in the pattern. The higher a Kleene star occurs in the AST, the larger the AST produced by unrolling and, thus, the more effort needed to encode. The automaton-based approach is not affected by this, as it does

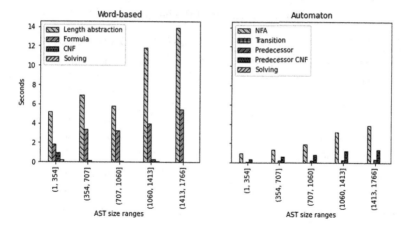

Fig. 7. Mean duration taken by each individual step, based on AST size.

not rely on unrolling. A plausible explanation for the increase in encoding time of the automaton-based approach is that Kleene stars introduce cycles in the automaton and thus generate more paths to encode.

Duration of Encoding Steps. We measured the time taken by the individual steps executed towards solving the predicates. For the word-based approach, these steps are the time to compute the length abstraction, the time to compute the formula, and the time to bring it into CNF. For the automaton-based approach, we measured the time to build the NFA, to construct the *Transition* and *Predecessor* constraints, and to bring the *Predecessor* formula into CNF (note that the other three formulae are already in CNF by definition). Additionally, we measured the time consumed by the SAT solver for solving the formulae. For comparison, we grouped the range of AST sizes of tested instances into five contiguous equally sized intervals and calculated the mean value for each of these steps per interval. The results are shown in Fig. 7. Interestingly, the time spent by the SAT solver to solve the formula is negligible compared to the encoding process. Regarding the encoding procedure, the bars agree with our findings discussed previously. The automaton is faster by a significant amount, and the performance difference amplifies with increasing expression sizes. The calculation of the length abstraction is the bottleneck in the word-based approach. However, if we were to omit it, the performance of the word-based approach would still lack behind its competitor, even when ignoring the fact that this would most likely increase the time to construct the formula. The duration to construct the formula does not increase as steeply as the time needed to calculate the length abstraction, which suggests a positive effect of the latter. Surprisingly, in the word-based approach, the application of the Tseitin algorithm [30] does not take any significant amount of time, independently of the expression size. Contrary to this, the duration to compute the CNF of the *Predecessor* formula behaves proportionally to the time it takes to compute the formula itself. However, most time is not consumed by the actual encoding but rather by constructing the NFA.

Table 1. Results of the benchmark.

	Automaton	Word-based	Z3seq	Z3str3	CVC4	Z3str3RE
sat	328	328	316	296	322	323
unsat	0	0	0	2	0	0
unknown	1	1	0	0	0	0
timeout	0	0	13	31	0	6
soundness error	0	0	0	2	0	0
program crashes	0	0	0	0	7	0
Total correct	328	328	316	296	322	323
Time (s)	71	80	2792	3800	88	765
Time w/o timeouts (s)	71	80	1232	80	88	45

4.2 Comparative Benchmark

In addition to the performance analysis, we compared our solutions to state-of-the-art string constraint solvers in a comparative benchmark. For this purpose, we used ZALIGVINDER [22], a benchmarking framework explicitly created for comparing solvers regarding their performance. The solvers we included are Z3STR3 (4.8.9) [6], Z3SEQ (4.8.9) [24], Z3STR3RE (4.8.10) [7], and CVC4 (1.9) [4]. The benchmark suite consists of a collection of benchmarks taken from JOACO [29], NORN [1], SLOTH [17], STRINGFUZZ, and Z3. We removed all but the regular constraints from the instances. That is, each instance contains one to many regular constraints and no other assertions. If a regular constraint includes a construct currently unsupported by WOORPJE, namely negations, intersections, complements, and wildcards, we omit the instance[4]. Further, as already mentioned, we only consider satisfiable instances. This leaves us with a total of 329 instances. We provide them in our evaluation artifacts to reproduce the results [21]. Each solver is executed with a limit of 2 min per instance. During this benchmark, we enabled the following preprocessing steps in WOORPJE. If a pattern has a constant prefix or suffix, we remove it employing *Brzozowski Derivatives* [12] for regular expression. For constraints of the form $x \in E$, if $E \in \Sigma^*$, we fix $x = E$. If otherwise E is a compound regular expression, but x does not occur in another constraint, we fix $x = w$ for some $w \in \mathcal{L}(E)$.

Results. The results of the comparative benchmark are shown in Table 1 and are visualized in Fig. 8 as a cactus plot. The plot shows the time needed per number of solved instances, ordered by increasing runtime for each solver. The further to the right a curve is, the more instances the respective solver solved (given the time limit), and the closer to the bottom, the less time was used.

Both of our approaches solved all but a single instance. That indicates that the range of tested upper bounds for the variables was set too narrow in this case.

---

[4] Additionally, we replaced the unescaped " occurring in the STRINGFUZZ set with dots.

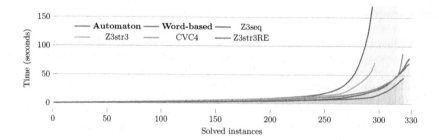

Fig. 8. Cactus plot of the results.

However, none of the other solvers managed to classify as many instances. For the correctly classified instances, it took the approaches 71 and 80 s, respectively. Thus, taking the number of solved instances as well as the runtime into account, WOORPJE outperformed the other solvers. CVC4 and Z3STR3 took a comparable amount of time, but managed to solve only 322, respectively, 296 instances. Considering only the SAT cases, Z3STR3RE scored highest, only needing 45 s and having timed out on six instances. Overall, Z3STR3 and Z3SEQ performed worst on this set w.r.t. both runtime and correctly classified instances. Additionally, Z3STR3 generated soundness errors on two instances, i.e., it decided two satisfiable instances to be unsatisfiable.

4.3   Threats to Validity

An inherent threat to the validity of the results we presented above lies in the sets of instances we used to conduct the evaluation. Foremost, the results of the performance analysis differ from the actual performance shown in the comparative benchmark. One reason is that the instances used in the former analysis were randomly generated and may not reflect the considered real-world applications. Additionally, we enabled preprocessing steps in the comparative benchmark that, likely, had a positive impact on the runtime. All of that has to be taken into account when valuing the results.

5   Conclusion

We dealt with solving string constraints, particularly regular constraints, using propositional logic. We presented two methods to achieve this. One of them takes advantage of the inductive structure of regular expressions, and the other works on nondeterministic finite automata. For both of them, we explored an approach to identify and omit substitutions that are nonviable only due to the length of the solution word they produce. For this purpose, we introduced the notion of the length abstraction of regular languages. To implement our approaches, we relied on WOORPJE as a framework. Our evaluation shows that the automaton-based approach is superior to the word-based. However, both are not only competitive to state-of-the-art solvers but also outperform them in many cases.

References

1. Abdulla, P.A., et al.: Norn: an SMT solver for string constraints. In: Kroening, D., Păsăreanu, C.S. (eds.) CAV 2015. LNCS, vol. 9206, pp. 462–469. Springer, Cham (2015). https://doi.org/10.1007/978-3-319-21690-4_29
2. Audemard, G., Simon, L.: On the glucose SAT solver. Int. J. Artif. Intell. Tools **27**(01), 1840001 (2018). https://doi.org/10.1142/S0218213018400018
3. Ball, T., Rajamani, S.K.: The SLAM toolkit. In: Berry, G., Comon, H., Finkel, A. (eds.) CAV 2001. LNCS, vol. 2102, pp. 260–264. Springer, Heidelberg (2001). https://doi.org/10.1007/3-540-44585-4_25
4. Barrett, C., et al.: CVC4. In: Gopalakrishnan, G., Qadeer, S. (eds.) CAV 2011. LNCS, vol. 6806, pp. 171–177. Springer, Heidelberg (2011). https://doi.org/10.1007/978-3-642-22110-1_14
5. Berzish, M., et al.: String theories involving regular membership predicates: from practice to theory and back. In: Lecroq, T., Puzynina, S. (eds.) WORDS 2021. LNCS, vol. 12847, pp. 50–64. Springer, Cham (2021). https://doi.org/10.1007/978-3-030-85088-3_5
6. Berzish, M., Ganesh, V., Zheng, Y.: Z3str3: a string solver with theory-aware heuristics. In: 2017 Formal Methods in Computer Aided Design (FMCAD), pp. 55–59. IEEE, Vienna (2017). https://doi.org/10.23919/FMCAD.2017.8102241
7. Berzish, M., et al.: An SMT solver for regular expressions and linear arithmetic over string length. In: Silva, A., Leino, K.R.M. (eds.) CAV 2021. LNCS, vol. 12760, pp. 289–312. Springer, Cham (2021). https://doi.org/10.1007/978-3-030-81688-9_14
8. Beyer, D., Henzinger, T.A., Jhala, R., Majumdar, R.: The software model checker blast. Int. J. Softw. Tools Technol. Transf. **9**(5–6), 505–525 (2007). https://doi.org/10.1007/s10009-007-0044-z
9. Beyer, D., Keremoglu, M.E.: CPACHECKER: a tool for configurable software verification. In: Gopalakrishnan, G., Qadeer, S. (eds.) CAV 2011. LNCS, vol. 6806, pp. 184–190. Springer, Heidelberg (2011). https://doi.org/10.1007/978-3-642-22110-1_16
10. Blotsky, D., Mora, F., Berzish, M., Zheng, Y., Kabir, I., Ganesh, V.: StringFuzz: a fuzzer for string solvers. In: Chockler, H., Weissenbacher, G. (eds.) CAV 2018. LNCS, vol. 10982, pp. 45–51. Springer, Cham (2018). https://doi.org/10.1007/978-3-319-96142-2_6
11. Boole, G.: The Mathematical Analysis of Logic. Cambridge University Press (1847)
12. Brzozowski, J.A.: Derivatives of regular expressions. J. ACM **11**(4), 481–494 (1964). https://doi.org/10.1145/321239.321249
13. Cadar, C., Dunbar, D., Engler, D.R.: KLEE: unassisted and automatic generation of high-coverage tests for complex systems programs. In: Draves, R., van Renesse, R. (eds.) 8th USENIX Symposium on Operating Systems Design and Implementation, OSDI 2008, 8–10 December 2008, San Diego, pp. 209–224. USENIX Association (2008). http://www.usenix.org/events/osdi08/tech/full_papers/cadar/cadar.pdf
14. Chrobak, M.: Finite automata and unary languages. Theoret. Comput. Sci. **47**, 149–158 (1986). https://doi.org/10.1016/0304-3975(86)90142-8
15. Day, J.D., Ehlers, T., Kulczynski, M., Manea, F., Nowotka, D., Poulsen, D.B.: On solving word equations using SAT. In: Filiot, E., Jungers, R., Potapov, I. (eds.) RP 2019. LNCS, vol. 11674, pp. 93–106. Springer, Cham (2019). https://doi.org/10.1007/978-3-030-30806-3_8
16. Ganesh, V., Berzish, M.: Undecidability of a theory of strings, linear arithmetic over length, and string-number conversion. CoRR abs/1605.09442 (2016). http://arxiv.org/abs/1605.09442

17. Holík, L., Janku, P., Lin, A.W., Rümmer, P., Vojnar, T.: String constraints with concatenation and transducers solved efficiently. Proc. ACM Program. Lang. **2**(POPL), 1–32 (2018)
18. Gerard, H., Checker, J.S.M.: The Primer and Reference Manual. Addison Wesley, Boston (2003)
19. Karhumäki, J., Mignosi, F., Plandowski, W.: The expressibility of languages and relations by word equations. J. ACM **47**(3), 483–505 (2000)
20. Kroening, D., Tautschnig, M.: CBMC – C bounded model checker. In: Ábrahám, E., Havelund, K. (eds.) TACAS 2014. LNCS, vol. 8413, pp. 389–391. Springer, Heidelberg (2014). https://doi.org/10.1007/978-3-642-54862-8_26
21. Kulczynski, M., Lotz, K., Nowotka, D., Poulsen, D.B.: Evaluation artifacts for: solving string theories involving regular membership predicates using sat (2022). https://doi.org/10.5281/zenodo.6384326
22. Kulczynski, M., Manea, F., Nowotka, D., Poulsen, D.B.: The power of string solving: simplicity of comparison. In: Proceedings of the IEEE/ACM 1st International Conference on Automation of Software Test, pp. 85–88. ACM, Seoul (2020). https://doi.org/10.1145/3387903.3389317
23. Matos, A.B.: Periodic sets of integers. Theoret. Comput. Sci. **127**(2), 287–312 (1994). https://doi.org/10.1016/0304-3975(94)90044-2
24. de Moura, L., Bjørner, N.: Z3: an efficient SMT solver. In: Ramakrishnan, C.R., Rehof, J. (eds.) TACAS 2008. LNCS, vol. 4963, pp. 337–340. Springer, Heidelberg (2008). https://doi.org/10.1007/978-3-540-78800-3_24
25. Plandowski, W.: An efficient algorithm for solving word equations. In: Proceedings of the 38th Annual ACM Symposium on Theory of Computing, pp. 467–476. STOC (2006). https://doi.org/10.1145/1132516.1132584
26. Plandowski, W., Rytter, W.: Application of Lempel-Ziv encodings to the solution of word equations. In: Larsen, K.G., Skyum, S., Winskel, G. (eds.) ICALP 1998. LNCS, vol. 1443, pp. 731–742. Springer, Heidelberg (1998). https://doi.org/10.1007/BFb0055097
27. Stanford, C., Veanes, M., Bjørner, N.: Symbolic Boolean derivatives for efficiently solving extended regular expression constraints. In: Proceedings of the 42nd ACM SIGPLAN International Conference on Programming Language Design and Implementation, pp. 620–635. ACM (2021). https://doi.org/10.1145/3453483.3454066
28. The SMT-LIB Initiative: The SMT Standard. https://smtlib.cs.uiowa.edu/standard.shtml. Accessed 17 Jan 2022
29. Thomé, J., Shar, L.K., Bianculli, D., Briand, L.: An integrated approach for effective injection vulnerability analysis of web applications through security slicing and hybrid constraint solving. IEEE Trans. Softw. Eng. **46**(2), 163–195 (2018)
30. Tseitin, G.S.: On the complexity of derivation in propositional calculus. In: Siekmann, J.H., Wrightson, G. (eds.) Automation of Reasoning. Symbolic Computation. Springer, Heidelberg (1983). https://doi.org/10.1007/978-3-642-81955-1_28

Correction to: Bounded-Memory Runtime Enforcement

Saumya Shankar, Antoine Rollet, Srinivas Pinisetty,
and Yliès Falcone

**Correction to:
Chapter "Bounded-Memory Runtime Enforcement"
in: O. Legunsen and G. Rosu (Eds.): *Model Checking Software*,
LNCS 13255, https://doi.org/10.1007/978-3-031-15077-7_7**

In the originally published version of chapter 7 "Bounded-Memory Runtime Enforcement" the Figure 3 was incorrect. The Figure 3 has now been corrected.

Owing to an oversight on the part of Springer Nature, Fig. 3 of this chapter was initially published with an error. The correct presentation is given here.

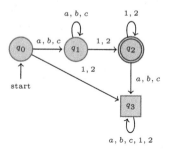

Fig. 3. A_{P_1}

The updated original version of this chapter can be found at
https://doi.org/10.1007/978-3-031-15077-7_7

Author Index

Printed in the United States
by Baker & Taylor Publisher Services